BETWEEN
◇ TWO ◇
CULTURES

THE ALEX CAMPBELL YEARS

To Bill + Denise,
The bond is strong!
With great affection,

Alex

by Wayne MacKinnnon

The Life of the Party

A History of the Liberal Party
in Prince Edward Island

"...this book has considerable value for students of Prince Edward Island and Canadian politics."

"Wayne MacKinnon possesses a rich sense of humour and a distrust of political cant. As a result he has given us one of the most useful and enjoyable party histories."

> - John English, University of Waterloo
> in *The Canadian Historical Review*

"...remarkably candid"

"MacKinnon has put us in his debt by producing an account which is frequently absorbing and usually reliable."

> - Ian Ross Robertson, University of Toronto
> in *Acadiensis*

"Traditional Island politics, as depicted so colourfully [by Wayne MacKinnon], often comes out looking at best like cynical comedy."

> - David A. Milne, University of Prince Edward Island
> in *The Garden Transformed*

"...Wayne MacKinnon, the trail-blazer for 20th-century Island political history."

> - Edward MacDonald, University of Prince Edward Island
> in *If Your're Stronghearted*

BETWEEN
◇ TWO ◇
CULTURES

THE ALEX CAMPBELL YEARS

Wayne MacKinnon

TEA •HILL
PRESS
Stratford
Prince Edward Island
CANADA

Published by
TEA HILL PRESS
80 Bellevue Road
Stratford
Prince Edward Island
Canada   C1B 2T8

Design & layout by Ken Shelton
Editing & proofreading by Daphne Davey
Printed in Canada

Front cover: Premier Alex Campbell, 1974

Library and Archives Canada Cataloguing in Publication

MacKinnon, Wayne E.
        Between two cultures : the Alex Campbell years / Wayne E.
MacKinnon.

Includes bibliographical references and index.
ISBN 0-9695400-5-1

        1. Campbell, Alexander B. (Alexander Bradshaw), 1933- 2. Prince
Edward Island—Politics and government—1959-1979. I. Title.

FC2625.M35 2005   971.7'04'092
C2005-903990-6

To Twilah

Between Two Cultures

"We, in this province, are caught between these two cultures. The culture of the past, with its problems of back-breaking labour, disease, child mortality, premature aging, inadequate medical facilities and limited educational opportunities, and the culture of the future as represented by modern industrial mechanized states ...

"We must be careful not to over-romanticize the past with the result that we only recollect or think of the finer aspects of an earlier Island life and reject or refuse to recall the more grim aspects of living in Prince Edward Island a century or less ago. Similarly, we must not forget that many Islanders today are not leading a particularly rewarding life ...

"What we must endeavour to do is to identify those advances which have helped in the past and can help in the future to eliminate a number of the debilitating and crushing problems we face and, at the same time, not lead ourselves into the mindless repetitive and de-humanizing aspects of the affluent society.

"Balance, to my mind, is the key word.

"I have considered and advocated for some time that we in Prince Edward Island must carefully examine change so that we are able to weed out those aspects of change which would be detrimental to our way of life, and, at the same time, take advantage of those aspects of change which will enhance and improve our quality of life.

"I firmly believe ... Islanders, given all the facts and an opportunity to study and think about the issues, can collectively achieve that balance and, in the process, build a better society."

Premier Alexander B. Campbell
"Between Two Cultures"
Charlottetown, May 28, 1973

!

CONTENTS

PREFACE

This is a story about what happens when a traditional society that has been stagnant for generations undergoes massive, fundamental change, when old signposts disappear but the way ahead is unmarked. It recounts how a society, clinging to the last vestiges of the old order, discovers its foundations are being eroded and swept away. The 1960s and '70s saw the world transformed; Prince Edward Island, one tiny corner of that world, was not immune to these changes in values, attitudes, beliefs and outlooks sweeping the rest of society.

According to Prince Edward Island historian Dr. Edward MacDonald, that period represented both a coffin and a cradle for the people of the province.

This is also the story about one of the first of a new generation of leaders who came to power in the midst of those changes. Premier Alexander B. Campbell, one of the most successful political leaders the province has ever known, not only presided over them, but rode astride them, spurred them on, and kept them in balance. Setting personal interests aside, he gave purpose and passion to the public interest with courage and conviction. He remains Prince Edward Island's longest-serving premier.

The Alex Campbell years were arguably the most important and productive in the Island's history. No other government in twentieth-century Prince Edward Island has played such a significant part in the daily lives of its people, nor left such a legacy.

Change has never come easily to Prince Edward Islanders. The more they are threatened with it, the more they cling to their habits and conventions. "Anne of Green Gables, never change," could well be their motto and mantra. The magnificence of the Island landscape itself, evoking mystic charm and transcendental magic, lulls those who inhabit it and imbues them with a sense of belonging and security. It also blurs and blunts them to its defects, and blinds them to its scars.

The ineffable "Island way of life" is the manifestation of a traditional society clinging to its identity and its myths during the process of modernization. The manner in which it dealt with change against the background of its traditional way of life illustrates one of the most distinctive characteristics of the province and its people.

But there is more to it than that. The Island is also full of surprises – which explains why so many people find it both frustrating and fascinating.

This is a story about many of the issues and events that marked Prince Edward Island during the Alex Campbell years.

I was privileged to serve on Premier Campbell's staff during part of those years. One could not imagine a better introduction to the world of Island politics and government. I was also fortunate to have the opportunity of working in the Premier's Office with Andy Wells, Campbell's closest political confidant.

That world also included political operatives such as Mike Schurman, Ned Belliveau, Frank Sigsworth, Sid Green, Jack Nicholson and Ben Crow; a host of others who gave colour and content to the Liberal Party, including party organizers Sterling Lane and Bill Morrison; and key policy advisors including Del Gallagher and Hector Hortie.

I want to acknowledge with sincere appreciation the many people who have helped with this book. Campbell himself was generous with his time and insights. Jack MacAndrew, John Eldon Green and Bill Morrison helped fill in some crucial blanks. John Brehaut read the early drafts and made invaluable comments and suggestions. I would like to thank Ed Frenette for his uncompromising critique of Island politics and for helping keep it in perspective.

Many thanks to Marilyn Bell and her staff at the Public Archives and Records Office; Nichola Cleaveland at the Government Services Library; and Simon Lloyd and Leo Cheverie at the Robertson Library of the University of Prince Edward Island. I am deeply indebted to Daphne Davey for her competent, creative and cheerful editing. I have gained a whole new respect and admiration for grammar, syntax - and editors. A very special thank-you is extended to Ken Shelton, designer and publisher at Tea Hill Press, who has so capably endowed this book with style and structure.

None of the aforementioned is responsible in any way for whatever errors, omissions or interpretations remain.

Finally, I want to thank Twilah for her love and support.

Wayne MacKinnon
Savage Harbour

PROLOGUE

It ended as it began, with a bare two-seat majority in the Legislature.

In between, the province was shaken to its very roots. It was a time of bold, dizzying, sweeping, breathtaking, convention-defying, awe-inspiring change, when cherished Island traditions and assumptions were flouted and when cherished mythologies were challenged to their very core. Expectations were heightened by a flurry of new ideas and often controversial new directions. For a time, the Island teetered on the very precipice of revolutionary change. And for a while the world watched, wondering what the outcome might be.

As the province found itself kick-started into the twentieth century, Islanders discussed, debated, deliberated, and not a few decried the sweeping changes to their way of life.

It was both the end of an era and the beginning of an era. The province, tottering through the last vestiges of the old order, was taking the first tentative steps towards a new and uncertain future. All of a sudden, politics mattered for those who dared to dream of brave, new possibilities. People raised ideas and engaged with their government. But the dream was clouded with ambivalence. Islanders, who wanted to gain more control over their lives, at the same time worried about abandoning familiar ways while embracing change. The past fought with the future over the present.

Prince Edward Island in the 1960s and '70s was caught "between two cultures."

The era started with promise, and ended in paradox and paralysis. A combination of anxiety, apathy, ennui, self-doubt, diffidence, guilt, resentment, inertia, evasion, and aversion to change trumped idealism and yearning. One of the most remarkable eras in the province in modern times eventually sputtered to an end, engulfed by fear mixed with longing, the people tempted by the vague promise of a return to simpler, less complicated times.

For a brief moment in the province's history, the shallow, superficial, often corrupt style of Island politics gave way to a new and deeper involvement in public life. Suddenly, politics mattered, government was important, and ideas could be debated. A new spirit of pride and place blossomed, along with a growing confidence in a vision of what the Island might become. Presiding over it all was Prince Edward Island's longest-serving premier, and one of Canada's youngest – Alexander B. Campbell. In that magical time, he inspired in Islanders the belief they that could take control of their own destiny.

Liberal leader Alex Campbell and 1ˢᵗ Kings Liberal candidates Bruce Stewart and Dan MacDonald spared no effort to reach voters during the deferred election campaign in July of 1966. This "life and death" struggle would determine which party would form the next government.

CHAPTER ONE

The Last Hurrah

It was easily the most infamous election in the history of Prince Edward Island politics.

The 1966 provincial general election campaign may not have been the most colourful, corrupt, controversial, or convincing, but it was easily the most cliff-hanging the province had ever experienced. The parties entered what was expected to be a close race – and indeed it was. One of the candidates died during the campaign so the election in that district was deferred; the general election ended with the opposition Liberals ahead by two seats; recounts made it a tie so the deferred election would decide the outcome; the Progressive Conservative government did all it could to hold on to power; the opposition Liberals did all they could to win; and as few as one percent of the votes made the difference.

Here's what happened. The Conservative government of Walter Shaw called the election for May 30, 1966. The standing at dissolution was seventeen to thirteen seats. The Conservatives had been in power since 1959, and were seeking their third term, while the Liberal Party had a new leader, Alex Campbell, first elected to the Legislature in a by-election just over a year earlier. Voters in the province's sixteen dual-member ridings once again turned out for a fierce contest to decide the outcome.

Five days before the election, William Acorn, the assemblyman candidate for the Liberal Party in the dual riding of 1st Kings, died suddenly, so the election of the two members in that district had to be deferred. After the votes were counted on May 30, the Liberals were declared the winners with sixteen seats against fourteen for the Conservatives. Recounts were held in four districts. In 4th Prince, the election of Max Thompson, the Liberal candidate, was confirmed. After the recount in 2nd Queens, the Liberal councillor candidate, Horace Willis, who was ahead by two votes on election day, finally lost by three votes to Conservative Lloyd MacPhail. In 5th Kings two recounts were held. On election day, both Liberal incumbents, George Ferguson and Arthur MacDonald, were declared elected. Following recounts, Ferguson's election was confirmed with a majority of five votes, while MacDonald lost to Dr. Cyril Sinnott, the Conservative assemblyman candidate, by the slimmest possible margin of just one vote, earning him the sobriquet "Landslide Sinnott" and confirming what Islanders knew all along – that every vote does count.

The 1966 election proved that.

After the dust from the recounts had settled, the province found itself facing a tie, with fifteen Conservatives and fifteen Liberals, and one district yet to vote. Both parties had won seats by the narrowest of majorities. For example, in the traditionally Liberal Belfast district of 4th Queens, the venerable J. Stewart Ross held on to his seat for the Liberals by a mere 25 votes, while his running mate, Harold Smith, narrowly won with 39 votes. In 3rd Queens, after a number of unsuccessful attempts as a candidate at both federal and provincial levels, Liberal Cecil Miller was finally swept to power with a 43-vote majority. Even Premier Shaw came close to defeat, winning by only 83 votes over upstart Liberal candidate Lorne Moase.

All told, a shift of a mere three votes in two districts on May 30 would have given the Liberals seventeen seats to the Conservatives' thirteen. On the other hand, a difference of three votes in one district would leave the Conservatives hanging on to power with two seats over the Liberals. On June 1, Premier Shaw declared that if the results of the recounts and the deferred election were not conclusive, he might call a new election.

The results were not unusual in a province where a shift in a few votes here and there tended to change the outcome of elections. In 1943, for example, the Liberals won twenty seats to the Conservatives' ten; a shift of 100 votes would have given the opposite result. Between 1893 and 1963, one out of every ten candidates was elected with a margin of 25 votes or less, and more than a third held office with a majority of less than 100 votes. The Liberals also led in the popular vote. In that same period, the provincial Liberals captured a total of 51.4 percent of the popular vote, with 47.75 percent going to the Conservatives. Other parties, never a factor to that point, accounted for the balance of less than one percent. Majorities had usually been close, although in 1935 the provincial Liberals made history by becoming the first political party in the British Commonwealth to win every seat in a general election.

The fate of the Conservative government would now be decided on July 11 in the 1st Kings by-election. All eyes turned to that district. For the next six weeks, no effort was spared and no stone left unturned to get every single able-minded, warm-blooded, living, breathing, sentient, eligible voter from East Point to Dingwells Mills out to the polls on election day. If for some reason, the district split its vote, electing one member from each party to the two seats, the province would be deadlocked, sixteen to sixteen. And that had never happened before.

The Liberals nominated Bruce Stewart, the popular former mayor of Souris, to replace the late William Acorn to join the incumbent, Daniel J. MacDonald, on the Liberal ticket. Stewart now faced a formidable challenge. Immediately after the May 30 vote, his opponent, Keith MacKenzie, had been appointed the newly minted minister of highways in Shaw's cabinet, although he did not have a seat in the Legislature. (The previous minister, Phillip Matheson, was defeated on May 30 and resigned.) On the other side of the ticket, Dan MacDonald, a distinguished war veteran and farmer who had held the seat for the Liberals since the previous election, was facing another respected local farmer, Peter MacAulay. Stewart and MacDonald, together with Campbell, campaigned door-to-door throughout the district.

The 1st Kings by-election, depicted as a "life and death struggle," was described by Hartwell Daley of the *Journal-Pioneer* as the most costly election per capita in the entire history of Canada. A sign at the entrance to the district blared, "Welcome to the promised land." Both parties competed aggressively for the minuscule percentage of undecided voters, calculated by one political observer at four percent. The price per vote – the best that money could buy – reached staggering proportions Even kitchen sinks were provided, no small treat in a district where less than half the households enjoyed the luxury of running water.

MacKenzie's appointment in the high-profile and politically attractive highways portfolio led to a flurry of road construction projects throughout the district. An estimated thirty miles of pavement was laid in less than six weeks, prompting repeated telling of the following story:

"Did you hear about the accident near Souris?"

"No, what happened?"

"Two road machines met in the same driveway."

In self-defence against the spate of paving taking place, one farmer erected a sign, "Please don't pave, this is my only pasture." It was said, so much road construction equipment had been moved to 1st Kings that the district was in danger of sinking under the weight.

And if the district did not succumb to the weight of road machinery, it would be floated away by liquor.

Liquor, money, and kitchen sinks were not the only inducements. Throughout the general election campaign, pensions had become a major issue, and during the by-election, the government's unofficial motto was said to be "If it moves, give it a pension; if it doesn't move, pave it." In fact, one of the Conservative commitments during the general election campaign was an increase in old-age pensions from $75 to $100 a month. (The Liberals made a similar commitment, which differed only in the details.) Although the pension increase was not scheduled to take effect until June 30, the Conservative government made the increases retroactive to April 1. Before the by-election campaign had ended, every eligible pensioner in 1st Kings received a cheque for the retroactive amount of $75.

People placed unrelenting demands on all candidates. Typical was the letter received by the Liberal candidates, pledging a vote in exchange for a job. One voter wrote to say he "controlled" 14 votes, which were available to the highest bidder. A woman wrote to Campbell asking him to pay transportation for her son to return home from Alberta – and, by the way, could Campbell further help by finding the son a job?

During the by-election, both Liberals and Conservatives continued to highlight the commitments they made during the general election campaign just ended. The Conservatives emphasized their record of largesse to the district over the previous seven years, and made a number of additional promises: they would establish a new crab- and shellfish-processing plant; a new vocational school; an all-weather highway to Elmira; ten new steel draggers to serve the existing fish plant in Souris; and a new national park for eastern Kings.

For their part, the Liberals reconfirmed their promised old-age pension program, pointing out the difference between theirs and the one being offered by the Conservatives. ("The Liberal $100 pension is not an election month payment. It is for every month!"). They also promised to reduce the down-payments on fishing boats from fifty to twenty-five percent and, playing on regional jealousies, they declared that Souris had been ignored while the Conservative government poured millions of dollars into the redevelopment of Georgetown.

Without the power of patronage at their disposal, the Liberals had to pull out all the guns in their limited arsenal. Campbell moved to the district, where he remained throughout the campaign, staying at Bruce Stewart's cottage in Red Point.

The Liberals grabbed every promotional opportunity they could. When a favourable mention about Campbell was made in the *Globe and Mail*, it was promptly copied and sent to every household in the district. Although not yet eligible to vote, every graduate from Souris Regional High School that year received a personal note of congratulations from the candidates and from Campbell. In all, some ten general mailings were sent out.

Party workers from across the province were pressed into service. Both Liberals and Conservatives made exceptional efforts to identify voters, real and potential. One list contained some 2,472 names, broken down by occupation, including 341 farmers and five barbers. Those requiring transportation to the polls were identified and assigned drivers. One enterprising driver, assigned to pick up a voter, parked in his driveway before sun-up to ensure his "vote" made it to the polls. Residents working outside the district who were eligible to vote were also identified and contacted, including patients in the Provincial Sanatorium. The Liberals ensured that on election day a lawyer was stationed at every poll to challenge voters suspected of being ineligible. In the end, so much help was mobilized that one of the biggest challenges facing campaign manager John Mullally was finding enough work for everyone to do.

Advertising by both parties was extensive – and expensive. It was calculated that the Liberals and Conservatives spent as much or more on advertising during the by-election as they had during the general election campaign itself.

Most observers suggested that the campaign was too close to call, with both parties scrambling to gain the advantage. One day, Campbell was in Souris getting his hair cut in the barber shop on Main Street when, as he described it, "the parade of government machinery went by." He realized the Liberals had to do something dramatic and substantive to counter the overwhelming weight of government patronage. He decided to play their federal card.*

Since having friends in Ottawa was always regarded as vital in a

---

* *Traditionally, the Liberals were the dominant party in Prince Edward Island, due in no small part to the hegemony enjoyed by their federal counterparts, dubbed the "natural governing party." Inspired by the belief that it was best to elect a provincial government of the same political stripe as the one in Ottawa to ensure more favourable treatment,*

province where two-thirds of its budget and much of its largesse came from the federal government, the provincial Liberals were anxious to demonstrate close ties with the federal Liberal government of Lester Pearson. Enlisting the tacit endorsement of the federal Liberals was now critical. In fact, federal politics was already playing a role in the by-election campaign. Mel MacQuaid, the Conservative MP for Kings County and a resident of Souris, was actively campaigning for his provincial party.

As the campaign entered its final week, the Liberals recognized they needed to gain an edge in what was likely to result in a dead heat. Demonstrating the benefits of close ties to Ottawa just might give them that advantage.

A Senate vacancy in Prince Edward Island was opened up in 1966, and local Liberals were pressing for the appointment of Tom Kickham, a resident of Souris West and a former Liberal MP for Kings County. Kickham was personally popular. He had been instrumental in securing much-needed markets for local fish and agricultural products in Newfoundland during the Depression so it was believed his appointment would be well received by the people in 1st Kings. Meanwhile, the Conservatives passed on rumours that the vacancy would be filled by Charlottetown resident Eugene Cullen, a former Liberal MLA and minister of agriculture in the Alex Matheson government. "Kings County will have to wait until the cows come home before it gets representation in the Senate from the federal Liberals," taunted the Conservative campaign literature.

To expedite matters, Campbell called Prime Minister Pearson urging Kickham's appointment, but there was little interest from the Prime Minister's Office. Other calls were made by John Mullally, himself a former Kings County MP, who lobbied hard among his contacts in Ottawa. Even Premier Louis Robichaud of New Brunswick lobbied on behalf of his counterparts in Prince Edward Island. Finally, with little sign of federal willingness to make the crucial appointment, Campbell dispatched Sid Green, the Liberal

Islanders typically cast their votes for provincial parties they deemed would be most acceptable to the federal government. Prince Edward Island, more than any other single Canadian province, boasted a record of "keeping governments in line" with Ottawa. Following on the electoral successes of the federal Liberal Party, the provincial Liberals had won eleven of the seventeen general elections between 1900 and 1962.

Party's fundraiser, to plead the case in Ottawa. Green was bluntly informed that Pearson was personally opposed to appointing Kickham. Several years earlier, Kickham (then MP for Kings County) joined a Canadian delegation to the United Nations in New York. Much to Pearson's embarrassment, Kickham was drunk for most of the time, and he did not forget the incident.

Eventually, however, the federal Liberals relented and came to the aid of their desperate provincial brethren. On July 8, three days before the by-election, Pearson announced that Kickham had been appointed to the Senate.

The next evening at the Liberal windup rally, before a boisterous crowd, the new senator joined a buoyant Campbell and the two Liberal candidates on stage, pledging federal co-operation and friendship with a new provincial Liberal government.

Monday, July 11, dawned warm and sunny. Before the day was over, Prince Edward Islanders would find out which party the voters of 1st Kings had elected to form the next government.

*   *   *

The 1966 provincial election was the first ever held under a formal set of rules. The new Election Act made history by introducing, for the first time, an official voters list, enumerators, revising and returning officers, and a chief electoral officer. Until 1966, provincial general elections on Prince Edward Island operated according to an informal and intricate set of rules, conventions, practices, and gentlemen's agreements. This electoral system was probably unique in Canada. Psephologists – those engaged in the arcane art of studying trends in elections and voting – would be hard pressed to provide rational explanations of its complexities, nuances, patterns, and proclivities. The electoral system had evolved in response to several distinctive characteristics of the province and its people – its rural backbone, religious cleavages, and intense partisanship. Despite the system's many flaws and anomalies, however, the privilege of voting was highly valued by the electorate; indeed, Prince Edward Island continues to enjoy the highest voting turnout rate in Canada.

The Island's electoral system, as it stood until 1966, traced its roots back to 1893 when the two original legislative entities were combined into a single legislative assembly. The Legislative Council and Legislative Assembly were both established in 1773, four years after the Island became a separate British colony, and enjoyed a lively and checkered past. The Legislative Council was a thirteen-member house elected by property owners; the Legislative Assembly, a thirty-member house with two representatives from each of fifteen electoral districts, was elected by all eligible males over the age of twenty-one.

The property vote was a hold-over from the days when it was believed that men who owned property had a greater stake in public affairs than those who did not. The Legislative Council was intended to serve as a check on the democratic impulses of the Legislative Assembly, or lower house. The property vote also reflected the Island's stormy past with the Land Question, when in the nineteenth century absentee proprietors owned the bulk of the Island and leased land to tenants who chafed under the often oppressive terms. Once the tenants had gained ownership of the land, however, they were quick to demand and exercise the same prerogatives associated with property ownership that their former landlords had enjoyed.

By the 1890s, in common with other jurisdictions across Canada, a move was afoot in Prince Edward Island to abolish the upper house, the Legislative Council, and establish a unicameral legislature. In 1893, both houses were finally amalgamated. The new legislature retained the fifteen dual-member ridings of the old assembly, with equal representation from the three counties. However, property owners, jealous to guard their privileges, demanded to maintain the property vote. As a result, one half of the thirty members of the new house – councillors – would be elected by those who owned property valued at a minimum of $325, and the other half – assemblymen – would be elected by property owners plus all other eligible males over the age of twenty-one.

Over the years, the property vote was gradually extended. Eventually, property owners could cast a vote in each district where they held property. It was theoretically possible for someone with extensive holdings to vote for councillors and assemblymen as many as thirty times in the fifteen dual-member ridings. Later, when women received the franchise, both husbands and wives could vote on property held jointly or in each other's name.

"Property" was loosely defined. In addition to the usual land and buildings, it could include recreational properties, gravel pits, blueberry bogs, fishing shacks, duck blinds – anything sworn to have a value of at least $325. One enterprising voter even attempted to cast ballots on the basis of a plot of land in the Floral Hills Memorial Gardens – a cemetery! The property vote was a great nuisance. Without a voters list, it was difficult to identify eligible voters, so abuses were widespread. Those who enjoyed the multiple vote were encouraged to vote early and often.

Other aspects of the electoral system were slow to evolve. The secret ballot was not introduced until 1913, reflecting the belief that no one should be ashamed of how he voted (even after the written ballot was introduced, voting behaviour remained an "open secret"). Then, after a long struggle, Prince Edward Island finally enfranchised its women in 1922, the second-last province in Canada to do so.

Finally, in 1966 a voters list was established along with other reforms. Prior to that date, enumeration was regarded as superfluous and extravagant in a poll where everyone knew everyone else.

There was little interest in changing the system. The 1950 throne speech under the Walter Jones government outlined plans to establish thirty single-member ridings, but the proposal was quickly buried under a barrage of dissent from government members. In 1959, the Liberal campaign platform hinted at abolishing the property vote and eliminating multiple voting, but the idea soon died.* As parties concentrated on "getting out the vote," the principle of voter parity was drowned under the practice of multiple voting. Prince Edward Island enjoyed its own brand of representative democracy.

However, in 1962, the Royal Commission on Electoral Reform, established in 1961 by the Shaw government and chaired by Judge J.S. DesRoches of the Kings County court, presented a number of important recommendations to modernize the electoral system. These included abolishing the property vote; establishing a voters list; appointing electoral officials; extending the franchise to aboriginals; and redistributing the seats to reflect shifts in the population since 1893. The abolition of the property vote would effectively end whatever distinction remained between councillors and assemblymen. But by now the distinction had come to serve another crucial function for political parties – that of accommodating religious

---

* There was a further attempt at electoral reform in 1974. A subcommittee of the Legislature recommended redistribution and the establishment of single-member ridings, but its recommendations were flatly rejected. The present system of twenty-seven single-member ridings, along with a major redrawing of district boundaries, came into place in 1996 after the Prince Edward Island Supreme Court ruled that the Election Act was unconstitutional because it failed to recognize the principle of voter parity as set out in the Charter of Rights and Freedoms.

differences. With councillors and assemblymen on separate ballots, parties could balance their slate of candidates along religious lines so that candidates of different faiths would not have to run against each another. And there was a further cogent reason for maintaining councillors and assemblymen on separate ballots. If the distinction between them were removed, members of the same political party would find themselves running on the same ticket, in effect competing against each other as well as their political opponents.

Representatives of both political parties recognized the pitfalls of a free-for-all if every candidate ran on the same ballot. In the 1953 federal election, when Queens County was still a dual-member riding, voters split their preferences between the candidates of the two parties. Liberal Neil Matheson and Conservative Angus MacLean topped the results. The other Conservative candidate, W. Chester S. MacLure, blamed his loss on MacLean, claiming that MacLean had not displayed sufficient solidarity on the ticket. Bitter to the end, he left instructions that MacLean was not to attend his funeral.

Faced with the religious and partisan implications of ending the distinction between councillors and assemblymen, both parties scrambled to find an acceptable alternative. Recognizing the potential pitfalls if DesRoches's recommendation was accepted, Opposition Leader Alex Matheson and Provincial Secretary David Stewart jointly developed a compromise: two ballots would remain, one for councillor and one for assemblyman, enabling parties to continue to accommodate religious differences and avoid the spectre of candidates of the same political party running on the same ballot. In effect, the political distinctions between councillors and assemblymen were removed and they would continue to enjoy the same powers and political status. However, retaining the two designation, would allow political parties to continue reflecting the underlying divisions among the electorate, and candidates for the same party could continue to work together to defeat their opponents.

The other major recommendation put forward by DesRoches concerned redistribution, which would prove to be more controversial. Major population shifts had occurred in the province between the 1890s and the 1960s, and both Charlottetown and Summerside sought increased representation. In a brief to the Royal Commission, representatives from the City of Charlottetown requested ten seats (a significant increase from the two it already had) while Summerside wanted its number doubled to four.

When the Election Act came before the house for debate, Alban

Farmer, Charlottetown MLA and Provincial Treasurer in the Shaw government, introduced an amendment creating an additional dual-member riding in Charlottetown. If the legislature were to remain a thirty-member house, that would mean the loss of a district elsewhere. Since Kings County had suffered the greatest loss of population, the decision was made to reduce its districts from five to four. The district of 5th Kings, which stretched around the coastline across several peninsulas in the southeast part of the county, and which included the town of Georgetown, was slated for elimination. The amendment passed. The district of 6th Queens was added, and 5th Kings ceased to exist. An immediate protest arose, not only from the voters of 5th Kings, who felt they had lost the right to representation, but from the entire population of Kings County. The age-old principle of county parity had been violated. Protests would continue long after the passage of the new Election Act.

As it happened, at this time the Shaw government was heavily committed to the development of new industries in Georgetown: a modern, integrated fish-processing facility, and a new shipyard. The developments – the centrepiece of the Shaw government's industrial development initiatives – promised to transform the economy in the Georgetown area. Then, just before the 1966 election, the Shaw government introduced an amendment to the Election Act, restoring the 5th Kings district, and raising the total number of MLAs to thirty-two. In the subsequent election, the close results in 5th Kings were interpreted as either reward or punishment for the government's tampering with the district.

The modernization of the electoral system represented a tangible and significant shift away from the shallow, often corrupt, old style of politics. The loose set of conventions and practices that had characterized the relationship between the people and their government in the past was now being codified and formalized. The political landscape was changing faster than the politicians who inhabited it. The province was breaking from the past and by the 1960s that change was finally catching up to the Island.

*   *   *

Change had always come slowly to Prince Edward Island. Often it was gradual and could be accommodated within the easy rhythms of life in the province. However, during the 1950s and '60s, as the rest of the country experienced the post-war boom, many Islanders feared they were falling further and further behind. While earlier governments had reacted to change, now they became more active; progress and development were the new watch words. In the process, the Island's mythical sense of place and identity lost its moorings.

Changes in the electoral system actually symbolized overall changes in the political and economic landscape. There was steady growth in government, and jobs in the service sector were beginning to replace those on land and sea. Some parts of the Island were becoming urbanized; for example, the villages of Sherwood and Parkdale now boasted populations of over 3,100 people, and in Summerside, the Hillcrest housing development had breathed new life into the town. On the other hand, rural areas were benefitting from paved roads and electrification, and young people were climbing on buses to attend new, local high schools.

Another sign of modernization manifested itself during the 1966 spring session of the Legislature. In what must have been a daring political move just prior to the calling of the election, the Shaw government finally ended the ban on the sale of margarine in the province (margarine had been banned decades earlier to protect the dairy industry). This was a sure indication that political power was slowly shifting from rural to urban Prince Edward Island.*

By the 1960s, the last vestiges of the old order were being eroded. Horses and buggies were giving way to televisions and cars; thanks to revolutionary changes in communications and transportation, the province no longer suffered from enforced insularity; technological advances were impacting its economic and social structures; and, as the province struggled to adapt to post-war realities, its political landscape was undergoing transformation.

Like many other predominantly rural areas, the Island's innate

---

* *Six years earlier, the Shaw government had risked the wrath of farmers when it introduced a highly controversial measure to implement daylight saving time. The scheme divided rural and urban Islanders, and was bitterly resented by farmers. (It also divided families. Dr. George Dewar was a member of the government that introduced the controversial change. His brother Lincoln was the secretary-manager of the Federation of Agriculture, which attacked the move.) Incidentally, margarine and daylight saving time were not the only undesirable intrusions on the status quo. Automobiles and alcohol had also been banned in peaceable Prince Edward Island.*

conservatism blunted the massive political, social and aesthetic changes sweeping across North America. But the post-war generation was coming of age, casting aside its moorings to authority and responsibility, and rejecting the values and institutions of the past. While the 1960s promised affluence, technological advances, liberation and idealism, they also brought about massive unrest, rebellion, and a counter-cultural movement. South of the border, the 1960s spawned the civil rights and anti-war movements, free love, and flower power – and young people everywhere joined in.

It was, paradoxically, an age of both hopefulness and helplessness. The world could put a man on the moon but it could not solve the problems it faced at home.

*   *   *

In many ways, Premier Walter Shaw embodied a rural culture that had changed little in decades. He was born in West River in 1887 on a farm originally settled by his great-grandfather in 1806, and inherited values and outlooks deeply rooted in the culture of traditional Island society. Yet, in other respects, he was a study in contradictions.

For almost twenty years, Walter Shaw had served as deputy minister of agriculture under successive Liberal governments and acquired the perspective of the rational civil servant. Although branded a Conservative, he got along well with all sides and even confided once that Liberal Premier Walter Jones had tried to recruit him as his successor while both were attending an agricultural fair in Halifax. He was well respected by the farming community, and following his retirement from the civil service continued his interest in public affairs. Although not previously politically active, he decided to run in the 1955 provincial election as a Conservative candidate in 3rd Kings, but was handily defeated.

However, when Reginald Bell finally retired as leader of the provincial Conservatives, Shaw entered the leadership campaign. He narrowly defeated Dr. George Dewar, one of the three sitting Conservative MLAs, by a slim margin – 524 to 522 votes.*

---

* *Dr. Dewar initially said he did not want to run, and had tried to recruit Dr. Frank MacKinnon, principal of Prince of Wales College and son of former Conservative MLA and lieutenant-governor, Murdock MacKinnon, to contest the leadership.*

Upon his election as leader, Shaw inherited a party stuck in the political wilderness since 1935, one that was largely bankrupt, financially and philosophically. Thus, he began the slow, arduous task of rebuilding the provincial Progressive Conservative party.

But the defeat of the federal Liberals in 1957 after twenty-two years in office, and the ascendency of the Prairie populist, John Diefenbaker, dramatically changed the prospects of the Island's Conservatives. Riding on the coat-tails of now Prime Minister Diefenbaker, Shaw led the rejuvenated provincial Conservatives to power in 1959, ending twenty-four years of provincial Liberal rule. In a province with a tradition of keeping government in line with Ottawa, the election of the Diefenbaker government now worked to the provincial Conservatives' advantage. Shaw invited Islanders to join him in clasping the "friendly, outstretched hand of John Diefenbaker."

Despite his advancing years, Shaw led an energetic government. Under his leadership, the government improved programs to primary industries; embarked on a program of school consolidation and upgrading; continued rural electrification and road-paving; pioneered the establishment of senior citizens' homes; and expanded the province's efforts to attract new industry. Shaw also made the Conservative Party the "Party of the Causeway." He had extracted a promise from Diefenbaker just prior to the 1962 federal election to finally announce construction of the long-awaited, much-promised project to connect Prince Edward Island to the mainland.

Shaw, the former civil servant, also introduced a note of rationality to the provincial government's creaking administrative structure. He introduced the first effective civil service act, which incorporated revolutionary (to Prince Edward Island) concepts such as the merit principle and security of tenure. Although Liberal critics decried the move as a blatant effort to protect recent Conservative appointees, the new act was generally well accepted by Islanders, who recognized the need for a better trained and more professional public service. Shaw also commissioned a comprehensive analysis of the province's social and economic conditions. The massive $340,000 study, carried out by the leading Canadian consulting firm Acres International Limited provided a wealth of data that was later used in the formulation of the province's Comprehensive Development Plan under Campbell's Liberal government.

Shaw was a highly popular premier. Given to soaring feats of oratory, peppered with Biblical allusions and barnyard metaphors, he resonated with rural Islanders. His progressive reforms also appealed to those who were interested in seeing the Island develop and modernize, but during his time in office, the fissures in Island society became more evident as the chasms between the old and new widened.

During the summer of 1962, however, Shaw's political future was in doubt. He had been hospitalized in August, but in October, following his recuperation, he declared he would continue until after the next election.

The Shaw government was re-elected on December 10, 1962, timing the election to occur just before the federal debacle which toppled Diefenbaker from power in early 1963. In addition to continuing the initiatives from its first term, the new provincial government embarked on an ambitious, multi-million-dollar program of industrial development in Georgetown. But by 1966, serious questions were being raised about the project.

By then, the provincial Liberals had elected Alex Campbell as their new leader, and the party was quickly rebuilding. The renascent Liberal Party, and the whiff of scandal emanating from Georgetown, prompted Shaw to call a snap election for May 30, 1966. The Legislature was dissolved on April 16, and that evening Shaw went on CFCY Television to announce the election, accusing the Liberals of vicious propaganda that threatened to undermine the government's progress.

For Campbell, who had been a member of the Legislature for just over a year and Liberal leader for less than six months, facing the venerable Shaw would be his first real test in politics.

PARO

Marilyn and Alex Campbell cast their ballots in the 1966 provincial general election.

CHAPTER TWO

"Let's Go For Action Now"
- Liberal campaign slogan, 1966

The 1966 provincial election was a study in contrasts. At the age of seventy-eight, Premier Walter Shaw was the oldest political leader in Canada. At thirty-two, Opposition Leader Alex Campbell was the youngest. Shaw was loquacious and folksy, given to soaring feats of oratory; Campbell was articulate and urbane, more rational than rhetorical. Shaw had a remarkable memory for names and faces, a fund of anecdotes, and a never-ending litany of nostrums; Campbell was emboldened by new ideas and possibilities, for whom politics was the art of the possible. Where Shaw was nostalgic, Campbell was unsentimental. Where Shaw exemplified the past, Campbell personified the future.

The contrast was not lost on Campbell, who kept referring to the Shaw government as "the horse and buggy boys." Campbell represented a new generation of Islanders unwilling to be captives of the past. Politically, he was a pioneer, among the first of his generation to set out in uncharted waters.

These personality differences were also augmented by an important contrast in style. A new generation was also coming of age, exuding youth, fitness and fun, far from the old, doddery and dour characteristics of the older generation of politicians. While young Islanders would continue to respect the old, they were ready to take charge of their own future.

In the light of such contrasting leadership styles, the 1966 election was a watershed in Prince Edward Island politics.

* * *

Alex Campbell was born into politics. His father, Thane, a former Rhodes scholar, led the province as premier from 1936 to 1943, in which year he was appointed Chief Justice of the Prince Edward Island Supreme Court. Twenty-three years later, he presided over the ceremony to swear in his son as premier.

The Campbell family was among the earliest settlers in Prince Edward Island. James Campbell arrived from Perthshire, Scotland, via London in 1775.* He came over on the ill-fated ship *Elizabeth*, which was wrecked off the north shore near Malpeque at the end of its voyage. He had come to look after the business affairs of Robert Clark, a merchant in the struggling new community that proudly called itself New London. Campbell was one of the few people in the new colony who knew how to read and write.

Alex Campbell's grandfather, Alexander ("Sandy") Campbell, along with William Callbeck, was one of the founders of a company set up during the 1880s to provide insurance for farm buildings in what became known as the Prince Edward Island Mutual Insurance Company. He served as secretary-manager until 1931. Following his death, Thane Campbell took over the job, which became one of his main sources of income while he was premier. Alex Campbell's family on his mother's side, the Bradshaws, were pre-Loyalists from New York who settled in the Bay of Fundy. Eventually, one member of the family make his way to Prince Edward Island.

Thane Campbell's rise to the premiership was remarkable. In 1935, when Liberal leader Walter Lea was too ill to take part in the provincial election campaign, he summoned Campbell to his home in Victoria and asked him to take over as leader during the campaign. Thane led the party to an historic victory in the Depression-ridden province, winning all thirty seats in the legislature, and devastating the Conservative government of Dr. W.J.P. MacMillan, who suffered personal defeat at the hands of his son-in-law, C. St. Clair Trainor. When Lea died in early 1936, Thane Campbell succeeded him as premier. After two busy terms in office, highlighted by the establishment of the first national park in Prince Edward Island and efforts to counter the effects of the Depression, he resigned in 1943 to accept the appointment of Chief Justice of the Supreme Court of Prince Edward Island.

The Campbell family lived in Summerside, where Alex attended school. Following graduation, he attended Mount Allison and Dalhousie University in Halifax, graduating with a Bachelor of Arts and a law degree. During those years, Campbell took little interest in politics. He busied himself with both his studies and campus life, but although he joined the debating society, by his own admission he failed miserably at it!

---

* *Today, a cairn at Cousins Shore commemorates the arrival of the Campbells to Prince Edward Island.*

One of his roommates, a fellow fraternity member and law student at Dalhousie, hailed from Hartland, New Brunswick – Richard Hatfield, but the two future premiers rarely discussed politics.

In 1959, Campbell returned to Summerside to set up a law practice. He articled with Richard Hinton and, following his admission to the bar in 1959, opened an office on Central Street. The first day he welcomed what he thought might be three prospective clients. Two turned out to be insurance salesmen; the third was a Liberal poll worker inviting him to contest the Liberal nomination in 2nd Prince in the upcoming provincial election. He respectfully declined the offer. Instead, he threw himself into community activities, joining the Board of Trade and other local organizations. In 1960, he married Marilyn Gilmour, whose father served with the air force at the military base in Summerside, and settled down to life as a small-town lawyer. But he was soon recruited by the Liberal Party.

In 1959, new lawyer Alex Campbell was admitted to the Prince Edward Island bar by his father, Chief Justice Thane Campbell. In 1966, the younger Campbell was sworn in as premier by his father, also a former premier.

Campbell's first foray into active politics came in the 1959 provincial election when he served as campaign chairman for the Liberal candidates in 5th Prince, Morley Bell and Edward Foley (both of whom lost). In 1962, he once again chaired the district campaign, this time for Bell and Leonce Arsenault (who replaced Foley), again losing both seats to the incumbent Conservatives. The late 1950s and early '60s were desolate years for the provincial Liberals. Having been in power since 1935, they were not used to sitting in opposition. The party suffered from low morale, it was broke, and having difficulty attracting candidates and campaign volunteers. Thus, young, capable and aggressive Liberals like Campbell played key roles in an otherwise moribund political organization.

The party also faced formidable challenges in federal politics. In 1957, Diefenbaker ended twenty-two years of consecutive federal Liberal governments; at the same time, the once-safe Liberal seat in Prince County fell to the Conservatives. Prince County had been a Liberal seat for most of the twentieth century, boasting some illustrious representatives. In 1919, MacKenzie King was elected there by acclamation following his ascendency to the national Liberal leadership. Then, Alfred MacLean served the riding continuously throughout the 1920s and '30s until his death. In the subsequent by-election to fill the vacancy, the Honourable James Ralston, a member of MacKenzie King's wartime cabinet, was elected by acclamation (bringing air bases to Summerside and Mount Pleasant with him). Following the war, Summerside lawyer J. Watson MacNaught succeeded Ralston, serving from 1945 to 1957 when he was defeated by dentist Dr. Orville Phillips, also from Summerside.

In 1962, however, Campbell's services were called upon in the federal election in Prince County where he chaired the campaign for the Liberal candidate, George MacKay, who was defeated by Phillips. However, two events took place the next year that would have a profound effect on the shape of politics in the years to come. The first was the appointment of Orville Phillips to the Senate.* With Phillips ensconced in the Senate, Lorne Monkley resigned as the Conservative MLA for 5th Prince in order to replace Phillips as the

---

* *Legend has it that the appointment was meant for Nathan Phillips, the mayor of Toronto, but a mix-up in the Privy Council Office over Diefenbaker's choice led to the appointment of Orville Phillips, the early-fortyish MP from Prince Edward Island, instead. The story may not be true, but Liberals took great delight in repeating it.*

federal Conservative candidate. The second event was the unceremonious fall of the Diefenbaker government, riddled by internal strife and constant bickering. A federal election was scheduled for April 8, 1963.

At that time, the federal Liberal Party held its national convention in Ottawa. Andrew Wells, a young Prince Edward Island Liberal attending the convention, had grown up in Ottawa in a political family with close ties to the Island. His father, James, had campaigned for Thane Campbell, and later worked in Ottawa with both James Ralston and Watson MacNaught. In 1959, Andy moved back to the family farm in Cascumpec.

There had been a great deal of discussion at the convention about attracting new blood to the national Liberal Party. At the party's ground-breaking Kingston Conference, when a bold new agenda was hammered out and adopted, its leaders recognized that they needed people to help revitalize it for the coming election. At the 1963 national convention, a group of Island delegates convened in provincial Liberal leader Alex Matheson's hotel room in Ottawa to discuss prospective candidates; the name of Alex Campbell came up. After they reached Campbell by telephone, Andy Wells left the convention early to determine what support a Campbell candidacy might garner. He picked Campbell up in Summerside, and together they drove to Alberton to contact local Liberals. It was a cold, windy, wintry day, and Campbell and Wells had to walk a mile and a half across the snow-covered fields to reach Wells's home in Cascumpec.

The next day, Campbell met with local Liberals to gauge potential support in the western part of the district. With relatively strong support already assured in the Summerside area, Campbell announced his decision to seek the nomination for the Liberal party in Prince County in the forthcoming federal general election. He was not the only one. As it turned out, a total of seven candidates emerged, including MacNaught and another Summerside lawyer, Bruce MacDonald. The nominating convention was one of the largest ever held in Prince County's history. The speeches seemed to last forever; the voting went on all evening; the respective balloting dragged out; and as candidates dropped off, their tired and dispirited supporters went home. At the end, only two names remained on the ballot: Campbell, the twenty-nine-year-old political novice, and MacNaught, the old Liberal warhorse. After the votes were counted, MacNaught received 212 votes, topping Campbell's 211 by just one vote.

MacNaught recaptured Prince County for the Liberal Party and was appointed Solicitor General for Canada by Lester Pearson, the new prime minister. Campbell went back to his law office in Summerside. But it was not long before public life beckoned once more.

* * *

The resignation of Lorne Monkley to run federally had created a vacancy in the provincial district of 5th Prince, and before long Campbell was approached to contest the by-election. But with a young family, Campbell was not anxious to re-enter the political arena. He was also concentrating on building up his law practice and had put any potential political aspirations on long-term hold.

Meanwhile, he received numerous approaches from people in the district, along with advances from Alex Matheson and several other prominent Liberals from across the province. Campbell, who until then had not professed a great interest in politics, admitted to being surprised by the support for his candidacy, and finally agreed to contest the seat.

The by-election, one of two taking place in the province, was held February 9, 1965. The other was held in 1st Kings, where the Liberal candidate, William Acorn, sought to replace Conservative MLA J.R. McLean, who had died. The provincial Liberals fought both by-elections vigorously with the hope of improving their standing in the Legislature. The 5th Prince by-election was a close race. Campbell lost in most of the Summerside polls but won in the outlying rural areas, finishing with a 73-vote margin over the Conservative candidate, Claude Ives.

Campbell joined a somewhat reinvigorated Liberal caucus for the 1965 session of the Legislature. In addition to the win in 5th Prince, the Liberals had also captured 1st Kings from the Conservatives with the election of William Acorn by just sixteen votes. The standings in the house now stood at seventeen to thirteen, and the Liberals, buoyed as well by the success of their federal counterparts who had been returned to power in Ottawa, were looking forward to the next election.

Then, in the midst of the session, Opposition Leader Alex Matheson announced his resignation. The announcement came with no warning. Matheson had been absent from the Legislature for several days on out-of-province business. As a veteran politician, he had had enough of public life and, unbeknownst to his colleagues, had entered negotiations to take over the management of the local

Premier Alex Matheson addresses a meeting of the four Atlantic provincial premiers in Halifax, May 1957.

branch of a trust company in preparation for retirement from politics. On the evening of his return to the province, he attended a meeting of the student Liberal Club at St. Dunstan's University and surprised the unsuspecting members with the announcement that this was to be his last official duty as Liberal leader.

There was a mixed reaction from the Liberal caucus. Some were shocked by the unexpected announcement, and others dismayed that Matheson had not informed his caucus first. Yet others welcomed the announcement. Matheson's leadership had actually been under question for some time. Several years earlier, in an attempt to quell dissent, he had called for a party review of his leadership. It was the first time that individual members of the Liberal Party had voted for a leader in open convention; previously, the decision had been made by caucus. In September 1961, Matheson's leadership was contested in a bitter convention fight at the Kennedy Coliseum in Charlottetown. Although he easily defeated his closest rival, Watson MacNaught, by a vote of 751 to 278 (a third candidate, Dr. W.E. Callaghan, garnered a mere 25 votes), the debate over the leadership left a lingering bad taste in the mouths of many Liberals.

While Matheson was out of province, Dr. M. Lorne Bonnell, his running mate in 4th Kings, took over as acting leader of the Opposition. When Matheson returned to the Legislature the day following his announcement at St. Dunstan's, he declared that he was prepared to resume his duties until such time as a successor should be chosen. William Acorn, the newly elected MLA from 1st Kings, interjected that Matheson should give up the leadership immediately. Acorn had been opposed to Matheson's leadership since the 1961 convention, and was one of several caucus members who had been agitating for a change in leadership.

Acorn's proposal set in motion a flurry of backroom maneuvering. George MacKay, the respected MLA from 4th Prince, appeared to be the best choice to take over from Matheson on an interim basis since he was not running again. His selection would mean that those caucus members interested in the leadership would have an equal advantage. However, MacKay declared he was not interested, but indicated he was prepared to support Bonnell continuing as acting opposition leader. Bonnell, a highly popular MLA representing 4th Kings, was first elected in 1951 and served in Matheson's government. He was also potentially heir apparent to Matheson, and enjoyed considerable caucus support.

Before the next caucus meeting, Campbell and Bonnell met briefly in a corner of the Confederation Chambers at Province House. Campbell, a newly-elected MLA, told Bonnell he would support his candidacy for the acting leadership. When caucus met, Acorn moved that Bonnell be appointed acting leader, and Campbell seconded the motion. In the absence of any other nominations, Bonnell was acclaimed in the position. With that, Matheson's tenure as leader came to an unceremonious end, although he continued to sit as an MLA for the remainder of his term.

A leadership convention was scheduled for later that fall. As expected, Bonnell announced his candidacy. At first, Campbell showed no interest in becoming leader, citing his relative lack of political experience, his lack of confidence as a public speaker, the demands on his law practice, and – more important – his responsibility to his young family.

Over the summer of 1965, Campbell received various approaches about the upcoming leadership race. Those from the western end of the province were to be expected, for regional loyalties were strong. But further to that, following the leadership reigns of Walter Jones and Alex Matheson from Queens and Kings counties respectively, Prince County Liberals now believed it was their turn. However, quiet entreaties also filtered in from the rest of the province. Reg Jenkins, Liberal Party president, encouraged Campbell to enter the race, while Matheson, who had been expected to support Bonnell, his old running mate, also urged Campbell to run. Other prominent Liberals pledged their support. In Prince County, Andy Wells and Mike Schurman headed a group of Liberals ready to help organize a campaign.*

Politicians, it is said, know themselves and their times. The 1960s offered a time of promise and change. The decade opened with the election of a young, vigorous and attractive United States president, John F. Kennedy, whose promise of a New Frontier exemplified a fresh vision and bold sense of adventure. His appeal to put country above self inspired a new generation of political activists. Meanwhile, in Quebec, federal Liberals were recruiting a young intellectual activist by the name of Pierre Trudeau for the forthcoming 1965 federal election campaign. And in Prince Edward Island, a young activist United Church minister, David MacDonald, was preparing to take on the old Liberal warhorse, Watson MacNaught, in the federal riding of Prince County. A new generation was coming into its own.

Alex Campbell – young, handsome and popular – also personified the promise and spirit of the times, but by late summer was still declining to run. With the leadership convention looming up in early fall, it was a foregone conclusion that Bonnell would become the next leader. But because of the upcoming federal election on November 8, the convention was delayed until early December. New pressures from a group of prominent Liberals in Charlottetown began to mount on Campbell to enter the leadership race. These included lawyers Jack Nicholson and Arthur Peake; Ernie Matheson,

---

* *Coincidentally, both Wells's father, James, and Schurman's father, Harold, had worked as key organizers behind Thane Campbell's successful campaigns.*

a contractor and the former leader's brother; and Sid Green, a tobacco and confectionary wholesaler.

Finally, following a late-night six-hour meeting at Nicholson's office in Charlottetown, Campbell agreed to enter the leadership race. With a formidable organization behind him, he threw himself aggressively into the campaign, visiting poll workers across the province, writing letters, and formulating his policy views. However, he lacked experience in one of the most primal of political functions – meeting and engaging voters. Throughout November 1965, and leading up to the convention, his handlers had him out on the Hughes corner at the intersection of Queen and Grafton streets in Charlottetown, introducing himself to passers-by, pressing the flesh. It was an art at which he soon learned to excel.

The leadership convention took place at the Confederation Centre of the Arts in Charlottetown on December 11. The location – modern, elegant, and sprawling – typified the new style of politics in Prince Edward Island. It also represented a more open style, in which party members themselves would decide the outcome. The 1961 leadership convention called by Matheson was a harbinger of that style. Now, it came to maturity in the 1965 convention when party members themselves gathered to elect their new leader. In the chilly December day, Campbell stood at the Queen Street door of the Confederation Centre, shaking hands with some 1,300 arriving delegates. "That was the first experience I had of carrying a wounded arm as the result of so much hand shaking," recalled Campbell.

Elmer Blanchard, a young Charlottetown lawyer, chaired the convention and welcomed the overflow crowd served by closed-circuit televisions set up in the lobby. It was the glitziest political gathering ever held in the province. The convention opened at 2:30 p.m. with tributes to Matheson and an address by guest speaker Gerald Regan, the new leader of the Nova Scotia Liberal Party. Then came the candidates' speeches.

Campbell delivered a rather uninspiring speech in which he outlined his views on party policy and organization. Bonnell's was the more lively speech – partisan in nature and poking much-appreciated jabs at the Conservatives.* But when the vote was counted, Campbell had won handily, with 765 votes to Bonnell's 592.

---

* *Bonnell later claimed that he had left home without his speech. Before coming to the convention, he changed his suit coat, leaving behind the one which contained the speech he intended to deliver.*

Campbell had turned thirty-two just ten days earlier on December 1st. He was now leader of a party with no policy, no money, and few candidates. The electoral outlook for the party was also bleak; the previous month, the four federal Conservative candidates had swept every seat on the Island in the national campaign, decimating and demoralizing the Liberals.

* * *

Within days of the start of 1966, Campbell began an exhaustive effort to rebuild the Liberal Party. He set up an office in the basement of his bungalow on Maple Avenue in Summerside, and unfurled a huge chart on the wall plotting his schedule over the coming months. As many as sixteen meetings were organized across the province, at least one in every district, to rally the troops. The meetings typically opened with a welcome from party president Reg Jenkins, followed by a rousing and fiery rant by Charlottetown lawyer Frank Sigsworth, easily one of the best "stump speakers" in the province.* After Sigsworth had delivered his partisan appeal, Campbell would then speak, combining the central message of the Liberal Party with one emphasizing the need to organize. The first meeting was held in Morell on a dismal winter evening in January, attended by about seventy-five people, mostly middle-aged and older men, all party stalwarts. Following Campbell's remarks, one supporter took him aside and told him he would never go far in politics unless he put more fire in his speeches.

---

* Sigsworth came to play a key role in helping Campbell rebuild the party. Flamboyant and loquacious, he grew up in a rabidly Liberal Charlottetown family. He once boasted the family was so fiercely partisan that he was twelve years old before he found out that "damn Tory" were two words. Behind the colourful personality and flamboyant loquaciousness was a formidable intellect. He had received a master's degree in English literature from the University of Montreal, putting himself through graduate school teaching math and physics at Loyola University; then went on to study political science and economics at the London School of Economics before attending Dalhousie Law School on a scholarship. Following graduation, he briefly joined a law firm in Charlottetown before deciding to enter the Oblate Order to study for the priesthood. By 1965, however, he had returned to the Island and set up his own law firm on Lower Queen Street.

The formidable task of fundraising fell to Sid Green, who was charged with rebuilding the Liberal coffers for the upcoming campaign, expected later that year or early in 1967. Under the previous leader, Alex Matheson, the conduct of the party's financial affairs was nothing if not tumultuous. Matheson had personally handled the finances, and was widely criticized for his secretive approach. Campbell, determined to separate party finances from the leader's office, arranged that Green would raise the funds and Summerside accountant Earle Hickey would keep the books. With assurances from Green that the necessary funds would be found, from that point on Campbell ended his involvement in party finances. Green went to Nova Scotia and met with Liberal Party officials there to find out how they raised funds. He never looked back. He was soon raising funds across the Island, around the region, and throughout Canada. The funds were invested prudently, with maturities coming due in time for the next election.*

The other challenging task was to find candidates. Campbell and his advisors knew they had to field a slate of candidates seen to be competent enough to form a government. In a marked departure from previous efforts to recruit candidates, and with the advice of local Liberals and other citizens, Campbell personally approached a number of people who had little or no prior affiliation with the party or even with partisan politics. In the process, he identified some high-profile prospective candidates, including Gordon Bennett, registrar of Prince of Wales College; Earle Hickey; Elmer Blanchard; and others including Jean Canfield in Crapaud, one of the first female candidates recruited by the party. The caucus also included people with prior cabinet experience such as Lorne Bonnell and Keir Clark, and MLAs George Ferguson and Dan MacDonald, who brought additional political experience and perspective.

The Liberal Party also introduced a new campaign style to Prince

---

* *The ever scrupulous and discreet Green committed only one gaffe. He once wrote to Emu Wines in Australia, reminding the winery that its contribution was overdue and, if it wanted to maintain its listings with the Liquor Control Commission, the funds should be forthcoming as soon as possible. The practice of extracting funds from companies doing business with governments, called "tollgating," was later found by Nova Scotia courts to be illegal, but at that time its use throughout Canada was widespread. Chastened, Green vowed never to write another such letter.*

Edward Island politics. Ned Belliveau, head of Tandy Advertising of Toronto, had helped New Brunswick Liberal leader Louis Robichaud with his party's strategy and advertising. He would do the same thing for Campbell and the Liberals on Prince Edward Island, playing a key role not only in crafting messages but also in packaging them.

As Leader of the Opposition, Campbell faced Shaw across the floor of the Legislature during the 1966 session. He would soon be facing Shaw in a provincial general election.

*   *   *

Leaving aside the deferred election, the 1966 provincial general campaign was a dull affair. On May 30, election day, the *Journal-Pioneer* observed that the campaign was "the quietest in years with both parties coming up with similar pledges." But in common with most elections in the province, if on the surface the issues appeared to be few and the differences slight, they did not lessen the ardour of political parties and their supporters to fight them to the finish.

On the evening of May 10, Campbell went on CFCY Television to unveil the twelve-point Liberal platform, which in part reflected the outcome of discussions he had held with Liberals across the district the preceding winter – what he called the party's "want list." However, its main thrust came from Campbell himself. Through New Brunswick Premier Louis Robichaud, Campbell met a young, energetic Charlie McElmon (later a New Brunswick senator). Campbell and McElmon spent a day at MacLauchlan's Motel in Charlottetown putting together the first draft of the election platform. The second draft was polished by Campbell, campaign worker John Mullally, and former Islander David Anderson of Toronto, who had played a key role in Mitchell Sharp's federal campaigns. Campbell completed the final draft of the platform at his home in Summerside one Sunday afternoon and evening, then presented it to the Liberal candidates at the Kirkwood Motel in Charlottetown on Monday afternoon.

The Liberal campaign platform consisted of a hodge-podge of promises and vague commitments. It promised to introduce free textbooks for students up to the tenth grade; increase the minimum wage to $1.25; lower the voting age to eighteen; expand senior citizens' housing and other services; introduce a five-year road-building program; and, as usual, support primary industries. According to Campbell, it was "a plan of real action."

As Campbell prepared to go on television to announce the platform, Mullally rushed in from Liberal headquarters with an additional paragraph, one which ultimately proved pivotal during the campaign. The Liberals had just learned that Allan MacEachen, Pearson's minister of health, was preparing to announce new cost-sharing measures for old-age pensions. Up to then, the basic pension stood at $75 a month for seniors over seventy years of age, while the federal and provincial governments cost-shared on a fifty-fifty basis an increase up to $100 a month for those in extra need. MacEachen now proposed an increase in the base pension to $100 a month, and an increase in the cost-sharing component up to $125 a month. As a result, Campbell inserted an additional paragraph in his notes: "To provide a better retirement for our senior citizens, a Liberal government will in co-operation with the federal government's Canada Assistance Plan pay to our people $100 a month and increased up to $125 monthly, where there is a need, but without a means test."

The Liberal promise caught the Conservatives by surprise. They had not heard about MacEachen's proposals and were unsure of the federal cost-sharing figures. They immediately committed to an increase in pensions for those in need to $100 a month, with the implied hope that those who needed it would apply for the additional amount. Campbell immediately branded the Conservatives' apparent change of heart as "vague and uncertain." He charged that they were exploiting senior citizens for political advantage. At a press conference on May 18, he stated, "I am appalled that our Premier should try to employ a political trick in which he uses our senior citizens as a foil for his political advantage." While welcoming the fact that the Conservatives were "attempting to get onto our bandwagon," he denounced their commitment as falling short of the Liberals' promise.

That evening at a campaign rally in Eldon, Campbell repeated his assertion that the Liberal commitment went further than the Conservatives. He declared that the additional funds required to pay for the increase would come from improved spending efficiencies in government. To the public, it appeared that the Liberals were promising a basic $100 a month in old-age pensions, while those in need could receive up to $125 a month; under the Conservatives, the most anyone would receive was $100 a month. Suddenly, old-age pensions took centre stage in an otherwise lacklustre campaign.

Much to Shaw's annoyance, the Conservative platform was not

released until the day after the Liberals released theirs. His platform was actually drafted by some outside help; campaign recruits Dalton Camp, Flora MacDonald, and Lowell Murray, active workers in federal Conservative campaigns, drafted the platform late into the night of May 10. Shaw unveiled it the next day at a news conference during which he hinted at the development of a "program to cost millions" with no tax increases. He was outlining ambitious new plans to increase the level of agricultural production threefold over the next five years. Shaw boasted that they were presenting "a pilot project that would be of international significance," although he did not elaborate.

Shaw was actually referring to the massive amount of work then underway by the team of consultants from Acres International to formulate a new economic development strategy for the province which would become a forerunner of the Comprehensive Development Plan. The announcement received almost no attention from the public, and even the Liberals failed to grasp the significance of his remark. Instead, the Conservative campaign concentrated on bread-and-butter issues: the creation of two new national parks, one east and one west; an all-weather highway from Tignish to Elmira; and the introduction of a new program for low-rental family housing. Henry Wedge, Minister of Health, also called for tenders for the construction of a fifty-one-bed special-care home in Alberton.

The day after Shaw released the Conservative platform, Industry Minister Lloyd MacPhail announced that the government would provide a grant of $225,000 for a new fish-processing plant in North Rustico. At a public meeting in O'Leary, Shaw also revealed that negotiations were underway for the establishment of a fish- and herring-meal plant in Alberton to employ one hundred and fifty people. Further announcements were forthcoming: an annual grant of $300 per student to be given equally to Saint Dunstan's University and Prince of Wales College; more programs for farmers and fisher-men; and expansion of the tourism industry. The Conservative election slogan, "Building an Island of Opportunity," figured promi-nently in newspaper, radio and television ads.

Another issue that surfaced during the campaign was the planned causeway between Prince Edward Island and the mainland. Construction of this massive project had commenced the previous fall, but the federal budget introduced in the spring of 1966 by federal Finance Minister Mitchell Sharp called for a delay, putting the provincial Liberals on the defensive. Its status remained ambiguous, even despite the fact that federal Public Works Minister, George McIlraith subsequently announced the project was proceeding on schedule. The uncertainty appeared to be settled on May 19, however, when tenders were called for the second stage of the project.

Both parties skirted warily around possibly the most volatile issue of the campaign, the Georgetown developments. The government had spent millions on the development of a new fish-processing facility and shipyard in Georgetown. The development was spearheaded by promoter Jens Moe and Fisheries and Industry Minister Leo Rossiter. Rumours swirled around about the alleged mismanagement of funds and the soundness of the projects. There were whiffs of scandal and corruption, but no evidence. During the 1966 spring session of the Legislature, Campbell had called for a judicial investigation and an external audit of the development, but the government rejected both. Yet, by early 1966 the government itself was growing increasingly uneasy about the financial soundness of the projects. In a cabinet shuffle, Rossiter had been quietly moved out of the industry portfolio and replaced with Lloyd MacPhail. The government was attempting to stifle any hint of problems until after the election. Anticipating this to be a big issue in the campaign, the media also suggested that the industries in Georgetown were on a shaky financial footing. There was some speculation in the *Guardian* and elsewhere that Shaw timed the election to avoid any potential embarrassment.

The Liberals were in a difficult position. Although they suspected all was not right, they had no hard evidence of wrongdoing. They did not want to jeopardize votes in Kings County by overtly criticizing the development, neither did they did not want to appear opposed to new industry. So instead they criticized the fact that all the developments were concentrated in Georgetown. In its platform, the party declared itself in favour of a more even distribution of industrial development across the province. In response to suggestions that the Georgetown industries were facing financial difficulties, Campbell stated at a party rally in Murray River that a Liberal government would continue to proceed with the initiatives, either under present or revised arrangements, or under a crown corporation.

Above all, the Liberals were anxious to avoid any direct criticism of Shaw himself. They recognized that he was popular and well respected; personal attacks would only backfire. Instead, they suggested Shaw was losing control over the more reckless members of his cabinet. "Poor Walter Shaw, a nice old man who cannot control some of the boys in his cabinet," became the Liberal party line.

The Conservatives countered by playing up the seventy-eight-year-old Shaw's vigour during the campaign, and accused the Liberals of trying to undermine confidence in the future of industrial development. In the dying days of the campaign, the Conservatives took out a full-page advertisement headed "Beware," which featured a response to the litany of accusations made by the Liberals. The handbook, issued to Conservative candidates by their party's organizers, underlined the message. "Steady progress on the Island takes capable and experienced leadership – men alive to their jobs, alert to seize opportunity and anxious to create opportunity," it intoned. "We mustn't let the Liberal wrecking crew succeed in trying to undermine the new spirit of confidence, the spirit that makes the big difference between the Island that *was* and the Island that *is* and *will be*."

The media viewed the campaign as a close race. According to the *Guardian*, the Liberals were up against the fact that "the Shaw government, despite some mistakes, has had an unexcelled record of concrete achievements to its credit." The Liberals largely ignored the Conservatives and concentrated instead on promoting their own platform. Their campaign team also recognized that Shaw's folksy, paterfamilias image would be difficult to counter. Campbell was not personally well known, and some worried that his image as a "sharp young lawyer" with little political experience would not go over well with voters.

In order to identify Campbell more closely with Islanders, prior to the campaign Tandy Advertising's Ned Belliveau, extensively filmed Campbell meeting Islanders in various locales across the province. These clips were used in television ads aired throughout the campaign, the first time any party had made such use of this medium. Belliveau, a pioneer of modern election campaigns in Prince Edward Island, had to adapt his techniques to the technology then available in the province. For example, the local newspapers lacked the technology to run the layouts Belliveau had devised, so adjustments had to be made to the look and feel of the campaign. And CFCY Television did not cover the entire Island; to reach the eastern and western ends, ads had to be run through stations in Sydney and Moncton.

Campbell spoke at twelve party rallies across the province, including the kick-off rally at the Murray River Hall in Lorne Bonnell's 4th Kings district. While Campbell campaigned door-to-door with every candidate, some strategists worried about him spending too much time away from his own riding. Since the by-election of 1965, the riding had undergone redistribution; the heavily Liberal areas surrounding Summerside, which had given Campbell his slim majority, now belonged to other districts.

To complicate matters, in the final week of the campaign, 1st Kings Liberal candidate William Acorn died. In accordance with the Election Act, officials immediately deferred the election in that district.*

On Friday evening, May 27, the Liberals held a "giant" rally at the Kennedy Coliseum in Charlottetown. The crowd was warmed up by Don Messer and his Islanders and the Buchta Dancers. During the evening, Campbell spoke to a large and enthusiastic audience.

On election night, Campbell huddled with his advisors in the Charlottetown Hotel to watch the returns. The results see-sawed all evening, and even though the Liberals eventually emerged two seats ahead, it was not clear who had won until the recounts took place. When these recounts were completed days later, both parties had won fifteen seats.

It now remained for the voters of 1st Kings to decide which party would form the next government.

*   *   *

On July 11, the greatest cliff-hanger election in the history of Prince Edward Island came to a close, and with it the old-style nature of politics: tribal, raw and raucous. For the vast majority of Islanders for whom political campaigns represented a great spectator sport, the 1966 election would be their last hurrah.

Neil Matheson, a former Liberal MP for Queens County, now worked as a reporter with the *Guardian*. Although provincial politics was not his usual assignment (he mostly covered agricultural and community-based stories), he was able to persuade the editor, Pius Callaghan, to send him to Souris on the night of the by-election to cover the results. He arrived in Souris to a delirious, celebratory crowd. "Cars and trucks loaded with happy, cheering passengers toured Main Street with horns blasting and the occupants cheering

---

* In a rare display of solidarity and unanimity, both parties turned out in force for Acorn's funeral.

34

and whooping in their hour of triumph," he wrote. "From the time I parked on Main Street and heard returns from the first two polls on Russell Perry's big transistor radio, until I left some two and one-half hours later, there seemed to be nobody but Liberals on the street. A group was just starting to gather at St. Mary's Parish Hall for the party celebration just when I was leaving."

On this night of nights, who wasn't a Liberal?

The celebration marked the election of the two Liberal candidates, Dan MacDonald and Bruce Stewart, by majorities of 207 and 158 votes respectively. The Liberals now held a two-seat majority in the Legislature and were set to form the next government. When the dust settled on the final votes from the 1966 election, the Liberals had won 50.5 percent against 49.5 percent for the Conservatives. Alexander Bradshaw Campbell became the twenty-ninth premier of Prince Edward Island.

PARO

Happy Liberals in Souris cheering the 1966 deferred election win in 1st Kings. According to a reporter covering the results, "Cars and trucks loaded with happy, cheering passengers toured Main Street with horns blasting and the occupants cheering and whooping in their hour of triumph."

PARO

Campbell greets former premier Walter Shaw following the defeat of the Progressive Conservatives on July 11, 1966. The two candidates offered a study in contrasts: Campbell was the youngest party leader in Canada, Shaw the oldest.

Campbell's first cabinet. (Left to right): Earle Hickey, Keir Clark, Elmer Blanchard, Lorne Bonnell, Campbell, Gordon Bennett, Dan MacDonald, George Ferguson, Cecil Miller.

PARO

Jens Moe (centre left) *with MLAs Keith Harrington* (left), *Walter Dingwell* (centre right), *and Georgetown Seafoods manager Cyril Davies during a tour of the seafood plant.*

The Georgetown Fiasco

For a time, Jens Moe could do no wrong. His ambitious projects to revive the fortunes of the moribund town of Georgetown and transform the area economy were aided and abetted by compliant politicians, lauded by an uncritical press, and feted by an unsuspecting public. When it all came unravelled, Prince Edward Island was left with one of the largest financial fiascos in its history. The Georgetown Fiasco would preoccupy the new government of Alex Campbell for much of its first term in office.

The ground-breaking projects in Georgetown came about at a time when governments across the Atlantic region were desperately scrambling to jump on the industrial development bandwagon. That sense of urgency proved easy pickings for fast-talking entrepreneurs who found vote-grubbing governments all too willing to open their arms and pocketbooks to a new generation of developers, especially those who promised to create jobs and growth through their get-rich-quick schemes and dreams. All across the region stand monuments to political corruption, greed, and blind ambition: an oil refinery in Come-by-Chance, Newfoundland; a heavy-water plant in Glace Bay, Cape Breton; a Clairtone stereo factory in Stellarton, Nova Scotia; a Bricklin automobile plant in Saint John, New Brunswick; and, on the Georgetown waterfront in Prince Edward Island, a ship-yard and fish-processing complex.

As the world entered the second half of the twentieth century, swept along with a wave of unprecedented progress and prosperity, the Atlantic region quickly became a haven for "capitalists with no capital," while unsuspecting governments learned only too late of the sometimes unwitting role they had played, naively betraying the public trust and squandering their limited resources. It was a time of hubris and hyperbole, when hucksters and politicians formed an unholy trinity with people's hopes.

During the 1950s and '60s, the people of Atlantic Canada saw their region falling further behind the economic growth and prosperity sweeping across the rest of North America. A spate of reports, commissions and entreaties to the federal government reflected the increasing frustration of Atlantic Canadians with lagging growth rates, low standards of living, and high unemployment.

Regional disparities had been a fact of life since Confederation. Despite transportation subsidies, grants to governments, and other forms of ad hoc federal intervention, the Atlantic provinces continued to fall behind. The belated recognition that federal policies actually exacerbated such disparities may have inspired in Atlantic Canadians a desire for fundamental change, but governments in the region lacked sufficient political will and leadership to follow through with a vision strong enough to confront the need for new solutions to the region's malaise.

Favouritism, cronyism and parish pump politics were the means by which Atlantic politicians extracted what little advantage they could from Ottawa to boost their economies. And then there were people like Jens Moe.

*   *   *

In 1963, Jens Moe was an ambitious thirty-four-year-old sales engineer with Brown Boven (Canada) Limited in Montreal, making a salary of $610 a month. He arranged a meeting with Patrick Cavanagh, then president of Premium Iron Ore, an investment and holding company based in Montreal, to explore backing for a new enterprise. Moe wanted to manufacture some of the equipment he was then selling, and was interested in acquiring a machine shop in Bathurst, New Brunswick.

Cavanagh recalled the first time he came into his office. "I was impressed by him," he said. "He was very friendly, and we became acquainted over the next six months." They discussed a number of Moe's ideas, including building steel stern trawlers in Bathurst. In the course of their conversations, Cavanagh shared with Moe the results of a feasibility study Premium had conducted on various growth industries. At that time, one of the fastest-growing markets was frozen fish in Europe, which Premium estimated was increasing by more than thirty-three percent annually.

In the meantime, the Prince Edward Island government, led by Premier Walter Shaw, was looking for industrial development opportunities. In the early summer of 1963, the government sent Deputy Fisheries Minister Eugene Gorman to the Scandinavian countries to search out foot-loose companies interested in relocating some or all their operations. Through Uniconsultants, a consulting engineering company in Norway, Gorman heard about Moe's interest in various business opportunities. By then, buoyed by Premium's projections on the rising demand for frozen fish, Moe's interest in building fishing trawlers had expanded into fish processing. On August 15, 1963, he wrote to Premier Shaw expressing his interest in constructing a fish-processing plant in the province, and relocating his shipyard from Bathurst to Georgetown, where he would build the vessels required to supply fish for the plant.

The Shaw government responded quickly. Through the Prince Edward Island Industrial Development Corporation, it loaned Moe $385,000 for the relocation of Bathurst Marine to Georgetown, with the shipyard scheduled to open in early 1965. Discussions quickly followed on the proposed fish plant. Moe envisioned what he described as the first fully integrated fish plant in Canada, with the capacity to process not only fish but agricultural products as well. The Shaw cabinet was duly impressed. In an agreement with the Industrial Development Corporation dated October 18, the provincial government agreed to advance $750,000 for the construction of the plant, to be called Gulf Garden Foods, with Moe and his partners putting up $250,000.

The Gulf Garden Foods plant was a disastrous undertaking. Final costs came in at more than double the estimates. It was also poorly designed and inadequately equipped. The plant was doomed from the day it opened.

Despite its earlier involvement in bringing the parties together, however, Uniconsultants was not mentioned in the agreement. Instead, Moe approached Cavanagh to provide financing, management, and other services through Premium Iron Ore. Impressed with

Moe's success in obtaining government assistance for both the ship-yard and the fish plant, Cavanagh agreed to provide Moe's share of the funds and take control of the venture. In exchange, if all worked out well, it would be turned over to Moe in five years. Cavanagh, however, was determined to keep Moe in check. "He did not under-stand the financial aspects of business," Cavanagh later testified. In 1963, for example, Bathurst Marine showed a net loss of $5,726.

To help secure markets for the fish plant, Moe travelled to Europe in early 1964 and signed an agreement to supply frozen fish to a small dealer in Hamburg, Germany. But Cavanagh rejected the deal and urged Moe to find a bigger buyer. In July, Moe returned to Canada bearing a signed agreement with Produits Findus, a Norwegian subsidiary of Nestlé Alimentana S.A., the giant Swiss-based food conglomerate. The agreement committed Produits Findus to purchase a specified output of the Georgetown plant. The Shaw government appeared to have pulled off a major coup, with the announced construction of a new, modern, integrated fish- and vegetable-processing plant in Georgetown; relocation of a shipyard to build fishing vessels to catch the fish to supply the plant; and a signed contract to supply frozen fish to Europe. Announcements during the fall of 1963 and the spring and summer of 1964 signalled a new era for Georgetown and eastern Prince Edward Island. Moe was even dropping hints of establishing a salmon farm and mink ranch to utilize by-products from the fish processing plant.

Awe-struck Islanders saw Moe as a swashbuckling entrepreneur who would help revitalize the Island's stagnant economy and were duly impressed. In March 1968, Harry Bruce wrote an article in the *Star Weekly* magazine titled "How to blow ten million in a few easy steps." Summing up how Moe was perceived on the Island, he wrote, "Moe was in his mid-thirties, a strapping, good- looking chap, a fam-ily man, an extrovert, enthusiast. He came, originally, from a respected Lutheran family and, once after he became better known on the Is-land, he demonstrated to several locals that he was masterful at playing a church organ." Despite the accolades, the *Globe and Mail* later observed, "Moe is still regarded as something of a mystery man in Prince Edward Island." Prophetic words.

*   *   *

On August 21, 1964, Leo Rossiter from Morell, the flamboyant, irrepressible, and popular forty-one-year-old minister of Fisheries and Industry in the Shaw cabinet, sent a letter of intent to Pigott Construction of Montreal authorizing the construction of the fish plant in Georgetown at a cost not to exceed $1 million, excluding refrigeration and other equipment. The plant would be owned by the provincial Industrial Development Corporation and leased to Gulf Garden Foods.

Preliminary plans for the plant were drawn up by Commercial Marine International of Montreal, a ship design company in which Moe had recently acquired an option to purchase a fifty-one-percent interest. The company had no previous experience in designing a fish processing facility, let alone the highly complex one enthusiastically envisaged by Moe. Jack Pigott, head of Pigott Construction, expressed doubts about the design firm after a visit to its Montreal offices found only two people there. He predicted that "if we continued with Commercial Marine International, we are heading for a total disaster." Pigott urged that the C.D. Howe Co. of Port Arthur, Ontario, be retained to design the plant, and later recalled that Moe was "highly disturbed over the recommendation." C.D. Howe was eventually brought in, but Commercial Marine was retained at the urging of Rossiter, who subsequently authorized a payment of $42,000 to the company.

Design changes, construction delays, and wildly miscalculated estimates led to cost increases. Produits Findus had also requested a number of major design and equipment changes. By December, 1964, the Industrial Development Corporation was advised that the plant's final cost would be $1.6 million. Further increases for equipment would drive costs even higher. On a call for tenders for refrigeration equipment, two bids were received from off-Island suppliers: one from Frick of Canada for $393,636, and another from Lewis Refrigeration for $607,000. Rossiter ordered Pigott to negotiate with Lewis, the higher bidder, as a result of which the equipment ended up costing $522,000. As titular head of the Industrial Development Corporation, Rossiter also authorized a number of other cost overruns.

In the end, Gulf Garden Foods cost the provincial government $2.3 million, more than double the original estimates. An official with National Sea Products later testified to a Commission of Inquiry, established to investigate the fiasco, that the plant suffered from poor design, wasteful expenditures, inadequate equipment, and other serious deficiencies.* For example, although the plant included a canteen, a laundry room, and a large executive suite, the processing lines were confusing and other defects hampered operations. Lack of attention to design showed up also in little flaws: a cubicle for a receptionist, but no room for a typewriter. When the plant opened in the late summer of 1965, it would require close to another $600,000 to upgrade its capacity.

Unfortunately, Gulf Garden Foods was doomed from the day it opened. Cyril Davies, the new president and general manager, had no experience in fish processing. He ran into difficulties keeping the lines operating properly, and encountered problems in obtaining raw product. The contract with Produits Findus to supply frozen product suddenly appeared elusive. Although Moe's agreement with Premium Iron Ore to provide capital and management assistance was contingent on a long-term contract with Findus, it appeared Moe had misrepresented Premium's involvement with the venture. Moe kept secret the contents of the contract with Findus, and when pressed for details by Eugene Gorman, Deputy Minister of Fisheries, Moe told him they were "very confidential." Industry officials later testified that the contract prices were substantially less than prevailing market conditions; the prices negotiated with Findus were said to be unrealistic. In the end, not a single fish was ever shipped to the company.

In the winter of 1965, fish had to be trucked from Shelburne, Nova Scotia, to supply the plant because Georgetown harbour had frozen over, preventing vessels from docking at the Gulf Garden wharf. The Commission of Inquiry later observed that it was "a ruinous affair and seems to have been done merely as a costly bit of window dressing to make the plant appear active." Not surprisingly, Gulf Garden Foods very quickly ran into financial difficulties. In an effort to keep the scheme afloat, Moe enlisted the support of Rossiter and the provincial government in a brazen attempt to conceal this flagrant wheeling and dealing.

---

* *The Commission of Inquiry into matters pertaining to Bathurst Marine Limited and Gulf Garden Foods Limited was established by the Government of Prince Edward Island in March 1967. The Commission was composed of Supreme Court Judge C. St. Clair Trainor of Charlottetown (chair) and members Ian M. MacKeighan of Halifax and Alexander E. Pierce of Montreal. It began public hearings on January 29, 1968.*

In the summer of 1963, the provincial Fishermen's Loan Board signed an agreement with Bathurst Marine to build three steel stern trawlers. Under an existing program to encourage shipbuilding, the federal government subsidized fifty percent of the costs upon satisfactory completion of the trawlers. The Fishermen's Loan Board would advance forty-five percent by way of a loan to Bathurst Marine, while Moe had to come up with the remaining five percent. Moe forecast that sixteen trawlers would be needed to meet the requirements of the fish plant. The trawlers would be owned by Leaseway Limited of Canada, a subsidary of Cavanagh's Premium Iron Ore, while Leaseway would handle the financing and construction of the trawlers and lease them to Gulf Garden Foods.

After the agreement with Moe was signed, A. Walthen Gaudet, the chair of the Fishermen's Loan Board and a respected lawyer and former Charlottetown mayor, went to Bathurst to inspect the operations which were slated to move to Georgetown. He could find only one hull in the shipyard, and was told the hull of the second was inside the facility, but no one had a key. Gaudet returned to Charlottetown, having learnt nothing about the company or its operations. Shortly after the agreement to build three trawlers was signed with Bathurst Marine, Rossiter called Gaudet into his office and told him to draw up a contract to build five more trawlers. Gaudet refused, citing problems with the first two trawlers then under construction. However, following pressure from Rossiter, he later agreed to a compromise, and gave Bathurst Marine approval to begin work on three additional trawlers.

Then matters began to spin out of control. At Rossiter's urging, the Fishermen's Loan Board signed agreements to build even more trawlers. In March 1964, Rossiter authorized installment payments on the yet-to-be-started new hulls over the objections of both Gaudet and Deputy Fisheries Minister Gorman. Nonetheless, by September agreements were signed to lay the hulls of the additional trawlers. In each case, Bathurst Marine was entitled to receive progress payments from the Fishermen's Loan Board.

Since Moe virtually controlled both Gulf Garden Foods and Bathurst Marine, no tenders were ever called for the construction of the trawlers. Problems soon surfaced at the shipyard. Payments could only be made after federal inspectors issued progress certificates, but inspectors had discovered that parts had been stripped from one hull to satisfy requirements on another. Claims were then made more than once for the same material.

Moe made certain that Rossiter received credit for his largesse. In the fall of 1964, he arranged for Rossiter to travel to the Scandinavian countries to promote trade relations. In a letter to Rossiter on November 20, he included a copy of the November newsletter of the Canada-Scandinavian Foundation, which, as Moe gushingly described, "will show you in the exalted company you keep." Moe expressed the hope that the trip had not been only interesting and memorable, but profitable as well. "With all the lovely herring, the pops, the Findus hostesses, and the Danish pie for dessert ... I wish we could go again," he wrote. Moe ended the letter with a personal request for assistance. "I have an unsettled account with a Danish nightclub and I feel I cannot go back until I have paid this bill, so will you please indicate to me what it is?" For his part, Rossiter appeared happy with the relationship, but the Fishermen's Loan Board was becoming increasingly concerned. If the trawlers failed to pass federal inspection, they would not be eligible for the fifty percent federal subsidy, and the Board would be left with the liability. Bathurst Marine was already a year behind in delivery of the first trawlers, yet the Board was being asked to commit even more funds for additional trawlers. Unable to obtain detailed financial or construction details on the trawlers that were then under construction, it was concerned about the absence of any safeguards, such as performance bonds or late penalties.

Eventually, in March 1965, Gaudet resigned in disgust as chair of the Fishermen's Loan Board. "I had a belly full of political interference with the job of the board and I got out," he later told the Commission of Inquiry. In his letter of resignation, Gaudet wrote that he was quitting "for a wide variety of reasons too numerous to go into in any detail herein, but borne out and developed this past year or more through a lessening confidence in the minister responsible for the operation of the Board [Rossiter] and his general lack of co-operation thereon." Gaudet also complained to the commission that Rossiter kept officials "completely in the dark" about the transactions involving Gulf Garden Foods and Bathurst Marine. (Gaudet, however, appears to have mended his differences with the government; he re-offered as a Conservative candidate in 5th Queens in the subsequent general election.)

There is some evidence that Gaudet was not the only provincial government official experiencing difficulty with Rossiter's free-wheeling style. In a letter dated December 23, 1964, Premier Shaw wrote to his industry minister expressing concern that, contrary to his directions, copies of agreements and contracts with the Georgetown industries had not been filed with the Provincial Treasurer and the Deputy Provincial Secretary. "I was rather amazed a few days ago that your office had not complied with these instructions," he complained. In the letter, Shaw asked for a list of the investors behind Gulf Garden Foods and Bathurst Marine. Shaw was also worried about rumours of problems at the shipyard, and asked Rossiter to send him an inventory of its equipment. "I think you quite realize that this Government could be brought into disrepute and trouble for its good record position if we are not able to provide not only full and complete answers but also answers that will indicate that our agreements and guarantees are supported by ample security," he warned.

In the meantime, Moe was taking advantage of his position in both Bathurst Marine and Gulf Garden Foods, drawing a salary of $800 a month from each company. Moe also controlled fifty percent of a company called M.K. International, which had been set up to collect a five-percent commission on the gross sales of Gulf Garden. Over a period of two years, M.K. International received close to $36,000 for various administrative expenses, including one invoice "for assistance to the economy." Moe set up yet another company, Moe Industries, which acted as agents and importers for equipment used in building the trawlers. Over a period of two years, Gulf Garden Foods paid $205,000 to Moe Industries for services rendered – not to mention the fact that eighty percent of the company's overhead costs were being paid by Bathurst Marine and Gulf Garden Foods!

Because of the complex web of transactions between the shipyard, the fish plant, and Moe's various companies, it proved impossible to trace the myriad of credits, debits and financial transfers. One estimate suggested that over this period about $600,000 ended up in Moe's hands. With many of the records not available to the Commission of Inquiry, it simply stated said "it was not possible to trace the destination of these funds." Premier Campbell voiced his own explanation about the disappearance of the funds. "We know where it is and it isn't on the Island," he remarked succinctly.

Meanwhile, Moe was running into difficulties with Cavanagh. Premium had agreed to pay Moe $50,000 for negotiating the contract with Produits Findus, but Moe demanded $250,000. There were more serious issues, however. As part of the original agreement between Moe and Premium, Premium would own eighty percent of

Gulf Garden Foods, while its subsidary, Leaseway, would lease the trawlers to Gulf Garden. According to the agreement, Moe would increase his share of ownership over a period of five years. However, in order to raise his own share of funds towards the construction of the trawlers, Moe had pledged one million shares to various Norwegian interests in exchange for $250,000, effectively reducing Premium's ownership to a mere twenty percent. Premium's lawyer wrote to Moe in February 1965 reminding him that his client was the beneficial owner of eighty percent of Gulf Garden Foods, and threatening to withdraw from the agreement if the matter was not resolved.

The dispute between Moe and Cavanagh came to a head in April 1965 when Premium was voted out of the company, at which time it was purportedly owed $5 million from Gulf Garden Foods and a further $525,000 from Bathurst Marine. At this point, Leaseway was committed to more than $2 million in payments. Its officials were also concerned that, with Premium out of the picture, they might have trouble collecting the lease payments from Gulf Garden Foods. In desperation, they wrote to the provincial government expressing doubts about the fish plant's solvency and asking for a guarantee. To the surprise and chagrin of both Premium and Leaseway, the provincial government ignored both the warnings and the loss of financial backing. It continued to pour money into the fish plant and the shipyard without any sign of new investors. In August 1965, with no new investment forthcoming, the Industrial Development Corporation took over financing of the trawlers and created a new company, Seaboard Trawlers International, to take over their ownership.

Moe was desperate for cash flow to keep the fish plant and ship-yard alive. Following the departure of Premium, he met with Torstein Foss of Connecticut, president of Fjell Navigation of New York, a subsidiary of shipowners Olsen & Uglestad in Oslo, Norway. Moe told Foss he was interested in obtaining ocean-going vessels to transport fish to Produits Findus in Europe, adding that he required an additional nine trawlers to be built by Bathurst Marine. Foss and his associates were impressed by Moe's ambitious proposals. They bought $50,000 worth of shares in Gulf Garden Foods, and Foss personally purchased an additional 1,200 shares. Commenting later on the deal, Foss remarked that "it looked like Christmas to us."

Then in November, a group of Norwegian investors agreed to loan Seaboard $360,000 to finance the new trawlers. Moe used the

$360,000 loan to finance his five-percent share of the cost of the additional trawlers, which solved some of his cash flow problems.

With those problems at least temporarily resolved, in May 1965, Bathurst Marine submitted a proposal to the Fishermen's Loan Board to lay the hulls for yet more trawlers. The Board of course expressed concern that the previous three were still under construction and suffered a number of outstanding deficiencies. Nonetheless, despite the failure of Bathurst Marine to provide the required statutory declarations to the Fishermen's Loan Board certifying that each construction stage had been completed satisfactorily, the Board continued to make payments, even though it harboured suspicions that the construction funds were being transferred from Bathurst Marine to Gulf Garden Foods, which was now in operation but experiencing financial difficulties.

Further trouble was brewing at Bathurst Marine – it was seriously behind in its delivery schedule for the trawlers. Moe told the Fishermen's Loan Board that he needed to start construction of new trawlers immediately or the shipyard would be facing an extreme shortage of operating capital. He proposed the construction of three new trawlers at a cost of $837,000 each. At this point, the Board dug in its heels, repeating its concerns about committing even more funding without safeguards, penalties or firm delivery dates. However, under pressure from Rossiter, it eventually agreed to authorize three additional trawlers.*

In December 1965, with temperatures hovering around zero and swirling snow squalls blocking the harbour, Bathurst Marine launched the *Gulf Grenadier* in Georgetown amid much fanfare, pomp and ceremony, in the presence of politicians, town officials, company representatives, and other invited guests. The *Gulf Grenadier* was touted as the first steel trawler ever built in Prince Edward Island. On December 23, Mrs. Jens Moe christened the second

---

In all, nine trawlers were under construction or completed at Bathurst Marine after it was taken over by Moe in 1963. The shipyard, first in Bathurst and then in Georgetown, completed the Howe Bay, Iceland II, Gulf Gull, Gulf Gallant, Gulf Guard, Gulf Grenadier, Gulf Gunn, and Gulf Gerd *before it went bankrupt. The* Gulf Georgetown *was under construction and several others were in the planning stages when the provincial government took over the yard*

completed trawler, the *Gulf Gunn*, at a similar ceremony. The celebrations would be short-lived.

*   *   *

In January 1966, Leonard Baisley, Gaudet's successor at the Fishermen's Loan Board, returned to his office after a short out-of-province trip to find his secretary busily typing up contracts for nine new trawlers to be built by Bathurst Marine. She informed him that she was preparing the contracts on Rossiter's orders. On January 17, Rossiter also told Eugene Gorman that he had authorization from cabinet to amend the contract proposed by the Board in order to cover the construction of nine trawlers, not the three earlier agreed to by the Board. The Board met in the Georgetown courthouse on January 20 to discuss the new agreements. In attendance were Leonard Baisley, Eugene Gorman, Leo Rossiter, Jens Moe, Cyril Davies (of Gulf Garden Foods), and other officials. Premier Shaw and other members of his cabinet, including Agriculture Minister Andrew MacRae, later joined the meeting.

The mood at the courthouse was tense. Gorman expressed his view that the contract was highly unusual, and that before it was approved the Board should have the "express pronouncement and authorization of higher authority" – meaning orders from cabinet – to sign the contract. "This contract involves higher policy decisions, not a mere disbursement of funds for the rehabilitation of needy farmers and fishermen," advised Gorman, in a not-so-veiled reminder of the original purpose of the Board. He reiterated the Board's reluctance to commit to the building of more trawlers in view of the poor progress of the existing hulls and the lack of financial information. Baisley also pointed out that Gulf Garden Foods was already behind in its payments to government. (Gulf Garden had agreed to forward fifteen percent of the gross value of the catch as payment on the trawler loans, and to provide what were called "settlement sheets" to indicate what it was owed – neither of which had been received.)

In turn, Rossiter produced a letter he had written to Premier Shaw recommending initial payments be made on nine new trawlers. He added that Gulf Garden Foods had the capacity to fillet between sixty and seventy-five million pounds of fish and needed the extra trawlers to land that quantity. Agriculture Minister Andrew MacRae supported his colleague, pointing out that since all the companies'

The December 1965 launching of the Gulf Grenadier, *the first steel trawler to be built in Prince Edward Island.*

assets were pledged to the government there was no foundation to the Board's concerns or reservations. Throughout, Gorman resented the fact that Rossiter was ignoring his advice. In turn, Moe resented what he saw as Gorman's interference, and had actually urged Rossiter to fire Gorman on previous occasions. During the meeting, Gorman asked to be relieved of any further responsibilities in connection with the Georgetown operations. But before the meeting ended, the Board drafted a minute to cabinet expressly authorizing the contract.

The contract was signed for the construction of nine new trawlers at a cost of $871,000 each, for a total of $7.8 million. A lone clause provided for the Fishermen's Loan Board to take over the shipyard if Bathurst Marine was unable to complete construction. Under the terms of the contract, the Board could issue progress payments following the basic laying of the hull. Immediately afterwards, Moe drew down advance payments of some $261,000 on the new trawlers.

* * *

With both fish plant and shipyard now in full operation, the Shaw government proceeded confidently into the 1966 provincial general election campaign. Given the tremendous publicity surrounding the developments in Georgetown and growing speculation about the amount of public funds involved, the Shaw government's industrial development policies became a central issue in the campaign. The *Guardian* speculated in an editorial that the issue surrounding the Georgetown industries was "one of, if not the, major reason for calling the spring election."

That opinion was practically confirmed by Premier Shaw himself on April 16 when he went on television to announce the election. He spoke at length about Liberal opposition attacks on the Georgetown industries. "I had no intention at this time of calling an election," he declared, "but I am convinced our people wish to stamp out this unfortunate and vicious propaganda and protect the interests of the province at large." When some Liberal MLAs were heard to say it "would be a good thing if the trawlers sank at sea," Shaw pounced on the comment, accusing the Liberals of being opposed to development.

If officials of the Shaw government complained about being left in the dark on the details of government involvement in the Georgetown industries, the public knew even less. The Liberal opposition had demanded a detailed accounting of government financial commitments, but little information was forthcoming. In April 1966, before the election was called, Opposition Leader Alex Campbell had called for a judicial investigation and an external audit of the Industrial Development Corporation and the Fishermen's Loan Board. Both demands were vehemently rejected by Shaw and Rossiter. When former opposition leader Alex Matheson criticized the government for "spending money like drunken sailors," Shaw shot back that the Liberals were "trying to kill industry." However, Shaw himself had earlier expressed concerns about the projects. In a letter to Rossiter in late 1964 he stated that if the government did not provide detailed information "we will be like sitting ducks under Matheson's investigation."

Despite whatever reservations it may have had, the Shaw government constantly boasted throughout the campaign of its success in attracting new industrial development to Georgetown, and promised this would lead to even further economic opportunities. In fact, during the election campaign, two Norwegian businessmen announced plans to establish a mink farm in Georgetown. They would raise mink for pelts, feeding them on fish offal from Gulf Garden Foods. They were looking for $150,000 to build the facility, and another $10,000 to fly 1,000 units of breeding stock from Norway to Georgetown.

Both Gulf Garden Foods and Bathurst Marine struggled throughout the spring of 1966. Since Moe controlled both companies, he was able to funnel advances on the trawler contracts to Gulf Garden and keep it afloat. By October 31, Gulf Garden owed Bathurst Marine $630,000 and was falling seriously behind on other payments to creditors, including the government. Not surprisingly, the funds transferred from Bathurst Marine to Gulf Garden were crippling the shipyard. The commission of inquiry later found that "while such switching of funds alleviated only temporarily the already desperate financial situation of Gulf Garden Foods, the loss of such monies by Bathurst Marine could only serve to weaken its financial position."

In fact, the financial health of the Georgetown industries continued to deteriorate following the May 30 general election, while public speculation mounted. As the July 11 deferred by-election in 1st Kings loomed, the Shaw government became desperate to keep it all from unravelling. The most pressing concern was the financial plight of Gulf Garden Foods. Under the original 1964 agreement, the Industrial Development Corporation was to construct and own the plant, and lease it to Gulf Garden Foods at a nominal cost until January 1, 1967. Following that date, the costs would be amortized over a period of twenty-five years at an interest rate of six percent. Gulf Garden was also supposed to make payments on the trawlers, based on a percentage of their landings. The company was seriously in arrears on both.

None of this was apparent from the glittering ceremony arranged on the Georgetown wharf on July 4, just one week prior to the deferred by-election. The occasion was the christening of the *Gulf Gerd* at the Bathurst Marine shipyards. Thomas Sanderson, president of Bathurst Marine, officiated at the ceremony, which was attended by Lieutenant-Governor W.J. ("Billy Archie") MacDonald; Premier Shaw; K. Graesdal, Managing Director of Norinvest AS of Norway; R.V. Richards, vice-president of Nestlé Canada of Toronto; F. Larsen, Vice-president of Schroden Banking Corporation of New York; Leo Rossiter; Jens Moe, and others.

After Mrs. Graesdal christened the new trawler, the official party attended a lavish reception presided over by Moe, who confidently predicted a positive future for the Georgetown industries. Just the week before, the *Gulf Grenadier* (the first trawler launched by the shipyard) had returned to Georgetown reportedly loaded with the largest catch of fish ever landed in the province. But the upbeat mood concealed the deepening crisis facing Moe's companies.

On July 8, three days before the deferred election, Rossiter authorized a new agreement with Moe in a final, desperate move. Legal ownership of the plant would be transferred from the Industrial Development Corporation to Gulf Garden Foods for the sum of $3,396,750. This would give Gulf Garden some assets with which to enter into negotiations with creditors, and allow it time to put its financial affairs in order. To sweeten the deal, Rossiter instructed that the fish plant be deeded to Gulf Garden Foods with no payments due until April 1, 1968.

Following the Liberal election victory on July 11, Alex Campbell's new government was sworn into office on July 28. For most of the next two years, it would find itself preoccupied with the fallout from the Georgetown Fiasco.

*　　*　　*

PARO

Leo Rossiter (standing) *with Premier Walter Shaw. "Poor Walter Shaw, a nice old man who cannot control some of the boys in his cabinet," became the Liberal party line when attacking the Georgetown industries.*

When Campbell arrived at the recently constructed Shaw Building on Rochford Street as head of the new provincial government, he found no files in the Premier's Office relating to Jens Moe, Gulf Garden Foods, or Bathurst Marine.* Searches through the files of the Industrial Development Corporation and the Fishermen's Loan Board revealed little evidence of what had transpired.

"It was very difficult to obtain information," Campbell told the Commission of Inquiry. "The files left in the Premier's Office revealed nothing about Gulf Garden Foods and we found it extremely difficult to find information on these companies except for a sparse smattering of documents and so on in the Industrial Development Corporation. In the Department of Industry, filing cabinets had been stripped almost bare and we had to start somewhere."

It did not take long for the magnitude of the problems to surface. Within days, the phones started ringing in the Premier's Office from anxious creditors of both Gulf Garden Foods and Bathurst Marine – as many as twenty a day. They sought assurances that their outstanding accounts would be paid, and confirmation that, if they continued to do business with the two companies, government would guarantee payments. Creditors appeared from everywhere. Maritime Electric claimed it was owed $23,000 (although, to keep the operations running, the Shaw government had guaranteed the account earlier that year on March 10); Island Telephone was threatening to discontinue service; the Workmen's Compensation Board was owed $50,000; Island Oxygen claimed unpaid bills totalling more than $10,000; and CN Rail was holding carloads of steel and equipment on its sidings waiting to be released upon payment. To compound the problem, late charges on the shipments were mounting daily. Those were just the small bills; millions were owed to various creditors, including the government and other investors.

The new Campbell government faced its first major dilemma. Failure to keep the operations alive or forcing them into bankruptcy – especially so soon after taking power – might be perceived as an attempt to discredit the previous government. On the other hand, Campbell was not anxious to extend the string of losses. On October 7, officials of both Gulf Garden Foods and Bathurst Marine met with

---

* *The outgoing Conservatives named the building after Walter Shaw. It was quickly renamed the more prosaic Provincial Administrative Building by the new Liberal government. The name reverted to the Shaw Building when the Conservatives returned to power in 1979.*

Campbell's cabinet to outline their financial requirements. Bathurst Marine required an immediate injection of $817,775, while Gulf Garden needed $596,117. Together, they were asking for more than $1.4 million to stave off bankruptcy. Between September 30 and October 19, the government provided Bathurst Marine with $67,590 in an attempt to keep it afloat, and covered the weekly payroll.

Jens Moe was rumoured to be back in Norway looking for new investors, so the cabinet tracked him down there and asked him to return to Charlottetown for a meeting. Moe responded that he was attempting to persuade his investors to attend as well. "Impossible to arrange meeting all interested parties earlier than Tuesday next," he telegraphed. The cabinet went ahead with its meeting on October 15th in the 5th floor cabinet chambers at the Provincial Administrative Building, but neither Moe nor his investors showed up. Moe telephoned the Premier's Office claiming that his flight to Charlottetown had been cancelled, but a check by Andy Wells (now Campbell's executive assistant) revealed no cancelled flights to the Maritimes that day.

Six days later, Campbell received a telegram from Norinvest AS and Olsen & Ugelstad, two Norwegian companies who claimed to be investors in Moe's operations. "In view of recent very serious developments and press releases bring situation to very serious head," it read, "we have instructed Mr. Moe to postpone any meeting with PEI government or any of their branches – stop – as Guarantors and having Mr. Moe's stock pledge to us and thereby representing major potential creditor interests we are opinion this now primarily our business to discuss this matter with you and therefore request that no meeting be held without our representation – stop –." This gave the Campbell government the first indication that others might be involved in backing Moe. On October 29, the cabinet met with officials from Norinvest and Olsen & Ugelstad They quickly recognized that additional funding alone would not solve the operational problems of the two Georgetown companies, and agreed to work together to find solutions. The cabinet proposed that the owners, "whoever they were," should come up with an additional $500,000, which the government agreed to match. It was generally agreed that this additional infusion of $1 million in equity would help stabilize the companies until a longer-term solution could be reached. But the putative Norwegian investors balked. They first wanted to examine the financial condition and prospects of the companies, and asked the government to pay their expenses. Cabinet refused, the issue was dropped, and the investors – "whoever they were" – returned to Norway.

Campbell never met Jens Moe. "Not only did I never meet him, we were never able to even find him," Campbell later said of the elusive, swashbuckling developer.

Within a few days, the government had taken over payment of the weekly payrolls for both companies, which daily faced more liens from creditors. With no assurance that additional funds would be forthcoming to help stave off bankruptcy, it was becoming increasingly impossible to advance further monies to keep the companies afloat, and concerns persisted about the way the funds were being managed. The situation could not have continued for much longer. With debts piling up, Gulf Garden Foods ceased operations on November 30, 1966. The ten trawlers used to supply fish to the plant were tied up at the Georgetown wharf. In accordance with the earlier performance agreement between the Fishermen's Loan Board and Bathurst Marine, the Board took over the shipyard on December 30 when Bathurst Marine was deemed to be in default.

The government now found itself in a legal quagmire over Gulf Garden Foods. Moe legally owned the plant by virtue of the July 8 agreement whose terms did not require him to begin making mortgage payments for another sixteen months. The government could only stand by and wait while shareholders and creditors quarrelled over ownership and assets. By March 1967, both companies had been placed into bankruptcy. The government tried to find buyers for the fish plant, and approached W.R. Grace of New York, a renowned fish plant operator, but it rejected the offer, stating that the plant would not be profitable even if it were acquired under favourable terms. The government then offered Bathurst Marine for sale at bankruptcy proceedings but received no bids, so it bought the assets and converted the company into a crown corporation, Georgetown Shipyards.

When the dust settled, the provincial government's investment into the two companies totalled $9.9 million. The assets were valued at $3.1 million, and creditors were paid about twenty cents on the dollar. The demise of the two companies, once regarded as the jewels of a new era of industrial development in Prince Edward Island, caused a political storm. The opposition Conservatives asserted that "a little more money" in 1966 would have saved the companies.

When the Legislature opened in the spring of 1967, the Conservatives demanded an emergency debate on the demise of the

Georgetown industries. Shaw and Rossiter in particular were unrepentant. Rossiter continued to defend Moe, declaring that "no man worked harder to make a business go." According to Rossiter, Moe was simply unable to obtain the funds when he needed them. The former minister of Fisheries and Industry also claimed that the loss to Prince Edward Island taxpayers was limited to less than fifty percent because, after all, the rest of the money came from the federal government (and presumably didn't count.) At one point during the heated discussions, Speaker Prosper Arsenault suspended Rossiter from the Legislature for his unparliamentary language in attacking the incumbent minister, Cecil Miller.

The controversy continued to dominate debate in the Legislature the following year. Cecil Miller, with help from Frank Sigsworth, lambasted the failure of the Georgetown industries as "a swindle on such a gigantic scale that it deprived the people of Prince Edward Island of sums of money unequalled in the whole economic history of the province." Miller blamed the failure on a "garrulous gaggle of galahads dedicated to Moe," and declared that the projects were "a monument to the genius of one man and the stupidity and complicity of others." The fiasco was, asserted Miller with partisan passion and one eye on the public gallery of the Legislature, "a grim reminder of the barbarous and limitless capacity of the Tories for mismanagement, maladministration, and the deceptive mis-construction of fact."

It was sheer audacity that "these miscreants, these betrayers of the public trust, should stand before you destitute, destitute of defence, naked of trust, shivering in the cold gaze of the accusing public," he charged. He went on to castigate them for their "consummate audacity to this very day to stand up and defend their actions, to stand up and defend the record of this sorry object of their affection, to defend the record of this international swindler [Moe]." Is it any wonder, he asked, that "such people do rant and roar and fulminate and furiously strive, all for one purpose."

Rossiter responded vehemently, charging that the issue "has been a story of a systematic relentless attack by the members of the provincial government acting in their own political self interests. This is a story of a purposeful strangulation by the P.E.I. Liberal Government of two companies that had a wonderful future in the development of this province." To divert attention from the issue, he accused Frank Sigsworth of writing Miller's speech as a personal vendetta against him. Sigsworth, acting as legal counsel to the Commission of Inquiry on the Georgetown industries, was unrelenting in his exposure of the events leading to the companies' demise. In a hopeless gesture of bravado, Sigsworth ran against Rossiter in 2nd Kings in the 1966 provincial election, baiting him constantly on the campaign trail and happily engaging in political *schadenfreude*. For his part, former premier Walter Shaw declared that if he had stayed in power, "I'm sure we could have gradually solved the money problems involved."

PARO

Frank Sigsworth was a brilliant, flamboyant, and loquacious advisor to Campbell, who served as legal counsel for the government in the inquiry into the failed Georgetown industries.

In response to the growing controversy, Campbell appointed the Commission of Inquiry on March 7, 1967. The commission heard from government and industry officials, industry experts, and others who testified to the litany of woes that ailed the companies from the beginning. Premier Campbell was the only politician who appeared before the commission. Jens Moe refused to appear unless the hearings were transferred to Montreal.

The commission released its final report in August 1969. It raised no questions about the motives of the Shaw government. "The

Premier of the day, along with the members of his cabinet, were sincere in their desires to promote new industries in the province," it found. It did conclude, however, that the Shaw government should have exercised more prudence in its dealings with Moe and in its management of public funds, stating that, "as members of government they should unquestionably have satisfied themselves that all proper investigations were made as to the reliability and capability of Mr. Moe to carry out the project." But it stopped short of condemning Leo Rossiter, the key political figure in the fiasco. It merely noted that "in matters where differences of opinion existed between Mr. Moe and others, Mr. Rossiter seems invariably to have supported Mr. Moe's viewpoint."

The Commission made a number of recommendations about government's future role in industrial development, including the undertaking of proper feasibility studies, greater financial controls, and more oversight. It ruefully observed that "those in government who dealt with Mr. Moe in respect of the project seem to have overlooked the necessity of adequate planning before committing the province to the project, and were obviously carried away by Mr. Moe's salesmanship."

*   *   *

Unfortunately, the failure of the Georgetown industries had tarnished the province's reputation among serious investors. When the Campbell government took office, it found not only the filing cabinets stripped bare, the province's bank account was also nearly depleted. Provincial Treasury officials forecast that, within a month, the government would be unable to meet its own payroll.

When the Shaw government came to power, the province's net debt stood at approximately $32 million. When the Campbell government came into office, it stood at an estimated $75 million, with more than $8 million of that incurred between March 31 and July 28, 1966, when government changed hands. Other figures were being tossed around, some people putting the debt as high as $99 million. Nobody could figure out the real total. Commented the *Guardian*, "There isn't an auditor on earth who could get to the bottom of the mystery."

Campbell and Provincial Treasurer Earle Hickey travelled to Montreal to meet the province's fiscal agent, Merrill Lynch. At that point, they began to realize the magnitude of the provincial government's financial woes. During most of the previous year, the Shaw government had raised short-term funds on the money markets in the form of provincial treasury bills. Some of these were now maturing, and the provincial government would be unable to meet its debt obligations.

Merrill Lynch officials curtly informed the two politicians that they lacked confidence in the government's ability to manage its finances, and were not about to send good money after bad. A subsequent meeting was arranged between Merrill Lynch and the provincial cabinet at which Merrill Lynch officials issued an ultimatum: Cut spending or see the Province's credit rating evaporate. They eventually reached an agreement to convert the short-term debt to a longer term. Merrill Lynch managed to put together a total of eighteen bond dealers to purchase the issue, but the Province's financial reputation was badly tarnished all the same. Its perilous financial state was destined to continue throughout Campbell's first term.

At this point, Campbell made the first of many visits to Ottawa to find out where the money was, as he put it. His first meeting with Prime Minister Pearson was warm and cordial, although not as formal as Campbell may have expected. He and Pearson sat around a semicircle of chairs facing a television set. (Pearson was a fanatical baseball fan, and rarely missed at least parts of games when he was in his office.) Over coffee Campbell and Pearson discussed the province's financial plight. As leader of the only provincial Liberal government in Canada at the time, Campbell felt he had Pearson's implicit support.

By 1968, the province was still exercising prudence. The fact is, Earle Hickey told the Legislature in March of that year, "We are in a bad financial state. We have trouble borrowing money and if we don't show reasonable financial responsibility we are going to be in trouble. We made certain commitments last year that we would reduce our debt over a period of three years ... But the point is, we are faced with a certain condition here and we have to do our best to resolve it."

Prince Edward Island and its people learned a hard lesson from the Georgetown Fiasco, and the new government of Premier Campbell was determined not to make the same mistakes.

*   *   *

Jens Moe quickly dropped out of sight and never returned to Prince Edward Island. In May 1967, he was reported to be operating a company called Malpeque Shrimp, with head offices in Saint John, New Brunswick. Moe originally incorporated the company in September 1965 as Malpeque Commercial Distillery with the stated aim to manufacture, distill, and sell whisky. Now living in Montreal, he was supposedly flying frozen shrimp to Scandinavia, but the rumour was never confirmed.

CHAPTER FOUR

The Causeway

Alex Campbell's new government had barely settled into its offices when it faced a most serious crisis – a strike by employees of Canadian National Railway (CNR), including its marine division, CN Marine, which operated the ferry service between Borden, Prince Edward Island, and Cape Tormentine, New Brunswick. The strike, scheduled for late August or early September, threatened to disrupt the province at the height of the tourist season. On July 28, the day Campbell was sworn into office, stories reached him from Ottawa that Parliament might be recalled to pass legislation dealing with the imminent strike by the CNR. While negotiations continued with the Canadian Brotherhood of Railway Trainmen and General Workers Union, which represented the 450 ferry workers, Islanders and their government anxiously watched developments. Campbell was about to face his first test as premier.

On August 12, Campbell sent a telegram to federal Transport Minister Jack Pickersgill expressing his concern about a possible disruption to the ferry service, and urging the federal government and the CNR to negotiate a special agreement to keep the ferries operating.* Faced with the prospect of a national rail strike, the federal cabinet met on August 17 to consider its options. In the event of a strike by the 100,000 non-operating workers – clerks, telegraphers, and shop trades – along with 20,000 members of the union representing conductors and brakemen, the Canadian economy would grind to a halt. As union organizers prepared to hold strike votes, wildcat walkouts occurred in Montreal and spread to Toronto, London, Windsor, and Sydney. On Monday, August 22, union leaders announced they would strike on August 26, at which Prime Minister Lester Pearson recalled Parliament for August 29.

A similar exception had been made in 1950 when CN workers went on strike demanding a wage increase and a five-day week, but Premier Walter Jones negotiated a deal with the federal government under which the ferries continued to operate.

Meanwhile, Campbell was engaged in furious, three-way negotiations with the federal departments of Transport and Labour and with Local 127 of the Union. Campbell wanted assurances that at least one ferry would continue to operate if a strike took place. Following a meeting with the Union in Borden on Monday evening, he stated he was "confident that should a nationwide strike occur a transportation link between Port Borden and Cape Tormentine will be maintained." With rising consternation from tourism officials about cancelled reservations – visitors already on the Island were preparing to depart early – Campbell made a plea that "our visitors will await the next decision before leaving the province ahead of schedule." The wait was short. On Tuesday at noon, following a meeting at the curling club in Borden, union officials announced they had rejected the proposal for at least one ferry to continue operating in the event of a strike. In a last-ditch effort to avert a complete shutdown of the ferry service, Campbell tried to negotiate with them again in Borden the next morning.

With no agreement in place, the provincial cabinet met that afternoon at two o'clock to declare a state of emergency. Under its provisions, the government hoped it would be able to take over the operation of at least one ferry. Other emergency provisions allowed it to set priorities for both ferry services carrying traffic to and from the Island. "When the lifeblood of our Island economy is in jeopardy and we are faced with a serious curtailment of vital services, such as movement of agricultural produce, livestock and other perishable goods," Campbell told the *Guardian* "we are left with no alternative but to resort to the powers and provisions of the Emergency Measures Act in the public interest."

While federal officials in Ottawa were examining the legal implications of Prince Edward Island taking over a ferry, pressure mounted on union officials in Montreal to arrange for a limited ferry service. By Wednesday afternoon, traffic at the ferry terminals was beginning to back up at an alarming rate as visitors lined up to leave the province. Upwards of 150 automobiles were left behind after each crossing. However, despite the escalating situation and efforts to relieve it, on Thursday, Local 127 voted unanimously in favour of strike action, set to start at noon the next day, August 26.

The provincial government was dealing with the first ferry strike in the Island's history. The pickets went up in Borden at one o'clock on Friday afternoon, and the four CN ferries – the *Abegweit, Scotia, Prince Edward Island* and *Confederation* – were tied up at the Borden terminal with skeleton crews left on board for security.

The Campbell government immediately moved ahead with its plans to implement the state of emergency. Although resigned to the consequences of a strike, officials kept in constant contact with the Prime Minister's Office and with officials in the departments of Ttransport and Labour. A cabinet committee chaired by Keir Clark, with support from Major Orin Simmons, the provincial civil defence co ordinator, set up a permit system based on transportation priorities to be used on the Wood Islands-Caribou (Prince Edward Island to Nova Scotia) ferry service. In addition, a control head-quarters in Charlottetown kept radio contact with the terminals at Borden and Wood Islands.

After a telephone call with Transport Minister Pickersgill, who confirmed that the federal government would not intervene to keep the ferry service operating, Campbell held a news conference on Friday afternoon in Charlottetown. He told reporters that "we must recognize the limited influence which the federal government is able to exert beyond the nation-wide appeal by the Prime Minister." At the same time, he expressed frustration that the federal government had failed to keep the ferries running, especially in light of assurances that it recognized its obligations under the terms of Confederation to provide "continuous communications" with the mainland. "Why they didn't do something already about this, I don't know," he commented in exasperation.

Over the weekend, rumours circulated that the Canadian Coast Guard was preparing to take over the ferry service. The CCGS *Tupper* was said to be on its way from the Magdalen Islands. Meanwhile, the ferry service at Wood Islands had stepped up the number of crossings and was coping reasonably well with the increased traffic (fortunately, traffic to the Island was extremely light). With the public demanding an end to the strike and tensions mounting on the picket lines in Borden, Campbell appealed for calm, asking people to act reasonably.

Meanwhile, on Sunday, August 28, as Parliament prepared to go back into session, union officials in Montreal took a significant step, making quiet overtures about the possibility of a limited ferry service. Maintaining that even a temporary transfer of ferry owner-ship to the provincial government would break CN's contract with the railway workers, union representative R.C. Smith said it was willing to consider continued operations for passengers, automo-biles, and trucks, but not trains. Although some confusion reigned about the offer – strike leader Everett MacLeod in Borden claimed to be unaware of it – speculation mounted that the strike would soon be over.

On Monday, August 28, Parliament introduced national back-to-work legislation. Local 127 called a meeting that afternoon at the curling rink in Borden with Barry Hould, a union representative in Moncton and a go-between for the national unions, to discuss Smith's proposal and the threat of legislation. Following the meeting, Willard Pickering, president of Local 127, announced that a limited ferry service would begin at eight o'clock on Tuesday morning. On August 31, as the national unions faced back-to-work legislation, the picket lines in Borden came down and full ferry service was restored.

The Prince Edward Island government had averted a major crisis, but the perennial issue of transportation between the Island and the mainland had been reopened. Under the terms of Confederation, the federal government was obligated to provide a "continuous and efficient" transportation service between the Island and the mainland, but Islanders never regarded the service as either continuous or efficient. The transportation issue had dominated and would continue to dog federal-provincial relations for more than a century. As Campbell told the news conference before the strike began, "I regard the maintenance of the transportation link between Borden and Cape Tormentine as the prime responsibility of the federal government as set out by the British North America Act under which the federal government is obliged to maintain a continuous transportation link between the Island and the mainland."

With just over one month of experience in office, the Campbell government had quickly learned just how far the federal government was willing to live up to those responsibilities.

*   *   *

For people living on an Island, getting on and off is important. Despite the constitutional guarantee of "continuous and efficient" transportation to the mainland, the federal government did not interpret the guarantee at the same level of expectation as Islanders. The perennial problem of travel was caused, as a former premier, Robert Haythorne, put it, "for want of means of getting off and on." Those means were very limited.

After the Island joined Canada in 1873, the first vessel supplied by the federal government to ply the Northumberland Strait was a wooden steamer called the *Northern Light,* which went into service during the winter of 1876. The steamer was not built to withstand the ice conditions; the first year the steering gear broke, and the following season the propellor was smashed. However, when the crew later discovered that its stern was better adapted than its bow for breaking through the ice floes, the *Northern Light* jettisoned its dignity and majestically navigated the Strait sailing backwards. On one occasion, she was ice-bound for three solid weeks. When passengers ran out of food and water – and patience – they disembarked and walked the perilous journey back to shore.

The early vessels assigned to the service were inadequate to meet the Island's transportation needs. For weeks on end, as Islanders would say, "the mainland was cut off again." In the winter of 1881, tons of merchandise destined for the Island sat in warehouses in Pictou, Nova Scotia, while large quantities of freight and produce destined for mainland markets sat on the Island for want of a means to ship them. In 1885, deeply frustrated with the lack of response from Ottawa for better service, the government of the time finally launched a desperate appeal to Queen Victoria. A committee of the Queen's Privy Council placed the blame simply and squarely on the practical difficulties of crossing the Northumberland Strait during the winter months. Canada, it proffered, could only provide "what science and experience might determine as the best and most efficient within the range of possibility."

A tunnel was suggested as the solution. In the 1890s, Island Senator George Howlan estimated that a tunnel (actually, an iron tube resting on the bottom of the Strait) could be constructed at a cost of $6 million. Howlan resigned from his seat in the Senate to run for the House of Commons, basing his campaign on the slogan "Howlan and the Tunnel." When both the tunnel and the seat in the House of Commons failed to materialize, Howlan accepted yet another appointment to the Senate, and the idea of a tunnel was put on hold.*

During the 1911 federal election, Conservative leader Robert Borden promised the construction of a tunnel between Prince Edward Island and the mainland. Following his election, Borden's enthusiasm waned as the cost estimates escalated (in 1906, engineers with the federal Department of Public Works estimated the cost of construction to be $10-20 million). But on January 3, 1912, in the midst of the provincial election campaign, he promised the establishment of a ferry service to connect the Island railways to the rest

---

* *Howlan later resigned from the Senate again to accept an appointment as the Island's lieutenant-governor.*

of the country. The *Guardian* was ecstatic, gushing that "no more important message has come to this province since Confederation than this." The local Conservatives won an overwhelming majority of twenty-eight seats to two, and the Borden government kept its commitment. It commissioned the construction of a new car ferry from a shipyard in Newcastle, England, and the Roger Miller Co. of Prince Edward Island commenced construction of the terminal in the community that, in gratitude, was renamed Port Borden.

The daily ferry service commenced on October 16, 1917. This connection to the mainland railway system revolutionized freight shipments, and when automobiles were finally allowed on Island highways, the ferry was able to accommodate them as well. But as demands on the service grew, so did the need for more and better ferries. Shipping costs represented yet another issue. In response to regional grievances, the MacKenzie King government introduced the Maritime Freight Rates Act in 1927, which provided for a twenty-percent reduction on freight rates within and out of the region east of Levis, Québec, and south of the St. Lawrence River. Ferry rates were also cause for concern. With the advent of the TransCanada Highway as a Depression-era construction initiative in the 1930s, the Island government viewed the ferry service as part of the system and constantly agitated for lower – if no – fares.

In 1928, as the federal government provided $1 million for the construction of a second ferry, the Department of Railways and Canals was re-examining the idea of a "fixed link." Rather than a tunnel, engineers studied the feasibility of a causeway, described as a "breakwater structure with a road on top and adequate facilities here and there for the passage of boats to and fro." The scheme was dropped, however, because of the prohibitive cost of approximately $50 million, and the fact that its durability could not be assured.

In 1937, to counter demands from residents of eastern Prince Edward Island, the federal government established a second ferry service between Wood Islands and Caribou, Nova Scotia, and undertook the construction of harbour facilities at Wood Islands with the full support of Queens County MP Charles Dunning.*

---

* *Dunning, who was not an Islander, served in King's cabinet as minister of finance, and was found a seat in Queens County during a by-election in 1935. For his part in helping establish the new service, one of its ferries was named after him.*

But as traffic volumes increased, along with a growing sense of isolation from markets, agitation continued for improvements in transportation infrastructure and capacity to the mainland. In 1938, Premier Thane Campbell resurrected the idea of a tunnel before the Rowell-Sirois Commission investigating federal-provincial relations. The Commission rejected the idea, while acknowledging Campbell's position. It concluded "that a reasonable ferry service has been provided and reasonable improvements have been instituted from time to time."

In the period following the Second World War, freight shipments doubled and automobile traffic rose dramatically. As a result, the MV *Abegweit* joined the Borden ferry service in 1947. But despite all these significant improvements, delays increased, costs rose, and the service proved less than efficient. The CNR, which operated the Borden-Cape Tormentine ferry service, was criticized for failing to pay more attention to the increasing volume of highway traffic, which was siphoning business away from the railways. Progress notwithstanding, the ferry service remained a lively and complex issue.

By the mid-1950s, the idea of a causeway had been revived. That idea came to dominate transportation discussions for the next fifty years.

*   *   *

In 1955, fresh from its electoral victory, Alex Matheson's provincial government requested Ottawa to investigate the economic and technical feasibility of a causeway linking the Island to the mainland. O.J. McCulloch, the engineer who had designed the recently completed Canso Causeway joining Cape Breton Island to mainland Nova Scotia, provided a construction estimate of $50 million. He concluded that forty million tons of rock fill would be needed, and federal Public Works Minister Robert Winters sent a team of geologists to Cape Tormentine to investigate the availability of supplies. The idea was picked up by John Diefenbaker's new federal government following its election in 1957. However, feasibility studies indicated huge engineering problems. Concerns arose about the impact on tides, water temperatures, fisheries, and navigation. The challenge was to design a causeway that would accommodate these concerns as well as resist the massive ice floes, which travelled through the Strait at four miles per hour in the winter months. Meeting those design challenges boosted costs and dimmed hopes.

Walter Shaw came to power in 1959, after an election in which the Conservatives billed themselves as "The Party of the Causeway." Shortly after his election, Shaw met with Diefenbaker at the Charlottetown Hotel, at which time the Prime Minister made a commitment to proceed with plans for the causeway. Nothing much happened in the next few years, however, but on the eve of the 1962 federal election Diefenbaker announced that his government had decided the project was feasible in both economic and engineering terms, and that construction would proceed at a cost of $105 million. A consortium of Canadian engineering consultants was organized, and established offices in Charlottetown to begin work on the project.

The 1962 federal election returned a Conservative minority government, which soon collapsed under the weight of Diefenbaker's ego and political squabbles with his cabinet. In the ensuing 1963 federal election campaign, both Conservatives and Liberals promised to continue with the causeway. The Liberals were particularly critical of the slow progress to date; Jack Pickersgill, campaigning for the Liberals from his riding in Newfoundland, dubbed the project the "Pauseway."

Following its win in 1963, the new Liberal government under Lester Pearson continued with the design work. Finally, after more than seventy-five years of dreaming, planning, and pleading, on July 8, 1965, Prime Minister Pearson announced a call for tenders to construct a combined tunnel, causeway, and bridge for a total estimated cost of $148 million.

Although many people feared the causeway would destroy the tranquillity and charm of Prince Edward Island and turn it into another Coney Island, the announcement was nevertheless greeted with widespread support.* The causeway would provide a major impetus to tourism (already the second-largest industry on the Island); boost manufacturing; and facilitate the shipment of produce – not to mention a number of other spin-offs.

As Canada once again prepared to go to the polls in late 1965, Solicitor General and Liberal MP for Prince County J. Watson

---

* *Coney Island, a pleasure ground located in Brooklyn, New York, developed into a highly popular, if relatively tasteless, tourist attraction.*

Bridge

The bridge section of the fixed link was close to four miles in length, consisting of 41 spans with an elevation of 100 feet. Like the causeway section, the rail tracks ran underneath the roadway.

Causeway

The causeway portion of the fixed link between Prince Edward Island and New Brunswick would begin at the end of Jourimain Island on the New Brunswick side and extend for over two miles into the Strait. It was designed as a rock-filled structure with a two-lane elevated roadway and a single track underneath for trains.

Tunnel

The tunnel was designed in two sections, beginning on the Prince Edward Island side and extending more than two miles from the shore. They would be joined by an artificial island.

MacNaught (uncharitably dubbed "J. Watson MacZero" by journalist Peter Newman) climbed on a bulldozer near Cape Tormentine on November 5, three days before the election, and turned the first sod on the approach road for the causeway. Despite the symbolic significance of the act, MacNaught was widely criticized for failing to invite Premier Shaw and other provincial dignitaries. The inauguration of the most important public works project in the history of Prince Edward Island, described as a "shabby, colourless little ceremony" by the *Canadian Annual Review*, nevertheless represented the translation of years of planning into reality.

Yet, visions of the long-awaited causeway would soon evaporate.

* * *

The ferry strike faced by the Campbell government immediately following its election in 1966 stiffened its resolve to see the causeway project proceed. In his first visit to Ottawa to meet Prime Minister Pearson, Campbell impressed on him the importance of proceeding with construction. That summer, the project appeared to be on target. The Northumberland Strait Crossing design team was hard at work; construction companies were gearing up for the massive task ahead; and the approach roads for both highway and rail traffic on both sides of the Strait had been started.

A briefing session held by the federal Department of Public Works on July 14, 1966, just days after the election of the Campbell government, translated the long-awaited concept into something people could now visualize. The causeway section – a rock-filled structure with an elevated roadway, a single rail track, and provision for the two vehicle lanes to be widened to four – would extend from Jourimain Island on the New Brunswick side some 11,560 feet out into the Strait.

The 18,300-foot-long bridge section would be carried at an elevation of 100 feet, its forty-one spans resting on piers founded on the bedrock of the Strait itself. On the Prince Edward Island side, the first section of the tunnel would begin in Borden and extend some 7,000 feet under the Strait to an artificial island, from where it would continue on to join the bridge section for a total length of 13,000 feet. The rectangular tunnel, constructed of reinforced concrete, would carry the rail line in the centre and two lanes of traffic, one on each side, in the outer sections.

On June 30, 1967, as work on the approaches continued, tenders on the first phase of the causeway section came in much higher than expected, and Public Works Minister George McIlraith announced that the design would be reassessed. To dampen growing doubt and scepticism, Pearson reassured the public that the project was only being rescheduled, not deferred. In an attempt to solidify the federal government's commitment and to demonstrate the widespread political support in Prince Edward Island for the causeway, Campbell took Walter Shaw along to a federal-provincial conference. He gently chastised Pearson for the on-again, off-again nature of the project. If Pearson were now to break his previous promises to Shaw, it would be tantamount to "highway robbery," as Campbell phrased it. But the federal government was not the only one having second thoughts. O.J. McCulloch, who had carried out preliminary work on the concept in 1955, submitted an unsolicited evaluation to Public Works in April 1967 which stated that "the purpose of the criticism was to induce the Government to halt proceedings long enough to have the whole scheme thoroughly studied and approved by an independent and competent board before going any further."

Meanwhile, Colonel Edward Churchill, who had supervised the widely acclaimed construction of the 1967 Montreal Expo, was appointed to take over supervision of the project. Federal officials were now working on a new design with construction targeted for completion by 1972. One proposal involved eliminating the rails, an option opposed by the provincial government. In a statement Campbell made in October, he emphasized he was interested "only in those designs which make provision for rail service unless and until a realistic alternative to our present rail service is established to the satisfaction of the government and the shippers of the province."

Churchill, aware of the potential difficulties, made a speech to the Charlottetown Board of Trade on October 25, expressing disappointment but not surprise that the original bids were rejected. "Large marine projects are usually more difficult to evaluate than land based projects because of the risks involved and the greater number of unforeseen difficulties," he explained. Comparing the causeway project to the construction of the St. Lawrence Seaway and the massive Churchill Falls hydroelectric facility, he extolled its potential benefits, hailing the causeway as "one of the greatest transportation links in the world."

By this time, the causeway was being touted as the economic salvation of Prince Edward Island; politicians and the public alike extolled it as critical to the Island's future prosperity. "I am tempted to believe that there can be no real improvement in income and in standards of living on the Island unless easy and continuous access to markets is arranged," Churchill told the receptive Board of Trade. "Significant economic growth will take place only after the crossing has been completed." Meanwhile, the Campbell government had entered into serious negotiations with the federal government on a massive development plan aimed at transforming the Island economy. Before it was over, the government was accused of abandoning the causeway for the development plan.

Work remained stalled on the causeway as summer – and a federal election – arrived in 1968. "Trudeaumania" had swept the country in June as the new prime minister, Pierre Eliott Trudeau, captivated Canadians with his vision of a "just society." To the chagrin of Islanders, that "just society" did not appear to embrace the causeway; it was not even mentioned during the Liberal election campaign. As summer turned into fall, the *Globe and Mail* and other national media began to speculate that the impending funding for Prince Edward Island's proposed Comprehensive Development Plan would come at the expense of the causeway.

Campbell was becoming increasingly frustrated with the continued delays and the federal government's failure to provide answers on both the causeway and the Development Plan. But these were not the only points of contention between Prince Edward Island and the federal governments; earlier in the year, Campbell had led a delegation to Ottawa, including Summerside Mayor George Key and the four Island MPs, to fight for the survival of CFB Summerside in Slemon Park, which was threatened with closure. Campbell had met with Trudeau on a number of occasions to discuss the causeway and other issues.* But the federal government's obstinate attitude fuelled his rising frustration that federal policies were failing to address regional economic problems. Publicly, he mused that a change of attitude towards Prince Edward Island was necessary "if

---

* *Campbell's relationship with Trudeau was not as close as it had been with Pearson, although they did become political allies. At the 1968 federal leadership convention, Campbell had supported favourite regional son Allan J. MacEachen on the first ballot; when MacEachen dropped out, Campbell threw his support behind Trudeau.*

Prime Minister Pierre Trudeau is interested in preserving Confederation."

Frustration continued to mount through the summer and fall of 1968. In October, Campbell sent a strongly worded telegram to Trudeau. "The daily barrage of rumours emanating from officials in departments at Ottawa suggesting the project already scrapped, too expensive and not justificd, most annoying to us here," he fumed. To press his point, he took his full cabinet to Ottawa to pressure the federal government into renewing its commitment to the causeway. By then, Campbell believed the federal government had always regarded the causeway as a purely local "Prince Edward Island project," not part of a grand nation-building enterprise. In the eyes of Islanders, it seemed as though the provincial government was being forced to choose either the Development Plan or the causeway.

The causeway had now attained mythological status; Islanders were convinced it represented the Island's economic salvation. But, as 1968 drew to a close, it became increasingly apparent that the project would not proceed. On October 11, Del Gallagher, general manager of the Economic Improvement Corporation, accused the federal government of trying to "squeeze" Campbell to free it of its promise to build the causeway. Although transportation links were an important component of the Development Plan, the causeway was never an explicit part of the province's development strategy. Finally, on March 5, 1969, Prime Minister Trudeau announced in the House of Commons that, in the process of "fixing the priorities of expenditure," his government had scrapped the causeway project. In his statement, Trudeau told the House of Commons that his government had decided instead to support the Comprehensive Development Plan as "the likeliest method of offering appreciable and lasting benefits to the economy of Prince Edward Island in the foreseeable future ... The government should have liked to be able to assist at the same time in the construction of a causeway linking the Island to the mainland but there is a limitation to the resources of Canada."

On March 6, Jean Marchand, Trudeau's minister in charge of regional development, arrived in Prince Edward Island to finalize details and officially sign the Development Plan the next day. At a meeting that evening at the Kirkwood Motel in Charlottetown, Marchand and his deputy, Tom Kent, demanded that Campbell inform reporters that the choice of the Development Plan over the causeway was made by the provincial government. If Campbell refused, Marchand warned that he might not attend the Development Plan signing ceremony scheduled for the next afternoon. Campbell called Marchand's bluff, and went out to the parking lot for a cigarette, leaving the federal officials to consider their options. When he returned to the meeting, Marchand had changed his mind.

On March 7, the Prince Edward Island Comprehensive Development Plan was signed during an impressive ceremony at the Confederation Centre in Charlottetown. No mention was made of the causeway. Following the signing, Marchand and Campbell appeared on CFCY Television and together extolled the virtues of co-operative federalism.

*   *   *

The provincial government continued to feel the sting of criticism that it had abandoned the causeway for the Development Plan. Yet Campbell never gave up on the project. Following Trudeau's discouraging announcement, he began to explore other options for its construction. For example, he approached Stanford University to conduct a feasibility study as a private-sector enterprise, and met with investment bankers in New York to explore the possibility of long-term financing. The Stanford University analysis revealed that the project would require an annual subsidy from the federal government, one that Campbell argued would be more cost-effective in the end than the ongoing – and mounting – costs of operating the ferry service. When he presented the analysis to Trudeau, the Prime Minister shrugged it aside, insisting that if the project were to proceed the federal government, not private enterprise, would construct and operate it.

Campbell always believed the project was feasible through a partnership between the private and public sectors and never gave up in his efforts to justify it on an economic basis. In 1976, the federal transport department carried out a Prince Edward Island-mainland transportation study that backed up Campbell's contention. It found that constructing a fixed link, based on the 1968 design, would cost twenty to thirty percent more than operating the ferries, but if the rails were eliminated, the difference would be reduced by a significant amount. The study also admitted that the economic analysis upon which the decision to cancel the causeway project had been based failed to foresee the high inflation rates that occurred in the early 1970s.

The study provided the first formal acknowledgment of what many Islanders suspected all along. It concluded that "the termination of the fixed crossing was contingent upon a comprehensive development agreement for P.E.I. as well as an upgrading of the ferry service." Islanders were mollified by neither.

*   *   *

Sometime later, *MacLean's* magazine asked Campbell what he would like to be doing if he were not premier. "A ticket vendor on the PEI causeway," was the reply. As it happened, thirty-two years after Watson MacNaught mounted a bulldozer to turn the first sod for the causeway, Alex Campbell chaired a panel to choose a name for the newly constructed fixed link – the Confederation Bridge.

CHAPTER FIVE

A Single University

O n April 2, 1968, Premier Campbell received the unanimous consent of the Legislative Assembly to make a statement at 10:00 a.m. at the opening of the day's session on the future of higher education in Prince Edward Island. Since the public had been notified in advance, the gallery was crammed and the tension was palpable.

In 1968, Prince Edward Island boasted two degree-granting institutions: Prince of Wales College, a publicly funded, non-sectarian university which had just achieved degree-granting status and was now preparing to graduate its first class in 1969; and St. Dunstan's University, a church-supported institution with deep roots in the province's Roman Catholic community, which had just gained access to public funding on the same basis as Prince of Wales.* Both offered programs in arts, science and education; both were struggling with operating debt, capital costs, and rising enrollment; and both had ambitious plans. Since the establishment of Prince of Wales in 1834 and St. Dunstan's in 1855, these two rival institutions had fought fierce battles over post-secondary education in the province, with both sides jealously guarding their prerogatives. The contentions were based largely on the wide-spread and pervasive religious bigotry and intolerance that divided Islanders, hindered progress, distracted attention from important issues, and even brought down governments. As a result, religion had become a pervasive and in-tractable issue in Prince Edward Island.

Meanwhile, changes introduced in the 1960s to the funding of post-secondary education made both institutions eligible for public funding. But despite efforts by the provincial government to encourage co-operation, decades of religious mistrust, hostility, bickering, divisiveness, and political interference flew in the face of progress. At the first meeting of a co-ordinating council established to encourage joint planning by the two universities, the members

---

* From its inception, Prince of Wales had been a junior college, but received full university status from the provincial government in 1965.

found themselves at loggerheads and resolved never to meet again.

The Speech from the Throne that opened the 1968 session of the Legislative Assembly announced plans to establish a grants commission to advise the government on the universities' funding needs, and to recommend ways to eliminate duplication of services and programs.* The legislation introduced on March 26 elicited a vehement reaction from Dr. Frank MacKinnon, principal of Prince of Wales College, who slammed the legislation as interference in the affairs of his college, and demanded it be withdrawn.** When Bill 57, the Act to Establish the Grants Commission, was finally tabled in the Legislature, MacKinnon immediately went into action. Section 15 of the act gave the Commission powers to approve or terminate any service or program provided by a university. MacKinnon described this section as a "jet engine on a bicycle" and accused the Campbell government of violating academic freedom. His challenge was not to be taken lightly. MacKinnon was a highly respected college principal, author and academic. To his far-reaching vision and enormous energy were also credited the establishment of the Confederation Centre of the Arts in Charlottetown despite the prevailing spectrum of public opinion, ranging from plain indifference to outright antipathy.

MacKinnon quickly organized strong protests against Bill 57. For instance, a student arrived at Prince of Wales College early one

---

In 1967, the federal government transferred control of funding for universities to provincial governments, largely in response to demands from the province of Quebec for greater autonomy over what it regarded as a primarily provincial area of jurisdiction.

*** MacKinnon spearheaded the impetus behind the elevation of Prince of Wales College. The son of a former lieutenant-governor, MacKinnon possessed impeccable academic credentials and a clear vision for the future of the college. He had been hired by former premier Walter Jones during an agricultural exhibition in Ontario, where MacKinnon was teaching at that time. (As he liked to joke, Jones hired him during discussions over the back of a prize bull Jones was admiring.) MacKinnon had consistently and successfully resisted any political interference in the operation of Prince of Wales, which was frequently subjected to demands from politicians on staffing and other issues. But he was hampered by the absence of a real board for the College, which only stiffened his resolve to firmly establish its status as an independent institution with full degree-granting powers.*

Dr. Frank MacKinnon (left), *the formidable principal of Prince of Wales College, with Queen Elizabeth, Premier Walter Shaw and Mrs. Shaw* (extreme right) *at the official opening of the Confederation Centre of the Arts in 1964.*

morning to be met by biology professor Tom Lothian leading a group of students out of the door. "The UPEI horse rides again," shouted Lothian in defiance, "and we're going to shoot it down." Student demonstrations took place at the Legislature; letters, and telephone and telegraph messages flooded the Premier's Office; and a rash of newspaper advertisements and petitions vehemently opposed what was portrayed as an affront to the new degree-granting Prince of Wales College. All demanded withdrawal of the legislation. Behind MacKinnon's strenuous objections stood a fierce belief in the educational superiority of Prince of Wales College. He regarded any attempt at co-operation with St. Dunstan's as a impediment to the realization of the College's aspirations. MacKinnon ardently maintained that a place could be found for both institutions in the province. "There are different courses offered, different standards, different instructors and different concepts of education," he argued.

The reaction from St. Dunstan's was more muted. It had only recently acquired eligibility for government funding, and was coming to terms with its eventual demise as a church-controlled institution. With rising enrollment, it also recognized the need for public financial assistance to meet the post-war demands for diversified programs. Given its past history of unsuccessfully pressing successive governments for public support, it now saw the Grants Commission as the vehicle that would at long last formalize and solidify response to its demands. At the same time, St. Dunstan's was being swept along on a wave of ecumenicism in the wake of Vatican II. For a number of years, a group of citizens composed of representatives of Protestant and Roman Catholic churches had been advocating for closer co-operation, if not outright federation or amalgamation, between the two institutions. But MacKinnon would have nothing to do with it. He rejected calls for co-operation with St. Dunstan's as "a 'sop' to unsuspecting Protestants."

As Campbell rose in the Legislature on that Friday morning in April, he faced not only the immediate crisis over Bill 57, but also a long-standing tradition stemming from two centuries of religious differences. Loyalties for the two universities lay deeply entrenched, making public reaction towards significant changes to higher education unpredictable. With less than two years in office, the government was still feeling its way through the intricate and complex nuances of Island politics; with a bare two-seat majority in the Legislature (one, after the election of the Speaker), its hold on power was only tenuous.* This would not be the first time that a government had faced the threat of being split apart due to religious divisiveness. Just four years earlier, the decision to confer degree-granting status on Prince of Wales College had threatened to destroy the Shaw government in the face of fierce opposition from its Roman Catholic members.

Campbell also recognized the formidable opposition from Frank MacKinnon. "Dr. MacKinnon's refusal to have a grants commission

---

* *Already, one cabinet minister – Robert Campbell, the verbose, voluble and volatile MLA from 1st Prince – had threatened to resign over relatively minor changes to the Lord's Day Act. His departure over such a seemingly inconsequential amendment would have brought down the government.*

meddling in the affairs of 'his' college, his refusal to collaborate with St. Dunstan's and the government's insistence on seeing the public interest represented where public funds were involved, were the essential issues at the crux of the dispute," he stated. At issue was the fate of the still-fresh Campbell government. "As premier of the day, and a young political neophyte, still wet behind the ears, I had little room to manoeuver in the house," he admitted.

As he commenced his one-hour speech, Campbell felt very apprehensive. "As I rose to deliver the government's response, I speculated on how opposition members might react," he later recalled. "How would the people of Prince Edward Island receive it? Would my own caucus remain unanimous or split as happened earlier in the session with the Lord's Day Act? Only time would tell."

As it turned out, this speech marked a defining moment in the history of post-secondary education in Prince Edward Island. It also represented one of the boldest and most courageous acts of Campbell's first term in office.

*   *   *

The rocky relationship between the province's two institutions of higher education, deeply rooted in religious bigotry, prejudice, and discrimination also reflected what was happening in the rest of society. There were "Catholic" communities and "Protestant" communities, including Catholic and Protestant hospitals, medical clinics, schools, colleges, nursing schools, orphanages, and social service and community organizations. The divisions manifested themselves in disputes over teaching religion in public schools, and erupted from time to time in violent outbursts such as the infamous Belfast Riot during a by-election in 1847, which resulted in serious injuries and death.

Religious differences also poisoned politics. During the infamous "Bible questions" of the 1850s and '60s, religious factions within political parties struggled for ascendancy following the achievement of responsible government in 1851. These differences could be contained and accommodated (with a few notable exceptions) in distinct geographic, social, and economic spheres, but they confronted each other head-on in the public school system over such practices as reciting the Lord's Prayer, reading the Bible, and teaching religion. In 1877, a coalition government finally resolved that issue in typical Island fashion – by sweeping it under the table. Henceforth, public school students could chant the Lord's Prayer or study the catechism discretely as long as the principle of non-denominational schools was upheld.

Paradoxically, in an elaborate effort to keep religion out of politics, it became of utmost importance to and an integral part of the political system. No one was elected to political office or appointed to cabinet, the courts, Government House, or any other post, without reference to religious affiliation. Religious and party affiliation constituted the two-headed political animal that ruled with a heavy hand the public life of the province. In election battles, Protestants opposed Protestants and Catholics opposed Catholics. All knew their place through the carefully crafted art of political accommodation. The Protestant hegemony, however, prevailed. Since the achievement of responsible government over one hundred years ago, only one Roman Catholic had been elected premier.* Inevitably, the religious divisions became inextricably entangled in the province's institutions of higher education.

The history of higher education in Prince Edward Island began in 1804 when Lieutenant-Governor Edmund Fanning set aside ten town lots in Charlottetown for the establishment of a college for "the education of the youth in the learned languages, the liberal arts and sciences and all the branches of useful and polite literature." In 1834, the Central Academy (later Prince of Wales College) was founded by Royal Charter of King William IV as a publicly supported non-sectarian institution – and, as it evolved, a de facto Protestant one.

The first Catholic institution of higher education, St. Andrew's College, was founded by Bishop Angus MacEachern in 1831. It was succeeded by St. Dunstan's in 1855, offering "a literary, moral and religious education to all who chose to avail themselves of it." In 1892, St. Dunstan's affiliated with Laval University, which granted

---

* This was W.W. Sullivan, who served as premier between 1879 and 1889, making him the Island's longest-serving premier until the advent of Alex Campbell. He was appointed following the breakup of the Louis H. Davies coalition government that had helped to resolve the school question. Two other Roman Catholic premiers served in the twentieth century: Aubin E. Arsenault and W.J.P. MacMillan. However, both had come to power following the resignation of their predecessor and both failed to win the subsequent general election. James Lea, who became premier in 1982, was the first Roman Catholic to be elected premier in the twentieth century.

its degrees, but from 1941 onward it conferred its own degrees. Over the years, St. Dunstan's attempted to gain access to public funding, but was unwilling to give up its sectarian affiliation in exchange. In the process, it resisted any efforts on the part of the provincial government to extend largesse to Prince of Wales College. The resultant impasse frustrated the development of higher education in Prince Edward Island for over a century.

Prince of Wales College, on the other hand, evolved from the Central Academy, and became a junior college offering the first two years of post-secondary education. In 1907, the College was presented with an unprecedented opportunity to affiliate with McGill University in Montreal, thanks to the largesse of native Islander Sir William Macdonald (of the Macdonald tobacco empire) who offered to finance the College's expansion as he had done with the universities in Victoria and Guelph. Island premier Arthur Peters welcomed the generous offer, reporting a "a strong sentiment among many of our people that the affiliation would be a good thing for our Province." He confidently predicted that Prince of Wales would become "one of the finest colleges in the Maritime provinces."

That same year, the provincial government drafted a bill designating "The Prince of Wales College of McGill University" and sent it off to McGill officials in March. Then opposition to the measure raised its head. An Island farm organization, the Farmers' Institutes, complained in petitions to the government "that more money should not be expended on University Education before we have expended some additional on Agricultural Education." It was widely rumoured that a well-organized Catholic lobby opposed to more public funding for Prince of Wales was behind the petitions, although the question was not pursued in public. At any rate, the opposition had its desired effect. On April 17, Premier Peters sent another letter to McGill about the petitions received from the Farmers' Institutes. "I am sorry to tell you that for the present year we do not propose to carry out this proposition," he wrote, and suggested it "stand over for another year." That was to be the end of the matter.

As the two institutions evolved separately, they developed distinctive philosophies of education: Prince of Wales, based on the classical ideals with a rigorous intellectual orientation; St. Dunstan's, based on Christian ideals with a humanistic social orientation. Over the years, the rivalry simmered but came to a head in the period following the Second World War when increasing enrollment and a growing demand for university graduates led to intensified competition for recognition. In 1957, the rivalry erupted when Keir Clark, Minister of Education in the Liberal government of Alex Matheson, announced a new certification policy to meet the growing demand for qualified teachers. As the only degree-granting university in the province, St. Dunstan's received Clark's endorsement of its graduates as eligible for teachers' licenses. Inevitably, Prince of Wales College viewed this as an invasion of its exclusive prerogative to provide a teacher training program. Militant Protestants also resented a sectarian university training teachers for public non-denominational schools (ignoring the fact that most other Maritime universities were also aligned along religious lines), and they mounted a fierce personal attack against Clark. A bitter debate ensued in the Legislature, dividing both Liberal and Conservative caucuses.*

By the 1960s, with the mounting importance of post-secondary education, pressure increased to extend degree-granting status to Prince of Wales College. Although enrollment was rising, its graduates were forced to leave the province to conclude their studies elsewhere because the College offered only the first two years of university. Many never returned to Prince Edward Island. In 1962, Dr. Paul Cudmore, a respected Charlottetown physician, chaired a committee to lobby the Shaw government to confer degree-granting status on Prince of Wales College, and issued a feasibility report supporting the proposal. During the winter of 1964, a local committee of private citizens, including Charlottetown lawyers Alan Scales and Arthur Peake, provided legal advice and helped draft the legislation.

Now the long-simmering dispute over elevating the status of Prince of Wales College erupted. On February 5, 1964, anticipating opposition from the Catholic members of caucus, Education Minister Dr. George Dewar told Frank MacKinnon that the government wanted to soft-pedal the issue, and asked him to refrain from public comment. When Dewar presented the draft Prince of Wales College bill to the Conservative caucus on March 5, the heated debate lasted two and a half hours but ended without resolution. When the bill was introduced to the Legislature on March 9, Provincial Treasurer Alban

---

* Clark later acknowledged that, had he not singled out St. Dunstan's, but extended the endorsement to the graduates of any other degree-granting institutions, he might have muted if not avoided the controversy.

Farmer broke ranks with his own government and immediately introduced amendments that would have relegated Prince of Wales to the status of a private institution on a par with St. Dunstan's. That evening, despite entreaties from Dewar, the Conservative caucus upheld the Farmer amendments.

On March 11, Dewar met with Shaw in the Premier's Office and warned him that the government could be defeated over the issue. The next day, Shaw called a secret meeting of Protestant members of his caucus to determine if they would support the government on the issue. Dewar had suggested meeting with Protestant members of the Opposition as well to see if a majority could be put together to support the bill, but Shaw did not trust Alex Matheson, so the meeting never took place. After a vicious fight in caucus and on the floor of the Legislature, the bill passed through first and second reading, but still faced possible defeat by government caucus members led by Farmer. Dewar later declared, "Most Roman Catholics, I feel, are reconciled to the Prince of Wales elevation but Farmer apparently threatened to resign or cross the floor of the House." Meanwhile, Protestant members on both sides were quietly urging Shaw and Dewar to proceed to third and final reading.

The Legislature stood at an impasse until Henry Wedge, Shaw's health minister, proposed a compromise. He introduced an amendment to establish a Royal Commission on Higher Education, delaying proclamation of the Prince of Wales College bill until after the Commission had released its recommendations. The amendment passed, ending the standoff but leaving a bitter taste. "I wish to God that I wasn't in politics after what went on last week," said Robert Grindlay, the Conservative MLA from 2nd Prince and Dewar's running mate. The Royal Commission on Higher Education, chaired by former Islander and Presbyterian minister Dr. J.S. Bonnell, was appointed after some jockeying on both sides to secure members sympathetic to their views. Members included Charlottetown physician Dr. J.A. MacMillan, and (following opposition to the appointment of Justice Walter Darby by some Roman Catholic members of caucus) Dr. Norman MacKenzie, retired president of the University of British Columbia.

The Commission presented its report to government in January 1965. It recommended that the Prince of Wales College bill be proclaimed, and in an effort to appease supporters of St. Dunstan's it also recommended that operating grants based on enrollment be provided to both institutions. The recommendations went even further: The boards of both institutions should study the feasibility of a federation and the provincial government should consider the establishment of a single university within which the two present institutions would be preserved as distinct components. Recognizing the sensibilities at stake, the Commission issued a cautious but hopeful suggestion about the respective ideals of the two institutions. "They will want to ensure that these ideals will be fully preserved if a federation should come," it demurred. "Both will want to make sure that it will not just be an appendage of the other, nor be swallowed up by the other and so lose its identity."

Prince of Wales College finally obtained degree-granting status during the 1965 session of the Legislature, and actively prepared to expand its programs. In the meantime, the Commission's report gave voice to a quiet but growing movement to put an end to years of rivalry between the province's institutions of higher education.

* * *

A number of leading citizens representing both Protestants and Roman Catholics and calling itself the "Group of Ten" started meeting to discuss the idea of a single university. This eclectic group, headed by Charlottetown psychiatrist Dr. Mac Beck and physician Dr. John Maloney, included clergymen of both faiths like David MacDonald, James Kelly, Kenneth Norris, William Simpson, and Edmund Roach; and lay members including Dr. Marvin Clark, Dr. John Gillis, John Eldon Green, Elmer Murphy, and Sheldon Campbell. In May 1965, the group released its report, which concluded that a single university be established to meet the growing post-secondary education needs of the province. "The academic advantages inherent in one larger institution of higher education cannot be questioned," it asserted. "The economic advantages will be apparent to all."

The report's underlying message targeted a more ambitious goal. "From the cultural viewpoint, this proposal has implicit within it a spirit of mutual self-interest, communication and understanding which could eradicate from our midst the unfortunate attitudes of religious bigotry and intolerance which have repeatedly impeded both our spiritual and economic progress in times past," it proffered. The report was greeted with derision in some quarters. Reflecting the perspective of a Catholic educator, St. Dunstan's philosophy professor Dr. Patrick J. MacInnis sent a sharply worded open letter to the

Group of Ten asserting that the respective divergent approaches to education of the two institutions could not be resolved by combining them into one. "Not only do I consider your basic assumptions false, but I energetically reject the tone and spirit which vitiates your published and oral pronouncements," he protested, "... a spirit which augurs ill for a fruitful solution of this complex problem under your pressures, guidance or inspiration."

The official response from St. Dunstan's was less clear. Earlier, Bishop Malcolm MacEachern had publicly supported the continuation of a religious education system along the lines of the traditional approach taken by St. Dunstan's. "In the interests of the young people of the province, as well as those who wish to further their own education as adults, St. Dunstan's must be the foundation on which the structure of higher education and adult education for the future is built," he maintained. Over at Prince of Wales, MacKinnon was not prepared to be reconciled to the concept. His dream had been to make Prince of Wales the pre-eminent educational institution in the province, and he viewed any level of co-operation with St. Dunstan's as frustrating that goal.

In June 1966, the boards of both universities met jointly to discuss a number of models for higher education. These included each continuing on their own; undertaking co-operation in some areas; establishing a federation; or outright amalgamation. From the beginning, it was clear that Prince of Wales – or MacKinnon, at least – was opposed to any relationship with St. Dunstan's. He believed ecumenism was a highly controversial and dogmatic theological concept and refused to have anything to do with further discussions. About this time, he received an invitation from Lieutenant-Governor W.J. MacDonald, a former math teacher who had worked for him at Prince of Wales. Over lunch at Government House, MacDonald conveyed a message from Bishop MacEachern: If MacKinnon would agree to either federation or amalgamation, the Bishop would support his nomination for president of the new university. MacKinnon politely but firmly declined.

Instead, he ploughed ahead with ambitious plans for his new university. The Weymouth Street campus underwent extensive renovations and expansion, and in November 1966, a group of Toronto architects arrived in Charlottetown to plan a "campus of the future," a downtown university consisting of a complex of buildings and open spaces extending from Prince of Wales College to Confederation Centre.

PARO

Architect John Arbeau (centre) shows a model of the new library for Prince of Wales College on Weymouth Street, Charlottetown, to former PWC principal Dr. G.D. Steele (right), and former MLA Don Campbell and Mrs. Campbell. Dr. Frank MacKinnon saw the new university as a mix of "town and gown," with the campus eventually tied into the Confederation Centre of the Arts.

The new government of Alex Campbell was anxious to promote greater co-operation between Prince of Wales College and St. Dunstan's University, while the federal government, concerned about the rising cost of post-secondary education, was also encouraging greater co-operation among Canadian universities. In 1967, it had changed its granting policy and transferred decisions on the financing of post-secondary education to provincial governments. It was now up to the provincial government to decide how the funds would be allocated. Each year, Campbell, Education Minister Gordon Bennett and Labour Minister Elmer Blanchard met with representatives of the two institutions – with MacKinnon and members of his staff in the small dining room at Montgomery Hall, and with Bishop MacEachern and his officials at the bishop's palace. While the meetings were cordial, little progress was made in achieving greater co-operation between the two sides.

Meanwhile, the government established the Universities Co-ordinating Council, with members drawn from both institutions, to discuss areas of co-operation in an effort to save costs, but the Council dragged its feet. Its first meeting ended with the decision not to meet again. In early November 1966, Dr. John Gillis, chair of the Prince of Wales College board of governors, informed a clearly disappointed Campbell that the College would remain separate from the proposed new university and pursue its own independent course. In fact, the two universities, acting independently of each other, drew up ambitious plans to expand programs and facilities. In early 1967, they presented separate submissions to government for financial support, requesting upwards of $10 million each for campus development. To the Campbell government, the inherent duplication of proposed library, science, and other facilities, and the overlapping of course offerings and services, was obviously wasteful. The cash-strapped government was simply not in a position to accede to their growing demands for funding.

Following the protests over Bill 57 to establish a University Grants Commission, Campbell was even more determined to get the two universities to co-operate, and decided to act. He called Del Gallagher, head of the Economic Improvement Corporation, to his office. The Corporation was drawing up details of the Comprehensive Development Plan in which education was considered a critical component. Could money needed for the creation of a single university be found in the framework of the Plan then under negotiation with Ottawa? he asked. Over the next week, officials of the Economic Improvement Corporation worked feverishly to draft a three-point program for post-secondary education. Campbell was taking a significant political risk. After MacKinnon challenged the government with his demand for the withdrawal of the Grants Commission legislation, Campbell concluded that the issue had escalated beyond a purely educational one. The question now was whether the future of higher education would be determined by Frank MacKinnon or the Government of Prince Edward Island.

Campbell also had to deal with his education minister, Gordon Bennett, who until then had strongly favoured the continuation of the two universities. In directing officials of the Economic Improvement Corporation to draft proposals for the future of higher education, he was effectively bypassing his education minister. Although Bennett was a former registrar of Prince of Wales College, he did not enjoy a close relationship with MacKinnon and could do little to keep the lines of communication open with College officials. MacKinnon, on the other hand, was in frequent contact with Lorne Moase, Bennett's deputy minister, attempting to forestall any forced moves towards greater co-operation, but by then the matter was out of the Department of Education's hands.

While Gallagher and his officials were drafting the statement on the future of post-secondary education, Campbell met with Bennett late into the evening after the Legislature had finished sitting for the day. Bennett was initially lukewarm to the proposal, but for Campbell the idea of a single university held strong appeal. Many other provinces, including Newfoundland, New Brunswick, Manitoba, Saskatchewan, Alberta, and British Columbia, had provincial universities – why not Prince Edward Island? Campbell's vision of a provincial university went well beyond the narrow confines of religious partisanship; a single university would resolve a host of other quickly intensifying problems.

A draft statement, vetted for politically sensitive wording by Andy Wells, was presented to caucus and cabinet on April 1. The next day, Campbell rose in the Legislature to present it to the people.

* * *

The outline of the government's proposal for the future of post-secondary education was presented during a one-hour address based on the "White Paper on Higher Education." The three-point policy included proposals for student aid, a new college of applied arts and technology, and a single university, all of which would fundamentally reshape the future of higher education in Prince Edward Island. Significantly, they represented a break with the past and its history of religious intolerance, placing the future of higher education squarely within the context of the Island's social, cultural and economic goals.

"The development of a well-rounded post-secondary education program is necessary to provide the widest possible opportunities to the people of the province and is crucial to the economic objectives of the Development Plan," Premier Campbell told the Legislature, adding that he was not forcing amalgamation onto the universities. "If either wishes to continue its existence as a private institution utilizing its own financial resources, the Government certainly will not interfere," he advised. "But let one thing be very clear: the

Government will support financially, with all the funds at its disposal, only a single public university in Prince Edward Island."

Campbell outlined his vision for the new university. "It must be considered to be the university of all religious faiths, the university of each and every ethnic group, in short, the university of all Islanders," he declared. "It will be our university, and our program – for the Island. A university that can grow as we grow and one that all Islanders can support, utilize and cherish." After he concluded his remarks, Shaw rose briefly to declare that, while the Opposition was not against the idea of a single university, the announcement would require further study. The statement, he respectfully conceded, was "comprehensive, far reaching and startling."

The Legislature then adjourned for the Easter break. Campbell left shortly afterwards for Ottawa to attend the national Liberal leadership convention (which would select Pierre Trudeau to succeed Lester Pearson). In his absence, officials went to work drafting new legislation to be introduced later in the session.

On April 8, Dr. Frank MacKinnon and sixteen of his staff at Prince of Wales College resigned. He claimed the government never consulted him about its plans or gave the College an opportunity to defend itself. Years later, from self-imposed exile in Calgary, he delivered a vitriolic assessment of the events of 1968. In a book on church politics and education he wrote, "[It] was my turn to speak for the record, as the last Principal of Prince of Wales College." The "forced union" of the two colleges "followed two centuries of turbulent church-state politics that retarded the Island," he asserted. "What little is known of this story is mostly fiction. Clergy and laity gave full rein to fantasy; the local bishop issued an authoritarian political decree; government had ferocious rows in closed sessions. But the public was not given the facts." Actually, hard-core supporters from both sides continued to debate "the facts" for years to come. But although the fight continued ferocious at times, the issue had lost its teeth.

The path to the establishment of a single university told a pathetic story of petty prejudice, blatant bigotry, false bonhommie, intellectual pretensions, insatiable egos, and unmitigated arrogance. Its conclusion represented a significant and indeed dramatic departure from the nature of the debate that had dragged on for decades, one that had elevated religious interests to an inviolable level. Campbell did not perceive the issues entangling religion and higher education as insurmountable or even significant. His generation was witnessing the dismantling of the barriers between the two major religious groups; in his home town of Summerside, for example, the separate high schools had been amalgamated without fanfare, and across the province – indeed across the span of an increasingly secularized Canadian society in general – religious prejudices were gradually evaporating. In one deft stroke, he shattered two centuries of taboos and religious differences. In a bold, pragmatic move, Campbell had confronted one of the sacred shibboleths of Island society – its hidebound religious core – and found it hollow. The blight of what had poisoned Island society for so long was exposed to the harsh scrutiny of a new era. Although religion would remain a factor in Island life to some extent, it could no longer threaten to bring down governments.

*   *   *

On April 23, 1969, the government proclaimed the charters for both the University of Prince Edward Island and Holland College. The first classes in the two new institutions commenced that September. In May 1970, the University of Prince Edward Island held its first-ever convocation at Confederation Centre. In his address to the graduates, faculty, and assembled guests, the university's first president, Ron Baker, stated that "the uniting of the faculty, students and staff of old and proud institutions that have been, in some ways, rivals, is a major achievement."

An understatement of profound proportions!

CHAPTER SIX

The Development Plan

"The year 1969 was the two hundredth anniversary of the establishment of Prince Edward Island as a political unit," wrote Dr. Frank MacKinnon in that year's *Canadian Annual Review*. "The occasion was not celebrated. There was little to celebrate because the year was one of the most difficult in the entire history of the province."

Not everyone shared that view, however. In 1969, Prince Edward Island struck out on a course which promised to make it economically self-reliant for the first time in its entire history. On March 7, Premier Alex Campbell and Trudeau's minister in charge of regional development, Jean Marchand, signed the fifteen-year, $725-million federal-provincial Comprehensive Development Plan. The Plan, as it came to be known, was designed to fundamentally revitalize the Island's moribund economy and reinvigorate its stagnant society. Bold and

Campbell with federal ministers Allan J. MacEachen (left) and Jean Marchand at the signing of the Comprehensive Development Plan on March 7, 1969.

97

ambitious in scope, it confronted head-on traditions and attitudes that had changed little since early times. It kick-started and completed the modernization of the province, and accelerated the dismantling of a traditional society already facing drift and dissolution.

It also represented the most massive effort of its kind ever under-taken in Canada. "In total," proclaimed the Development Plan document, "the measures incorporated into the Plan are designed to substantially increase the capability of people, businesses and other institutions of the Province to guide and take full advantage of opportunities provided by the rapidly changing social and economic environment of Canada and the world at large." Thus, the Campbell government embarked on arguably its single most important policy initiative.

Although the common aim of the various programs was "to create conditions in which the people of Prince Edward Island can create viable economic enterprises for themselves," MacKinnon and many others were highly skeptical. According to MacKinnon, in 1969 the province faced the spectre of bankruptcy, and the Plan represented the loss of effective responsible government. In his view, the Plan (which would come to an end, ominously, in Orwellian 1984) was synonymous with the take-over of the Island. "The provincial government asked for help; the federal government responded with the Plan and a large task force moved to the Island and literally took over the government," he wrote.

*   *   *

Controversy inevitably clouded the Plan. What Islanders saw as a way of life based on traditional values, survival, and sense of place, others regarded a society suspicious of new ideas and characterized by stubbornness, apathy, and parochialism. A 1961 study commis-sioned by the federal government on life and poverty in the Maritimes noted with aspersion that "in these isolated areas, where the average age of farmers and fishermen is 50 years, the world of aspiration is limited and the universe itself is small." Both views came to resonate in the hearts and minds of Islanders. They may have wanted progress, but were unwilling to give up the familiar patterns of their lives. It was not a fertile ground for the uncompromising politics of develop-ment.

Throughout the Atlantic region, governments were struggling to develop their economies, and some were taking radical measures to confront decades-old customs and conventions. In New Brunswick, the government of Louis Robichaud was spearheading an "Equal Opportunities" program to reduce disparities within the province (especially between the anglophone and Acadian communities) and equip the provincial government with the powers it needed to undertake other economic and social reforms. In Newfoundland, in one of the most controversial initiatives ever undertaken in that province, the Joey Smallwood government was resettling hundreds of outport communities, disrupting a way of life centuries old. In the words of Nobel Prize winner, Swedish economist Gunnar Myrdal, "Often it is not more difficult but easier to cause a big change rapidly than a small change gradually." The Atlantic provinces of the 1960s were ripe for big, rapid change.

In Prince Edward Island, the Development Plan represented the province's response to its own distinctive economic and social challenges. For the first time since the debates over Confederation one hundred years earlier, the people were engaged in a fundamental debate to consider what kind of future they wanted for themselves and their province. By the time the Plan had ended, the province had shaken off much of its past and was venturing warily into the future, but without the support of the past's familiar signposts. The ensuing experience of being caught between two worlds, which engendered feelings of ambivalence, self-doubt and schizophrenia would haunt Islanders for years to come.

*　　*　　*

Prince Edward Island was always a "have-not" province, first as a colony of the British government, then as a province dependent on the Canadian government. Its short-lived "golden age" of the 1850s and '60s dissipated rapidly in the face of the federal government's National Policy, which shifted trade and investment patterns away from and to the detriment of the entire Atlantic region. Following Confederation, the Island lost confidence in its ability to survive on its own. In addition, thousands of Islanders fled the province in a mass exodus to the "Boston states" and elsewhere; those that remained looked to Ottawa for help.

Yet, despite increases in federal transfers to the provincial government, the Island could not keep up with the progress enjoyed by the rest of the nation. The great national enterprises of expansion, industrialization, and railway building – the fulfillment of the national dream – bypassed the Island, which lingered at a semi-subsistence level in a state of continuing dependency. The elusive goal of self-reliance was obscured by the resignation of Islanders to a fate of dignified dependence. The Island's official motto, *Parva sub ingenti* (the small under the protection of the great), was also its political mantra.

Since Ottawa caused the problem, it was up to Ottawa to fix it. Successive governments all the way back to 1873, when Prince Edward Island reluctantly joined Confederation, attempted to improve on the terms of that union. Premier Thane Campbell best expressed the position of Island governments in his presentation in 1938 to the Rowell-Sirois Commission, established by the federal government to examine the entire scope of federal-provincial relations. "The people of Prince Edward Island seem to have had an almost prophetic view of what the result of the union would be," he told the Commission during its hearings in Charlottetown. "Yet once committed to the union, there never was, nor is there now, any question of withdrawal. The citizens of this province have borne with patience a national policy which has been distinctly not beneficial; they see the citizens of other provinces grow rich at their expense; they see the best of their youth attracted to other provinces, just as they are entering the period when they might become an asset to the community. The only protest has been an occasional request for 'better terms.'"

The Commission was quick to recognize the dilemma faced by the province. "In spite of the fact that Prince Edward Island is the most perfect geographical entity of any Canadian province, it does not form a satisfactory unit from the point of view of public finance, and particularly for raising revenue," the report observed. The Commission went on to recommend the establishment of a system of financial equalization from which the Prince Edward Island government subsequently derived as much as two-thirds of its total revenue through this and other federal payments.*

Yet, despite equalization and other measures, the post-war boom

---

* *The concept of equalization, established after the Second World War, involved financial transfers from the richer to the poorer provinces under a complex formula; thus Canadians would receive roughly the same level of services while incurring roughly the same level of taxation, regardless of in which province they lived.*

---

left Prince Edward Island further behind. By the 1960s, the provincial government carried the highest per capita debt in Canada; the unemployment rate stood between fifteen and twenty percent – the second highest in Canada, next to Newfoundland; per capita incomes were slightly more than half the national average; and output per worker was measured at just half the national average. The Island's population of 109,000 had never recovered from its pre-Confederation levels and now suffered from the effects of aging, as well as out-migration of its young and better-educated citizens. The economy depended heavily on the land- and sea-based resource industries of farming and fishing. What limited amount of manufacturing there was relied almost entirely on the primary resource industries. The province's leading industry, agriculture, was caught in a downward spiral, losing a farm a day.

These deeply ingrained problems plagued every provincial government. During the1940s and '50s, Premier Walter Jones sought to defend and promote rural interests, but was unable to reverse the tide that was eroding the traditional farm economy and way of life of Island communities. While boasting in his 1948 "State of PEI" address that there was "no area anywhere that provides as good a chance to make a living as Prince Edward Island," even his ardent defence could not obscure the fact that the Island was sliding into precipitous decline, with as many as four in ten Islanders leaving the province in their productive years.

In 1955, Premier Alex Matheson told the Royal Commission on Canada's Economic Prospects that federal policies worked to "the great detriment and disadvantage of Prince Edward Island."* In a familiar refrain, he told the Commission that "the economy of Prince Edward Island has, from the earliest times, been directly affected by general policy determined outside the Province for enterprises not affecting the Province, or affecting it adversely." The Commission agreed. In its 1957 report, it remarked on the province's lack of development and progress. "In essence the story is one of difficult adjustment to changing economic circumstances," it noted. "Included in these circumstances were those which developed at least in part from economic policies designed to create the Canadian nation."

*　　*　　*

---

* This commission was chaired by Walter Gordon, an ardent Canadian nationalist, who later served as finance minister in the Pearson government.

Other governments and agencies in the Atlantic region also clamoured for a more effective response to its long-standing and deeply rooted economic malaise. "At the end of the 1950s it became clear that the rapid expansion of the Canadian economy as a whole had not improved the relative position of the Atlantic region," concluded the Atlantic Development Council. By this time, the federal government was coming to the realization that federal transfers and equalization alone would not adequately address the underlying structural problems associated with regional disparity. The Atlantic Provinces Economic Council observed that the 1960s represented a decade of growing awareness and changing attitudes on the part of the federal government to the problems associated with regional economic disparities. In a landmark report on regional disparities in Canada published in 1968 in its Fifth Annual Review, the Economic Council of Canada stated that "policies have evolved with increasing awareness of the long-term persistence of regional imbalances and their economic, social and political implications." As the 1960s unfolded, the Economic Council noted with approval a number of federal initiatives for improving regional balance, along with a shift to greater innovation in policy responses.

Emboldened by its experience in economic intervention during the Second World War, buttressed by Keynesian economic theory (which made the case for state intervention in the economy through spending and taxation), and advances in the social sciences in social and economic planning, the federal government realized it had the ability to devise strategies that would address the underlying structural weaknesses of regional economies. As a result, during the 1960s it poured out an alphabet soup of federal programs to address economic development problems: ARDA (Agriculture Rehabilitation and Development Act); MMRA (Maritime Marshlands Rehabilitation Agency); ADB (Atlantic Development Board); ADA (Atlantic Development Agency); and FRED (Fund for Regional Economic Development).

At the same time, provincial governments across the Atlantic region increasingly demanded action to deal with the lingering problems of regional economic disparity. At the 1960 Premiers' Conference, Walter Shaw called for a "bold, ambitious and coordinated approach to the underlying problems of the region." In 1965, the Shaw government signed an agreement to undertake a broad range of sectoral studies of the Island economy, and commissioned Acres International to undertake the studies. The detailed analysis was in the final stages when the Campbell government came to power in 1966.

During the election campaign, Shaw kept referring to major structural changes in the Island economy and a significant increase in output and activity, but his government's industrial development policies, including Georgetown, overshadowed the "bold, ambitious and coordinated approaches" to deal with development needs. If Shaw had a development strategy, it did not surface during the campaign. Meanwhile, the Campbell campaign team seemed oblivious to the comprehensive analysis that Shaw was conducting on the Island economy, and equally oblivious to the possibilities it presented. The Liberals campaigned on issues such as free textbooks for students; higher pensions for senior citizens; and the usual promises of more support for primary industries and highway construction. The ambitious program of economic development hinted at by Shaw was hardly mentioned by either party.

The first inkling of the magnitude of the development strategy under consideration came the day following Campbell's election as premier. As he was leaving the Charlottetown Hotel, he ran into Hartwell Daley, Charlottetown bureau chief for the *Journal-Pioneer* and an economic advisor to Shaw. Daley told him that an economic development agreement with the federal government was about to be signed. Despite Hartwell Daley's hint, Campbell quickly discovered on moving into the Premier's Office that little more than a shopping list of potential economic opportunities actually existed. The Acres International studies had compiled masses of data on the various economic sectors in its eleven-volume, $340,000 report, but had formulated no specific proposals.

This was his introduction to what would become the centrepiece of his administration.

*　　*　　*

Following completion of the Acres report, a federal-provincial steering committee recommended that Prince Edward Island take the initiative in putting specific development proposals in place. A confidential memorandum prepared by the federal Department of Forestry and Rural Development offered the opinion that if the Prince Edward Island government took the lead in formulating the proposals, it would avert the perception that a federal plan was being imposed on the province. More importantly, the memorandum also concluded that the provincial government lacked the capacity to implement development programs; thus taking a key role in formulating a development strategy would help it acquire much-needed experience. Such experience would be crucial, given that unlike past sectoral strategies this plan would be comprehensive in scope, touching all sectors of the economy in a co-ordinated and integrated way.

To help move the proposals forward, Campbell turned to Del Gallagher, an experienced and energetic economist. Gallagher was flamboyant, chain-smoking, and goal-driven, with previous experience working for governments in Nova Scotia and New Brunswick, and came with a strong recommendation from New Brunswick premier Louis Robichaud. He demonstrated an impressive facility for developing concepts and formulating them into practical approaches, and quickly became one of Campbell's closest advisors.

Campbell presented his blueprint for development during the 1967 session of the Legislature. The White Paper on Economic Planning and Development, drafted by Gallagher, underlined the need for

Del Gallagher, chief architect of the Comprehensive Development Plan, was one of Campbell's closest economic policy advisors.

PARO

expansion of the provincial economy "to bring to the population the full measure of the benefits of economic growth which prevail generally in the Canadian society." It called for an approach that was at the same time comprehensive, substantial and dynamic – one which would lead to rising standards of living; an improved level and quality of government services; and local participation. "It is these principles upon which Government policy in the field of economic development will be based and as such, they reflect the Government's interpretation of the requirement of our society," Campbell declared in the Legislature, promising that "in due course they will be as well reflected in the specific goals of the plans and the development strategies to be utilized."

Converting the masses of data into development strategies and programs was a huge undertaking, involving intensive and ongoing discussions and negotiations between politicians and planners. The process of preparing a comprehensive development plan for an entire province was unprecedented in Canada. Quite simply, no precedent existed in any government in Canada for this kind of activity. The emergence of a new "technocratic class," based on a belief in the possibilities of rational political and economic action, made planning a science. Planners dreamed and attempted to determine the limits of the possible. Politicians decided from among the alternatives. And the people of the province would have to live with the consequences.

The White Paper set out the relationship envisaged between politicians and planners as they prepared to embark on this new and untried endeavour to turn the provincial economy around. "The specification of economic development goals therefore becomes the first means of applying government responsibility," Campbell told the Legislature, describing cabinet's role, but conceding that the process involved an interplay between planners and politicians. "While such goals must inevitably arise from social, economic and political considerations, they are at the same time influenced by technical considerations of the various planning alternatives which are available." Most importantly, in an era when governments were gaining confidence that they could make a difference in the lives of the people they served, the White Paper reinforced the role of the Prince Edward Island government as a central player in the economic life of the province. Campbell pointed out that he recognized "the potential role which [the provincial government] can play in influencing the rate at which the provincial economy develops and expands over the years." In so doing, he was gambling the future of his government on the success of the development strategy.

The federal government had pressed for the establishment of a separate agency to lead the planning process, believing that the limited level of skills, knowledge and expertise available within the provincial government departments would prevent them from conducting the high level of analysis required. At the same time, both federal and provincial governments agreed that it was difficult to adapt existing government administrative machinery to a planning and development process, especially when that process would inevitably confront the need for change in the programs and direction of government itself. As a result, with federal funding under the five-year planning agreement from the Shaw government already in place, Campbell's government set up a crown corporation, the Economic Improvement Corporation, and appointed Gallagher as general manager. Gallagher moved quickly to bring together a cadre of skilled planners, economists, sociologists, and other specialists to whip the Acres International studies into a comprehensive economic development strategy and to undertake further research and analysis. But to do so, he needed to search for expertise outside the province.

Although not quite the task force that MacKinnon had predicted would move to the province and take over the government, Gallagher's team was nonetheless a formidable one. Its members came from across Canada, the United States, Great Britain, and Australia. Some of its early members included Robert Blakely, a sociologist from Minnesota; George Dargie, a graduate in agricultural economics from the University of British Columbia; Michael Lane, an economist with a graduate degree from Oxford; James Lovering, who studied land economics at Cornell; Richard Higgins, an economist from New South Wales; and Harold Verge, with a background in planning studies from the University of Toronto.

The EIC soon exceeded two hundred people, functioning in relative isolation from the provincial government staff. Inevitably, the perception soon developed that the planners were taking over the future affairs of the province, a view strengthened by the fact that Gallagher and most of his immediate staff occupied most offices on the ground floor of historic Province House, the seat of government. Added to this, the EIC quickly attracted the distrust and jealousy of many government officials because the team brought together skills and qualifications that were severely lacking in the province's mostly rudimentary public service. All the EIC senior staff had been recruited from off-Island, arousing suspicions about "outside experts," and because they were not civil servants in the normal sense their salary levels greatly exceeded those of most provincial public servants. Thus, from the beginning, an unfortunate enmity developed between the EIC staff and the provincial government departments with which they dealt. On the one hand, the EIC tended to regard provincial government employees as deficient in the skills, understanding, and knowledge required for development planning. On the other hand, provincial government employees regarded EIC staff as aloof, lacking in knowledge of local conditions, and having little appreciation of the practical realities of life in the province. Both were partly right. As Gallagher later confessed, "You could probably conclude that overall, the relationship with the civil service was bad."

Gallagher's easy access to Campbell, and the significant support he was receiving for the work of the EIC, even attracted a degree of resentment and exasperation from within Campbell's cabinet and caucus. From the outset, many in cabinet did not understand the planning process, others did not want to understand it, and still others did not support the massive changes being considered.

But critics lacked the ammunition to deal with the sheer rationality of the process. The Development Plan was seamless, each component interdependent on the other. But even among this disparate group, one aspect of the Plan was of unanimous and paramount interest: the prospect of a massive infusion of federal dollars. Keir Clark, Campbell's health minister, later said of his cabinet colleagues, "I don't think they had any particular views. They just thought it was Santa Claus or something."

Soon Gallagher and the EIC were attracting public attention as well. As the profile of the planning process and the key role Gallagher was playing increased, Walter Shaw jokingly referred to the province as "Gallagher's Island" (a reference to a television comedy series popular at the time called "Gilligan's Island"). He criticized the staff as outsiders with little knowledge or understanding of the problems faced by the province. "Not one of the members belongs to the province of Prince Edward Island," he complained in the Legislature during the spring of 1968, "and I am wondering whether they are familiar with the difficulties and the problems that affect the farm people." Shaw was not the only politician with reservations. One of Campbell's own ministers described the Plan's provisions as the result of "unrealistic thinking of a bunch of far-out dreamers and intellectuals." Even Angus MacLean, the Conservative MP then representing Queens County, chimed in with his criticism, referring to the plan developed by the EIC as "a hair-brained one which was dreamed up by formerly unemployed economists."

Campbell found himself constantly having to defend the EIC against its critics, including some from his own party. "We found that within our own party there was this conflict between traditional approaches and the newer approaches, and not so much within cabinet perhaps as it was between the cabinet and the caucus," he recalled. "We found that our elected representatives within the caucus were deemed closer to the grass roots organization of the party desirous of reflecting the political facts of life than the cabinet itself dealing with the more important issues of policy."

Campbell also recognized the new demands being place upon the Island's traditional political structure. The cabinet faced a two-fold challenge: not only to obtain professional, expert advice on how best to direct the development of the province in this relatively new field of public endeavour, but also to interpret that advice in the light of practical – and political – considerations, based on the most feasible course of action and the extent to which voters would support it. "There is a limit and it will continue to be the very vital and important responsibility of the elected representative to balance what the experts will determine to be the need for change to be brought about by government programs, and on the other hand the desirability of those changes in the first place, and the possibilities for those changes," explained the Premier.

It was a risky political strategy. While Campbell was acutely aware that the presence of the planners was creating a number of political problems for his administration, nevertheless he continued to defend the planning process and the advice he was receiving from Gallagher and his staff. With a two-seat majority in the Legislature, and with one minister, Robert Campbell, already threatening to resign over changes to the Lord's Day Act, Campbell could not afford to squander any political capital he may have gained after just one year in office. To add to his problems, his cabinet was also divided. Not all its members shared Campbell's confidence in the outcome of the planning process, and others, such as Lorne Bonnell, were content to carry on with their own agendas, political or otherwise. It made for a tenuous, sometimes tense, atmosphere around the cabinet table. On one occasion, Campbell called a special cabinet meeting on a Saturday afternoon. Keir Clark objected, protesting that he had a business to run and would be in his store in Montague on Saturday afternoon. Campbell agreed to hold the meeting in Clark's office above the store – at which Fisheries Minister Cecil Miller refused to go to Montague in order to accommodate Clark.

As Campbell succinctly put it, "We walk a rather precarious political tightrope while in office here."

*　　*　　*

Throughout the remainder of 1967 and into the early part of 1968, Gallagher and his staff worked feverishly to put together a draft plan that would meet Ottawa's demands and the provincial government's priorities. The federal presence on the Island was largely confined to one person, Hector Hortie of the Department of Forestry and Rural Development, who kept the lines open to federal officials in Ottawa. The stage was now set to undertake what had never before been tried in Canada.

The planning process took place under the Fund for Regional Economic Development (FRED) legislation, a special federal fund to finance development and adjustment programs not covered by other government programs, federal or provincial. It largely circumvented questions related to the constitutional division of powers, thereby enabling the development of comprehensive strategies regardless of how they were financed or which level of government was responsible. Under the FRED legislation, the entire Island was designated a "special area" for development, the first and only province to be so identified. Some federal officials regarded the Prince Edward Island plan as a test case for the models they themselves espoused; the Island, with its distinct geographic boundaries and the relatively stable population, provided an ideal laboratory. Tom Kent (the first deputy minister in the new Department of Regional Economic Expansion that succeeded the Department of Forestry and Rural Development) told the House of Commons Standing Committee on Regional Development in April 1970 that the purpose of FRED was to provide "have-not" provincial governments with the resources to achieve the same level of development normally attained by those provinces that could afford to pay their own way.

In June 1967, as the planning process was just getting underway, Campbell told the *Financial Post* that the process represented a major departure from past practices when provincial governments sought increased federal largesse and ad hoc solutions to its problems. "For the first time in history," he noted, "we are able to face problems of regional development with federal programs designed for the basic needs of the region – not piecemeal solutions." Later, in November 1967, when the *Financial Post* interviewed him again, he commented on the great promise held out by FRED. "It is designed for the province to use as a gap-filler between existing programs and the development of an overall, comprehensive plan to cope with our problems over the long term," he explained. "We think it is the key to breaking our traditional budget and handout approach."

Although the Campbell government made such assurances of flexibility early in the planning process, it would never fully escape the criticism that the Comprehensive Development Plan was foisted upon it by the federal government, and effectively amounted to the loss of provincial autonomy. The criticism stung Campbell and stuck with him throughout his term in office.

* * *

By early 1968, a draft plan was ready for submission to the federal government. It grew out of sometimes spirited, sometimes acrimonious discussions in cabinet over the winter. Although they agreed on the broad objectives, ministers ran into difficulties when they got down to details. But, said Gallagher, "It wasn't the kind of plan that a cabinet would be able to change a great deal." Throughout the process, both Campbell and Gallagher tried to maintain the fundamental integrity of the planning process. Campbell kept the critics at bay while Gallagher and his officials prepared for negotiations with the federal government.

The first draft plan was submitted to the FRED board in Ottawa in May 1968. Despite overt assurances that the process would cut across federal departments, the proposal soon ran into major roadblocks. The FRED board, which consisted of representatives from federal departments such as Agriculture, Fisheries, Industry, Health and Welfare, and Forestry and Rural Development, immediately raised a number of objections. They were concerned that the proposal went beyond the FRED legislation in a number of constitutional areas, setting a dangerous precedent. In particular, they had reservations about the major component in the Plan dealing with education – a purely provincial responsibility, as well as the section dealing with provincial government reorganization, which was considered beyond the purview of the legislation. The board also raised concerns about the province's fiscal capacity to pay its expected share.

From the outset, Gallagher approached the planning process in the spirit of the FRED legislation, not worrying about who would pay for what but about developing the best response possible to the problem. The silence from the FRED board offered the first indication that federal government officials may have seen things differently. Despite its reservations, the board sent the draft back to the province without comment, even though a confidential memorandum to the federal cabinet from Forestry and Rural Development Minister Maurice Sauvé warned that failure to make a substantial commitment to the Prince Edward Island government would result in a breakdown of the planning process and a loss of momentum.

The timing could not have been worse. The federal government was facing a general election under its new prime minister, Pierre Trudeau, so federal officials were reluctant to make any long-term commitments. They also suffered from infighting, and some departments were reluctant to reallocate portions of their budget to the Plan. In fact, the federal election in June 1968 virtually halted all negotiations. But Campbell was reassured by comments made throughout the campaign by Trudeau, who expressed the view that the underdevelopment of the Atlantic region presented as much a threat to the unity of Canada as the French-English confrontation. Following the re-election of the federal Liberals in a wave of Trudeaumania, Campbell received assurances that the Plan would continue to receive consideration. As he put it, if the Plan was not given the green light, it at least got the amber.

After the election, the populist Jean Marchand was put in charge of regional development policies, and Tom Kent, Pearson's former chief advisor and a no-nonsense bureaucrat, was appointed his deputy. Despite such high-powered leadership, and Trudeau's supposed commitment to regional development, the new Department of Regional Economic Expansion (DREE) was not yet fully operational. It was a frustrating time for the provincial government, facing growing political pressure at home to show some results from all the planning activity.

In all, the Development Plan went through a total of thirteen drafts in an effort to secure agreement from Ottawa. Following the failure of the FRED board to fully respond in May, the provincial government submitted a new draft on August 30 after the federal election and the establishment of DREE. The board rejected that draft too, citing its continued reservations over the inclusion of education and its refusal to budge on the level of federal contributions.*

In September, following the rejection of the August 30th draft, Campbell telephoned Marchand and formally notified him that the provincial government had decided to withdraw from negotiations. Earlier, Gallagher had advised Campbell that the changes the federal government wanted were tantamount to removing "the guts of the whole plan," especially the section dealing with education, which was considered crucial to the achievement of its overall goals. Marchand agreed privately that the Island government had been squeezed too hard. Speculation was also rampant that the federal government was applying pressure on the province to free itself from the commitment to build the causeway, for which cost estimates were spiralling out of control. In late September, Marchand and Campbell met in Ottawa at which time Marchand agreed to take the issue to the federal cabinet to resolve the issues raised by the FRED board. He also agreed to the inclusion of education and government reorganization as components of the Development Plan, and to extend its implementation period from ten to fifteen years to accommodate federal financial contributions. Marchand took the proposal to the federal cabinet on October 25. Cabinet ministers agreed with his recommendations, but expressed strong reservations about the level of federal financial contributions. The new finance minister, Edgar Benson, argued that the federal government should contribute to the Plan or the causeway, but not to both.

In early November, an increasingly frustrated Campbell protested the lack of any meaningful negotiations between the federal and provincial governments to resolve the outstanding issues. In a strongly worded letter to Marchand, he wrote, "Once again I must emphasize that we feel considerably handicapped in these negotiations since there is little, if any, prior consultation on the main issues." On November 19, the problem was referred to the federal cabinet's Committee on Planning and Priorities, and sent back to full cabinet the next day. The federal government still worried about

---

* *The original request was made for approximately $425 million from Ottawa over ten years, but DREE was reluctant to commit more than $225 million, and wanted the provincial government to contribute a larger share.*

how the province would raise its financial share of the Plan, now estimated at approximately $725 million. Finally, with some changes in the phasing related to federal and provincial financial contributions, and the arrangement of a development loan to the province, the two governments reached agreement on February 18, 1969.

*   *   *

Premier Alex Campbell and the Honourable Jean Marchand signed the Comprehensive Development Plan at a ceremony in Memorial Hall at the Confederation Centre of the Arts on the dull, damp and chilly day of March 7. In his remarks on this historic occasion, Campbell magnanimously declared that "this is an agreement like none other witnessed in Canada before, and we are indeed privileged at having the opportunity to engage in it."

The tough part was about to begin.

PARO

"Be Sure Of Your Future"

- Liberal campaign slogan, 1970

The Prince Edward Island Comprehensive Development Plan represented the boldest and most ambitious effort ever made in the province to reverse its economic decline, reduce its dependency on federal support, and enable Islanders to become more self-reliant. It encompassed every sector of the economy and every person in the province. It represented nothing less than an attempt to overhaul and reshape the entire province and its people; in so doing, it would inevitably undermine the existing hierarchical and oligarchical power structures. At its heart was the need for fundamental change in the way Islanders saw themselves and their prospects. "The P.E.I. plan is a most interesting and important event in the evolution of economic planning in North America," wrote noted regional economists Thomas Wilson and W.Y. Smith in 1970. "The Plan's detail, its comprehensiveness, its ambitious targets, the involvement of both federal and provincial governments, all ensure that it will be watched with great interest by civil servants and scholars through-out the western world." The Plan was not only the "most interesting and important" event of its kind in North America, it was also the only one.

With reformist zeal, the Campbell government proceeded in a radical departure from the past to move Prince Edward Island into the twentieth century. Speaking on the Development Plan in the Legislature on March 18, 1970, Campbell acknowledged that it was based on some revolutionary ideas. Canadian journalist Peter Desbarats, writing in the *Toronto Star* in May 1972, even playfully compared Premier Campbell with another politician who was busy reshaping his island – Fidel Castro of Cuba. At first glance, he suggested, both Campbell and Castro had little in common apart from the fact that they both governed islands, that Campbell favoured cigarettes over cigars, and that he never harangued listeners on Marx and Lenin. "But in his own way, and in the quiet style of this smallest of provinces," he wrote, "Premier Campbell is a revolutionary

Alfredo Manto, AAA

It's not Campbell's soup ... but! An article in the Toronto Star *compared Premier Campbell with Fidel Castro of Cuba, saying both were taking revolutionary approaches to reshaping their respective islands: "But in his own way, and in the quiet style of this smallest of provinces, Premier Campbell is a revolutionary politician."*

politician." His views were echoed by UPEI political studies professor David Milne, who agreed that "in terms of Island conventions, the Campbell men can only be described as revolutionaries."

The blueprint was laid out carefully, rationally, and logically. Its overall goal was to give Islanders for the first time the means to take charge of their own future. In its scope, the Plan intended to inject a new level of flexibility into an economy that had been stagnant for most of the century, and increase its capability to grow and develop. From an economic growth rate of just 2.2 percent the year Campbell came to power, the Plan aimed to achieve 7.0 percent by the end.

The Plan's radical approach was manifested the strongest in the province's economic foundation – agriculture. In its own words, the Plan would bring about "full economic exploitation of the Island's large and potentially profitable resources for agriculture." In the process, this "full economic exploitation" would challenge all the nostalgic rhetoric related to the much-vaunted family farm. Henceforth, farming was to represent more than just a way of life; now it was a business.

The agriculture strategy included the creation of some 2,500 commercial farms. Of the more than 6,000 farms then in existence, less than one-third were classified as full time. Although the industry had increased its productivity through mechanization and other advances, profit margins were still on the decline. Farmers produced twice as much to earn half as much. The Plan aimed to put the industry on a firm footing so that farmers could improve productivity and earn higher returns. Small, part-time, and older farmers would be "rationalized" through a land adjustment program that encouraged the reallocation of land to its most profitable use. Through this scheme, retiring farmers could sell their land to the newly created Land Development Corporation, receive a pension, and stay in their farm home for life if they desired, while their land would be reallocated to commercial farmers. Marginal lands could also be converted to other uses, such as forestry, tourism, and wildlife conservation. In this way, some 270,000 acres of unused or underutilized agricultural land would be added to the 550,000 acres then under cultivation.

Flying in the face of two hundred years of struggles for ownership of the land (the Island's infamous Land Question), the Plan now asserted that "*the historical pattern of land ownership is badly suited to the needs of modern technology*" (author's italics). Walter Shaw grandiosely described the scheme as "the most insidious way of separating a man from his land and his liberty" the province had ever experienced. Others viewed the Plan's goal of 2,500 family farms not as a sign of progress in agriculture, but as a blatant attempt to reduce the total number of farms in the province.

The concept of "rationalization" would also be applied to the fisheries. The Plan called for a reduction in the number of "marginal" fishermen in an effort to match the limited resource with the demands of an emerging commercial fishery. Most of the small, inadequate port facilities around the shoreline would be closed down and the remainder consolidated and upgraded, leaving some twenty harbours to benefit from the latest in fish-handling and -holding facilities. Strengthened fisheries management would prevent the overexploitation of some species and encourage improved utilization of others. New technological advances in processing would lead to greater efficiency and productivity, improved incomes for plant workers, and higher returns to fishermen. The Plan approached the fisheries as an economic opportunity for the province, a rewarding career for participants, and a resource to be rescued from decades of chaos and mismanagement.

Fishermen rejected much of it. They refused to abandon the harbours their families had fished from for generations, and few agreed to participate in efforts to reduce the numbers of participants, despite the attraction of a lobster licence buy-back program.

Major plans were also in the works to make tourism an integral and growing part of the Island economy. In 1965, the province attracted 249,000 tourists who spent $6 million. With this in mind, the Plan proposed to support and broaden the potential impact of the industry, forecast to triple revenue by its tenth year. Strategies would be designed to distribute tourist numbers more evenly beyond the Charlottetown-Cavendish-Summerside triangle. This would involve establishing resort complexes in Brudenell and Mill River and developing other higher-end facilities; extending the season; and preventing unsightly development. Since people were already concerned that the burgeoning tourism industry threatened to destroy the Island's tranquil and charming character, in response the tourism strategy would "assist the development that must take place in the face of pressures of demand and provide the degree of regulation necessary to optimize the returns to the Island's economy." Faced with a growing proliferation of billboards and a plethora of tacky roadside advertisements, the government instituted a province-wide, standardized signage program.

The strongest critics lambasted the tourism development strategy for turning the Island into a "cute little theme park" and converting it into just one more commodity or product to be managed. They did not have to look far for their suspicions to be confirmed. A tourism study undertaken by an off-Island company, Project Planning Associates, outlined a vision for the future of the industry. "We believe it will be increasingly useful to think of the whole of Prince Edward Island as a park," it recommended. "As this view becomes generally accepted, the Island will be seen in a new and important context. Every part of the Island will be appraised in terms of its international tourist and recreational potential. Every activity will be considered as a function of a living park, where a variety of socio-economic activities take place."

The Plan also turned its attention to other economic and social priorities. The manufacturing and processing sectors would receive increased emphasis in order to diversify the economy and create employment for those leaving farming and fishing. Efforts would be undertaken in this sector to achieve a ten-percent growth rate through improved productivity, training and technology, although the Plan barely hinted at the controversial industrial parks later established in West Royalty and other communities across the province. Then, to accommodate the expected shift in populations to more urban areas, the Plan foresaw the need to support new municipal sewer and water projects, and create an ambitious grant program for first-time homeowners and the upgrading of housing standards throughout the province. But although health and welfare programs were incorporated into the Plan, no agreement was ever reached to involve the federal health department; failing its refusal to participate, these proposals ended up in limbo. Worse than this, however – and to the dismay of local MLAs according to the Plan, decisions over highway construction priorities would be made by transportation planners based on complementing development strategies, not securing votes.

Throughout the Plan ran a steel thread of opposition to the status quo. Credit Union Central, the provincial association for Island credit unions, received support under the Plan to extent its loan programs, and a new provincial lending authority was established. These crucial supports bore out the Plan's vision for new investment and spending in the Island's primary and secondary industries. When Del Gallagher met with credit union representatives from across the Island to discuss the provision of new sources of financing for farmers and fishermen, they asked him if he thought the thrust of his proposals might be construed as a threat to existing power structures, in which farmers and fishermen were sometimes held captive through trade credit and other forms of economic pressure. "I sure as hell hope so," was the terse reply.

As a further affront to the existing power structures in agriculture, the Plan established a new market development agency; more importantly, it made legislative provision for the establishment of producer-controlled marketing boards. The Campbell government was not hesitant in attempting to give people more power over their economic lives. "In the process of development, if it's true and effective development," explained Campbell, "you're going to bring other people to a measure of control over their own affairs."

Despite subsequent successes in establishing producer-controlled marketing boards, and giving farmers and fishermen greater access to independent sources of credit, one development project never did get off the ground. As part of the new marketing agency, the Plan proposed a central grading, packaging, and warehouse facility to improve the quality of potatoes destined for market. At that time, a small group of powerful potato dealers and shippers exerted a virtual stranglehold over producers. As an alternative, the central marketing facility would "make possible the marketing of high and consistent quality of potatoes, *produced and marketed by farmers in the province*" (author's italics). This project, like many others, never materialized.

Fundamental to the entire Development Plan was education. Development planners were acutely aware that education would have to play a major role in unlocking the potential of Islanders. In 1966, the Economic Council of Canada published a trail-blazing study that looked at the contribution of education to economic growth. It concluded that "an increase in the skills and knowledge of a population through education raises productivity and real income in the same manner as an increase in the stock of physical capital or advances in technology." The Campbell government had already moved to establish a single university (the University of Prince Edward Island) and a college of applied arts and technology (Holland College); it was now poised to revolutionize primary and secondary education across the Island.

Throughout the Development Plan negotiations, the provincial government had fought hard to make education an integral part its strategy, to the extent that at one point it withdrew from negotiations until the educational component was reinstated. There were good reasons for such insistence. Prince Edward Island suffered from one of the worst school systems in the country: including per capita spending on education that was less than half the Canadian average; one of the highest school drop-out rates in Canada; poorly qualified teachers; antiquated school facilities; and an out-of-date curriculum. Educational administration was also highly decentralized and somewhat informal. In 1966, no less than 403 school boards supervised 412 schools. Although the province boasted fifteen district high schools, the rest of the system consisted of a nineteenth-century network of one-room schoolhouses operating out of more or less primitive facilities.

Obviously, there was an urgent need to provide greater equality, improve access to educational opportunities, and streamline the system. The Development Plan's education strategy envisioned an extensive program of school consolidation, teacher upgrading, and modernization of the curriculum. It would also involve a radical shift in the governance and financing of education. The establishment of five new school boards would provide a more centralized educational administration, and the provincial government would take over responsibility for financing.

The fundamental reform of the school system involved a brand new approach to education. Traditionally, people regarded the education system as an extension of the family and the community. They treated the schools as integral social institutions where the local trustees, parents, and teachers reflected the norms and values of the community. The new view, however, placed education in the position of a powerful engine for economic development. The stage was being set for more than just an evolutionary reform of an anachronistic school system; it represented a revolutionary leap forward from the nineteenth to the twentieth century, with a new philosophy and a new orientation.

Of all the Development Plan programs, arguably the most controversial was education, principally because people equated the consolidation of schools with loss of local control. As Verner Smitheram, one of the consultants engaged to evaluate the first phase of the Plan, later observed, "The consolidation of schools is the most complete and socially significant transition to occur in Prince Edward Island since the Second World War." The issue soon divided Islanders.

Overall, the Plan introduced a hard-nosed industrial model of development, based on the full exploitation of the province's physical and human resources, leaving little room for sentiment or tradition. Writing in the *Toronto Telegram* in March 1970, Dalton Camp caustically observed that "Prince Edward Island has damn well got to progress, populate and pollute just like the rest of Canada." According to Camp, "Ottawa has proclaimed a Plan to save Prince Edward Island from its natural state." He wondered why "scrambling, vote-grubbing politicians" could not understand that the obsession with progress was destroying the very fabric of the Island's existence – its environment, its values, and its distinctive prospects. "Why, for example, does Ottawa want to make pastoral Prince Edward Island more like industrial Ontario?" he asked.

That question would be raised over and over again. The future of the "Island way of life" cut across all debates, discussions and diatribes. Campbell's greatest challenge was to convince Islanders to take a headlong leap into the future.

* * *

A more fundamental issue was embedded in the Development Plan – the very question of Prince Edward Island's autonomy as a province. Frank MacKinnon's later accusation that a large task force moved in and took over the government resonated with many Islanders. The issue would plague the Campbell government throughout its mandate.

The rest of Canada was largely indifferent to the fate of Prince Edward Island. After all, the Island economy accounted for less than one half of one percent of the national Gross Domestic Product. In fact, since the province's inception, outsiders viewed it as overgoverned at best, undeserving of provincial status at worst. Repeated calls for a union of the three Maritime provinces or for annexation of Prince Edward Island to one of its neighbouring provinces had been made prior to 1864, more than a century earlier when representatives of the three provinces met in Charlottetown to discuss the idea. On the day the Development Plan was signed, the *Calgary Herald* was moved to declare that "this island is not really a province anymore and should not go on being treated as [if] it were."

But the people living in Canada's smallest province rejected these assaults. According to UPEI history professor Fred Driscoll, they pay little attention to these arguments, "secure in the knowledge that their history has made them a distinct economic and political unit, and innately aware that size, population and wealth are not the only determinants of the appropriateness and legitimacy of the existence of British parliamentary institutions, and secure also in the knowledge that their representation in Parliament is guaranteed by the Constitution." Reviewing Prince Edward Island's legislative history, coloured by the close ties between Islanders and their political representatives, Driscoll remarked that "instead, they take some pride in being the closest thing to a direct democracy that exists in Canada."

A bleaker – and blunter – assessment of the future of provincial autonomy was raised by the *Financial Post* in May 1970. The Toronto-based newspaper reviewed the terms of the Plan and concluded that the federal government had, in effect, assumed control of the province and its finances. "When Islanders assess the impact of all this federal cash there is a tendency for many of them to wonder how much control over Prince Edward Island's destiny remains in the hands of the provincial government," it charged, then asked, "How long can provincial autonomy function effectively in such an environment?"

The debate over the threat to provincial autonomy stemmed from the Plan's structural and operational framework. From the outset, federal officials (especially in the Department of Forestry and Rural

Development, but more particularly in Finance) adamantly insisted that this untried approach to economic and social development of the magnitude being contemplated for Prince Edward Island required a whole new set of administrative arrangements. Not without justification perhaps, they convinced themselves that the Plan could not be entrusted to the present provincial governmental structure. After all, the province's new civil service reforms had been in place for less than five years, so the level of expertise was still limited. Federal officials recognized that the development and implementation of the Plan would necessarily involve a level of professional and technical expertise as well as fiscal and administrative structures and controls that they knew were practically non-existent within the provincial government.

Faced early on with the decision to overhaul and upgrade the entire provincial administrative structure or impose new management arrangements for the Plan, officials in the federal departments of Forestry and Rural Development and of Finance chose the latter. Under the five-year planning agreement signed with the Shaw government, the provincial government had therefore established the Economic Improvement Corporation with the sole focus of putting together and negotiating an agreement with the federal government. This approach made sense to the Campbell government, which clearly recognized the need for expertise beyond that currently available within its provincial departments. It also appreciated the advantage the new agency would have with no vested interest in existing programs and no turf to protect – an ideal starting point from which to come up with a new comprehensive development strategy.

Federal officials also believed the Economic Improvement Corporation to be the most appropriate body to implement the Plan, functioning at arm's length from the provincial government, and free from the day-to-day interference of politicians. In the meantime, some parts of the Plan's programs could be administered by provincial government departments; over time, as they gained experience and expertise, they might take over more responsibilities. For now, however, an independent agency, working closely with the federal government, would direct the activities. In addition, an independent, grassroots organization such as the Rural Development Council – non-partisan and non-political – would serve as the extension arm of the EIC. The RDC comprised a loose collection of clergymen, academics, members of the co-operative movement, and others who shared concerns about the Island's development prospects. In the role envisaged for it, the RDC would carry out community development and public participation programs away from the hurly-burly and complications of established political structures.

The Development Plan document explicitly spelled out the new approach: "Essential to the successful implementation of the Plan are a central coordinating body [the Economic Improvement Corporation], high capability in the operating departments of government [to be achieved over time], and strong, competent local organizations [such as the Rural Development Council], able to stimulate and make effective the widespread participation of the people for whom the development process exists and who, in the last analysis, are the people who will make it work." This process would clearly bypass the Island's long-established structures and traditions, and as much as possible it would avoid compromises between planners with their economic models and politicians with their pet projects. If the whole enterprise was ever to succeed, Islanders would have to put aside their differences, jealousies, loyalties, prejudices and parochialisms and work together in a new spirit of co-operation. Furthermore, with the Plan accounting for about twenty-five percent of provincial government spending, its pervasive influence would affect most other programs.

The approach by which federal and provincial governments were to oversee the Plan also led to criticisms that the provincial government was surrendering its autonomy. Reconciling political, bureaucratic and public agendas would prove an elusive exercise, as an organization called the Joint Advisory Board would reveal. Overall, the Plan was to be directed by this board, which consisted of senior federal and provincial government representatives. The federal representatives included senior mandarins, the deputy ministers of some of the key participating departments. To counter criticisms that provincial politicians were losing control, the provincial representatives on the board included the Premier and four of his senior ministers. That meant that federal bureaucrats and provincial politicians sat around the table as equals – the optics and import of which could not be ignored by those who insisted that the province had relinquished its autonomy.

The relative lack of open consultations during the Plan's development stage also deepened Islanders' suspicions about who was really in charge. During debates in the Legislature in the spring of 1968, Walter Shaw openly voiced concerns expressed by many people. "God knows how long it is going to be up there," he said in reference to the protracted negotiations with Ottawa, "and then the plan is going to be dumped on the people of Prince Edward Island." This accusation was reiterated by George Key, Shaw's successor as Leader of the provincial Conservative Party. Key complained vigorously about the Plan's "empire-like" structure. In an interview with the *Guardian* in September 1969, he said, "It can be seen that in order to carry out this long-term plan we have surrendered to the government a tremendous amount of our right to self-determination. I don't feel we should allow our people to become guinea pigs for the new breed of government economists in either Charlottetown or Ottawa." Key went even further in an interview with the *Globe and Mail* in May 1970, during the height of the provincial election campaign. "It's the mathematician, the economist, the planner, the bureaucrat, who will soon control Prince Edward Island," he warned. Throughout the campaign, Key maintained that the province was on the verge of losing its autonomy. "It's a deal conceived by Ottawa mandarins and it is they, not your elected representatives, who will decide your future," he charged.

Just prior to the calling of the 1970 election campaign, in his final appearance in the Legislature, Shaw continued to insist that the province would lose its right to self-determination. Conveniently ignoring its long history of dependency, he lamented its imminent fate. "Our people will have surrendered their pride, their independence and their future to become vassals of a commission administration," he mourned during the Throne Speech debate. Although Campbell publicly dismissed the allegations as "doom and gloom prophesies from the horse and buggy boys," in private he was growing increasingly concerned about the perceptions that his government was no longer in charge and that the Plan was being conceived in secrecy, which added to suspicions about the decision-making process. The provincial legislature might ask for details, Shaw complained in the spring of 1968 as negotiations continued with the federal government, "but we are not going to know the first thing about it."

For its part, the EIC did little to assuage concerns. In its second annual report to the Legislature for the year ending March 31, 1969, it explained its policy not to announce or otherwise make public details of the program as they might apply to the various sectors until they were finalized. With agriculture the subject of two or three sector plans, it asked rhetorically, what would be the point of making them all public, given that most of those interested were already aware of the general thrust in any case. "It was felt that to do so prior to the time when the Federal Government actually entered into an agreement with the Province would be dangerously irresponsible and prejudicial to provincial policy processes," explained the report. The EIC may have been correct in its assessment of the protocol, but that did little to relieve the political pressure on the Campbell government to be more open about what it had in mind.

The attitudes of some people within the EIC did little to reassure Islanders that their opinions mattered. Kingsley Brown, a journalist hired by the EIC to provide communications services, offered his own explanation of the lack of public awareness of what the Plan involved. "We have the worst newspapers in the country and yow-yow radio stations," he told a local reporter. "Little wonder Islanders are intellectually asleep." In response, John Brehaut, a news reporter at CFCY Radio, took to referring to Brown's communication *apparatchik* as the "ministry of propaganda." One afternoon, he received an angry call at the radio station from Dulcie Conrad, Brown's assistant, threatening to destroy his career unless he dropped his criticism of secrecy and his allegations of a high-handed public relations campaign.

As the development process moved from the planning to the implementation stage, Campbell became more acutely aware of the issues of accountability and autonomy. Throughout the planning process, Campbell and Gallagher worked closely together. Hardly a day went by when they did not meet or talk, while Gallagher and his officials attended part of most cabinet meetings throughout the summer and fall of 1968. The two men came to have great personal respect for one another, and for their respective roles and responsibilities. Campbell, who recognized clearly the need to protect the planning process from political interference, gave Gallagher full control over day-to-day operations at the EIC. For his part, Gallagher intuitively understood the political challenges Campbell faced in gaining public support for a concept so unfamiliar to most Islanders. Despite allegations by Shaw and others that the planners were dictating to government, Gallagher simply stated that, "unless asked, I didn't tell the government how to practice politics."

As the time approached to launch the Plan, Campbell moved to exert more political control over its implementation. In September 1968, he met with Robert Blakely, the EIC official responsible for the public participation component, and expressed his desire to attend the public meetings the Rural Development Council would be organizing to explain the various programs. With Campbell's endorsement, the EIC was preparing to sign an agreement with the RDC to carry out the public participation and community development components. Blakely resisted, reminding Campbell of the need to insulate the RDC from any overt signs of political interference. It was an awkward and uncomfortable meeting for both, exemplifying the subtle distinction that needed to be drawn between politics and planning.

Naturally, Campbell was concerned about gaining much-needed public and political support for the Plan. The document itself was written by the EIC planners using vocabulary most familiar to them, but not readily comprehensible to the average Islander, especially given that as many as one in four were functionally illiterate. Terms such as "viable human beings" would hardly resonate with most people. Other words used in the planning documents, such as "dictate," "control," "outmoded," "ineffectual," and "mismanage," failed to lend themselves to stirring political rhetoric. In October 1968, as federal-provincial negotiations were moving into their final stages, Campbell wrote to Tom Kent, Deputy Minister of DREE, reminding him that a major selling job was essential if the Plan was to be understood and accepted. "It now seems clear that a major re-writing job is needed on the program guide," he pointed out. Campbell dispatched Andy Wells to Ottawa to help federal officials put the Plan into plain language. In an effort to break through the mandarin-like mindset, Campbell lightly suggested to Kent that it would be desirable to "select a language which will warm the cockles of all Island hearts and will inspire their efforts to renew, restore and revitalize the Island they love so much." But despite the intervention, and the offer of help from Wells, the officials insisted it was a planning document, not a political manifesto; as a result, few changes were made. Ironically, much of the final version retained in the text was drafted by Campbell's own officials at the EIC in the first place.

By the early days of 1969, as final agreement with Ottawa drew near, Campbell turned much of his attention to the problem of how to administer and implement the Plan. The federal government wanted to retain the EIC as a central co-ordinating body, retaining control over the budget and authority to approve projects, with line departments of the provincial government delivering the various elements as they acquired the necessary experience and expertise. Maintaining the EIC at arm's length from government, insisted federal officials, would preserve the Plan's integrity and protect it from day-to-day political interference. Faced with growing criticism about the threats to autonomy and the effective loss of responsible government, Campbell wrote to Jean Marchand in Ottawa, proposing that a separate provincial government department with its own minister would provide a more effective means of ensuring control and accountability. However, Marchand had been in his position as minister of the newly created Department of Regional Economic Expansion for only a few months, and was hesitant to meddle with his officials.

As the two governments massaged the final details of the agreement, Campbell realized that Gallagher shared the federal view; once the Plan was signed, Gallagher – with the blessing of the federal government – would become head of the arm's-length administrative agency. Up till now, Campbell had believed that the work of Gallagher and the EIC would end once the planning was complete. If the EIC were to be given responsibility for the implementation of the Plan, then it, not the government, would be in control. Frustrated by his stalemate with Marchand, Campbell flew to Ottawa where he met with Don Jamieson, Trudeau's political minister for the Atlantic provinces. Jamieson was an astute and powerful politician, with a sharp wit and a down-to-earth political style. He met Campbell at his hotel room and they talked well into the night. By morning, Campbell emerged with Jamieson's tacit support to put a provincial government department in charge of the implementation of the Development Plan.

On his return to Charlottetown, Campbell met with Gallagher and informed him he would not be running the Development Plan. It was an intense, difficult meeting between two men who had toiled so long and hard side by side to put the Plan in place. Not unexpectedly, Gallagher strongly rejected turning over the EIC's mandate to a provincial government department, and further made it clear that he opposed leaving politicians in charge. Campbell offered to appoint Gallagher as his economic advisor, but Gallagher demurred and quietly left the province.

On March 11, 1969, four days after the Development Plan was signed, the spring session of the Legislature opened. During the Speech from the Throne, the government announced that a new Department of Development would be established to replace the Economic Improvement Corporation and, with Campbell as its minister, would direct and co-ordinate the implementation of the Development Plan.

Ironically, those who had been critical of the fact that planners had taken over the role of politicians now suddenly raised alarms that the process was becoming too political. The Rural Development Council demanded that the government take a non-partisan approach to the Plan's implementation, while others questioned its political motivations. Writing in the *Globe and Mail*, Lyndon Watkins accused the government of taking away the independence anticipated in the formulation of the Plan. The argument for doing so seems solid, he conceded, " but in an Island as political as PEI there is concern that political considerations might enter decisions that should be based on other factors."

Campbell had tackled head-on the thorny question of provincial autonomy. For him, the question was clear-cut. "It boiled down to who, in fact, was going to preside over the governing of this province," he said. "And to pass the responsibility for the implementation of such a plan to the manager of a given corporation who, no doubt, would have insisted on legislative protection of their autonomy, would have been tantamount to throwing the key of the Premier's office away."

Campbell was not prepared to throw that key away. Now, he had to face an election which would determine whether or not he could keep it.

* * *

By the spring of 1970, the Campbell government was heading into its fourth year in office. The preceding four years had been tumultuous and nerve-wracking. Controversies over the Georgetown developments; amalgamation of the two universities; cancellation of the causeway; the threatened elimination of CFB Summerside; and the protracted, seemingly secretive negotiations leading to the Development Plan – not to mention the thorny, day-to-day issues that plague politicians – had kept his government on a perpetual tight rope.

With just a two-seat majority in the Legislature, Campbell's government held on by its fingernails. The caucus was restive and the Cabinet divided. One minister, Robert Campbell, had threatened more than once to resign, while other ministers remained skeptical about the massive reforms being contemplated. Another minister, George Ferguson, although loyal to Campbell, suffered from serious health problems and was forced to miss some of his duties in cabinet and in the Legislature, where every vote was needed. That razor-thin majority hung like the sword of Damocles over Campbell's entire first term in office. During the special session of the Legislature that followed the 1966 election, 4th Prince MLA Max Thompson was confined to hospital, although his doctor gave him permission to leave at a moment's notice if his vote was required in the Legislature. (It was a fortunate coincidence that the party whip, Sinclair Cutcliffe, operated an ambulance service. It might have been needed to rush Thompson from the hospital to save the government!)

As final negotiations for the Plan approached the wire, Keir Clark – long-time Liberal MLA and Campbell's health minister – resigned in protest. In his letter of resignation, Clark told Campbell that in his view the power of cabinet ministers was being eroded by the planners, and he could no longer remain part of government. Then, as the Legislature opened in the spring of 1970, Clark announced that he was quitting the Liberal caucus as well. On March 3, Clark rose in the Legislature to announce his intentions. "I am no longer connected with the party of the plan," he said tersely, and asked the Clerk of the Legislature to move his desk across the floor to the opposition benches. Now the Legislature was evenly divided, sixteen to sixteen, but with the Speaker in the chair (voting only in the case of a tie) the government benches were reduced to fifteen members, two short of a majority.

On March 18, during his reply to the Throne Speech, Campbell delivered a wide-ranging review of his government's achievements since its election in 1966. Referring to his party's platform, he talked about the forty-seven planks which the government had success-fully initiated or were in the process of carrying out. "However, Mr. Speaker," he added, "we do believe that we have, in addition to all these programs, instituted yet another program for the people of Prince Edward Island, another program for the future of this Province, another opportunity for the people of our Province, another brighter prospect for our younger people who love this Province as much as our senior citizens, who want to remain here in this Province, and who express the hope that our economy will develop at a rate fast enough to provide industrial development, to provide jobs for our working people ... I am referring to the Development Plan, Mr. Speaker."

After all the studies and analyses, discussions and debates, negotiations and controversies, after all the hype and hoopla, Campbell tried to demystify the Plan. "The Development Plan, in two minutes to me, as I interpret it," he told the MLAs, "is a program of cost-sharing with the Government of Canada which to this Province, this year, will introduce $23 million of investment by the people of Canada in the people of Prince Edward Island." Then, turning to the opposition benches, he declared, "I am tempted to hope that our Honourable colleague who sat with us formerly in the Cabinet will vote against us so that we may go to the country and get a mandate and come back."

The vote failed to materialize. With few options remaining, Campbell dissolved the Legislature and called a provincial general election for May 11.

*　　*　　*

This time, Campbell faced a new Conservative Party leader. George Key, a former mayor of Summerside, was elected to succeed Walter Shaw at a party convention in September 1968. Ironically, Key and Campbell were considered to be friends. They both came from the same town, went to the same United church, were both members of the local YMCA, and in 1964 the Key and Campbell families had even taken a camping trip together.

Following Key's election, Campbell invited him to his office where he briefed the new leader on a number of provincial issues, including a detailed overview of the Development Plan then still under negotiation. With the lines on both sides now drawn, the two skirmished intermittently in the media and at various public meetings, but the 1970 election would provide the first real test of the style of leadership each offered. As the campaign got underway, the predominant issue – not surprisingly – was the Development Plan.

Key made it clear from the beginning that he was opposed to the Plan in its present form. At the Conservative Party campaign kickoff held at the Basilica Recreation Centre in Charlottetown on Friday, April 10, Key condemned the Plan, predicting it would destroy many family farms; crowd fishermen into designated ports; force families to leave their homes, or worse, the Island; and remove control of provincial affairs from elected representatives. "We do not accept the plan in its present form," he told the cheering party faithful. "We now call for a clear mandate so that we can immediately renegotiate the plan." The Key team, according to its election advertisements, "puts the Island first."

The Liberals held their kickoff rally at the vocational school in Summerside a week later on April 17, attended by a huge and enthusiastic crowd of more than two thousand supporters. In his keynote address, Campbell made the Development Plan a central issue. The Plan, he told the cheering Liberals, would result in a standard of living and a quality of life equal to the rest of Canada. In his address, he also acknowledged a major challenge facing his campaign; quite simply, most Islanders did not understand what the Plan was all about. Although it had been in place for just over a year, many of its programs were not yet launched or had only just started. Added to this, the Plan's sheer scope made it difficult for most people to grasp.

The government had in fact published a brochure explaining the major provisions of the Plan, but little tangible evidence existed to show what impacts could be expected. As the Campbell campaign team under the chairmanship of Mike Schurman put together the campaign's key messages, it faced a formidable hurdle in explaining the Plan in the short time available. "Make no mistake, the development programs are at work now," the campaign reassured Islanders. A subsequent Liberal campaign newspaper advertisement picked up on the theme, referring to some eighty programs included in their list of campaign promises. "People talk a lot about plans," declared one ad in an attempt to squelch criticism that the Plan was nothing more than a set of vague proposals, "but the early planning period of the Prince Edward Island Development Program has been completed. Many of the most important programs are now in effect." It went on to ask voters to trust in a new Liberal government which would deliver on the balance of the programs. "The next [programs] will come on schedule when you re-elect a Liberal government," it read. "They are programs for the people of PEI, programs to bring a better life to Islanders."

It was an ambitious pledge, based on a vague premise and an unproven concept. In effect, Campbell was asking Islanders to take a huge leap of faith; in so doing, he confronted an electorate unaccustomed to expect great things of its political system. Acres International had revealed this problem when it conducted its survey in 1967, concluding that "doubt and skepticism characterize the present attitudes toward the prospects of the Prince Edward Island development program." This view was endorsed by Del Gallagher who, as a result of his discussions with various organizations during the planning process, privately reported to Campbell that he encountered a feeling of disbelief among Islanders that anything was ever going to get done right in the province.

Campbell himself recognized this pervasive skepticism. In an interview with the *Financial Post* in late 1967, he talked about the province's low level of expectations in light of Islanders' historic sense of dependency on others. "This severely limits our ability to influence major changes in the economic course and development of the province," he conceded. "We have lacked confidence in our own ability to seek opportunities for development." Although he noted that those sentiments were gradually changing, he added that "depression attitudes have been with us for too long."

A private survey conducted for the Liberal Party by Ben Crow and Associates early in 1970 also revealed a set of conflicting attitudes about the economics of the province – past, present, and future. The survey concluded that, while people were generally satisfied with life in the province, they still harboured concerns about a host of economic problems. "This economic concern is the jarring note in the pastoral symphony," Crow reported to the Liberal campaign team. The survey also found little to comfort the Liberal strategists, who were fighting the campaign on essentially one issue, the Development Plan. Only four percent of respondents saw the Plan as something that affected them personally; forty-one percent were generally favourable to the Plan's overall thrust; and more than twenty-five percent were neutral or not sufficiently aware of the details to give an opinion. A further forty-two percent believed that the cause-way had been sacrificed to the Development Plan, while two out of every three resented the role of "outsiders" in formulating the Plan. Most troubling to campaign organizers, however, was the finding that seventy-five percent of Islanders believed the present lifestyle was "good" and that a change was "wrong." The survey also reported that sixty percent of Islanders admitted they feared change.

Crow's analysis did nothing to reassure Campbell's strategists as they prepared for the campaign.

"The Development Plan has not caught the attention or imagination of the people," said Crow in the understatement of the campaign, adding that "it is approved by some but considered a threat by many, especially to the basic lifestyle." Crow's survey identified one other disturbing fact of life in Prince Edward Island – an overwhelming sense of dependency and reliance on the federal government. "The two things looked for from Ottawa are interest or attention and money," stated the report. "Contribution of the province to the national interest does not seem to occur to many Islanders."

Political journalist Charles Lynch, writing in the *Winnipeg Tribune* on April 2, 1970, summed up the public mood. "Islanders generally seem to view the development plan in much the same light as they viewed the causeway – they'll believe it when they see it, and up to now they ain't seen much," he observed. For his part, Campbell was concerned about running too far ahead of public opinion. "Islanders who want the development plan are going to have to help me fight to get it going," he told the *Guardian* in a candid interview in November 1969.

For the Liberals, the 1970 election campaign hinged on selling the merits of a development plan that few among the public understood, and fewer still were prepared to accept. For the Conservatives, it came down to creating sufficient doubt and fear in the public mind to defeat the government. The choice was starkly presented in a *Guardian* editorial on the eve of the election. "After six weeks of electioneering, Islanders are left with a choice," it read. "Support or reject the comprehensive development plan." The Conservative campaign, on the other hand, attempted to strike at the heart of concerns about the impact of the Development Plan and Islanders' innate fear of change. In a direct response to Key's promise to renegotiate the Plan if elected, Campbell told the Liberal wind-up rally at the Kennedy Coliseum in Parkdale on May 8 that "I cannot see any reason to re-negotiate a standard of living and a quality of living second to none anywhere in Canada."

Few other serious issues surfaced in the 1970 campaign. To strengthen his hand, Campbell quietly reminded voters that the Liberal government had kept all the promises it made in 1966, and had dealt with a number of troubling and controversial issues. The list was impressive. In April 1969, H.B. Nickerson and Sons of North Sydney had purchased the assets of Gulf Garden Foods for an undisclosed price. With the Bathurst Marine shipyard now operating as a crown corporation, the trouble that had plagued the government over that particular inherited industrial development fiasco was now laid to rest. The new University of Prince Edward Island was preparing to graduate its first class. Provincial Treasurer Earle Hickey was forecasting the first balanced budget in a decade. His colleague, Health Minister Bruce Stewart, announced that medicare, which would pay eighty-five percent of all medical bills, would go into effect on December 1st. Federal Defence Minister Leo Cadieux had announced the previous December that CFB Summerside would remain open until at least April 1973. And Liberal campaign ads boasted of 570 miles of new paving – "paved roads for farmers and fishermen."

In the end, the Conservative campaign (which Campbell described as "warmed-over mackerel") never took hold. Despite the fact that the future of the Development Plan was at stake, the election was characterized by the usual hoopla, hyperbole and hype. *Journal-Pioneer* editor Elmer Murphy, who was not unaware that the fate of the Development Plan loomed over the outcome of the election, nevertheless characterized the campaign as "a dull, hard-working, dull, serious, dull, apparently honest campaign." As Campbell wound up the Liberal campaign during a boisterous rally at the Kennedy Coliseum, he asked Islanders to give him a mandate to continue with the job. And on Monday, May 11, they responded with the largest popular majority ever received by a political party in Prince Edward Island.

PARO

Campbell congratulates Gilbert Clements (left) *and Lorne Bonnell following the 1970 election campaign.*

Prime Minister Pierre Trudeau (left) *with Campbell.*

The Liberals captured an astounding and unprecedented fifty-eight percent of the popular vote, winning twenty-seven of the thirty-two seats, and sending a number of long-time Conservative MLAs into political oblivion. Even leader George Key failed to get elected, losing to his opponent (and cousin) Josh MacArthur by 12 votes. All of Campbell's cabinet ministers were re-elected. The campaign also earned a seat for Jean Canfield, the first woman ever to be elected to the provincial legislature. The people of Prince Edward Island had taken a leap of faith. They may not have known much about the Development Plan, there may have been much in it they were concerned about, but they were willing to give their youthful premier a chance.

During negotiations over the Plan, Campbell had expressed his hope and confidence that it would be the means of ending the province's historic dependence on the federal government, and for the first time bring the province a degree of self-reliance. "I submit that the Prince Edward Island Development Program presents the best opportunity, if not the last opportunity, for rational social reform and resource development in this Province," he wrote to Jean Marchand.

Only time and subsequent events would tell.

PARO

"From then on he was king," said the Guardian *after the sweeping election victory of 1970. "He formed what came to be known as one of the strongest ministries the province ever had and he was its undisputed master."*

* * *

The 1970 election represented a triumphal victory for Alex Campbell. He was attempting to set a new direction for the province, and the people seemed prepared to follow. He later described his first term as a "path finder," a period of discovery. What are our possibilities, he had asked? What do we do? What are our goals and objectives? Now, he and his government were prepared to move forward. "From then on he was king," said the *Guardian* in a later editorial. "He formed what came to be known as one of the strongest ministries the province ever had and he was its undisputed master."

But on the day following the May 11 election, Campbell was characteristically modest. At an impromptu victory rally at the vocational school in Summerside, he announced to supporters and well-wishers that he was going to get a haircut and go back to work.

Campbell at home with his family: his wife, Marilyn, and (l-r) Graham, Heather and Blair.

CHAPTER EIGHT

Junction '71
and Other Atrocities

This much is clear. During the Easter weekend of 1971, three young Prince Edward Islanders – Doug MacArthur, Ron Cameron, and Cuyler Cotton – organized Junction '71, a rock concert to be held at the Kennedy Coliseum in Parkdale. Headlining the concert was an up-and-coming Canadian musician, Bruce Cockburn. Other local, regional, and national groups were booked to make an appearance: Edward Bear, whose song "You, Me and Mexico," had reached the charts; Ocean, noted for its rendition of "Put Your Hand in the Hand," written by Islander Gene MacLellan; Pepper Tree, with its hit single, "Love is a Railroad;" and legendary Maritime rocker Sam Moon and the Universal Power. The concert would be promoted across the Maritimes and was expected to attract upwards of five thousand fans. The promoters said fifty percent of the proceeds from the two-day event would be donated to the Rotary Easter Seals fund.

Then all hell erupted. The spectre of thousands of drug-crazed, sex-starved, draft-dodging, fucked-up, long-haired hippie weirdo freaks, high on cocktails of dope, speed, acid, booze, raging hormones and testosterone, rampaging out of control through the quiet streets of Parkdale, leaving a trail of wanton destruction, engaging in random acts of violence, committing unspeakable acts of sin and debauchery, and despoiling young innocents, was too much for the good people of Prince Edward Island to accept – especially on one of the holiest weekends of the year. In an unprecedented display of solidarity, Liberals and Conservatives, Protestants and Catholics, town and country, rich and poor – every red-blooded, law-abiding, right-thinking, God-fearing, Jesus-loving, hippie-hating, holier-than-thou citizen of this fair and peaceful province – joined in a unanimous and uncharacteristic display of hostility and inhospitality. Even the moribund Women's Christian Temperance Union, which promoted total abstinence from alcohol (and presumably other mind–altering substances as well), was re-energized by the crisis, sensing that its uncompromising position had finally been vindicated.

Junction '71 evoked visions of Woodstock, where an estimated half a million people in the flowering of the youth culture converged on Max Yasgur's farm in Bethel, New York, in August 1969 for one of the greatest rock concerts of all time, and Altamont, California, where in December 1969 a group of crazed Hell's Angels, acting as security guards for the Rolling Stones, killed a black man on camera during one of the most violence-prone and drug-ridden concerts in the history of rock and roll. Not surprisingly, the good people of Prince Edward Island did not want to see their province similarly despoiled and desecrated. They demanded a stop to Junction '71. The "summer of love" would not come to pass on this peaceable Island if they had anything to do with it.

Junction '71 exposed the raw nerves, atavistic attitudes, festering sores, bitter resentments, and acute sensibilities of Islanders – not to mention the widening gap between generations and cultures. The thin veneer of civility and tolerance was shattered by the hidebound histrionics of the comfortable majority and their deep-seated but simmering paranoia. The first shot came from the village commissioners of Parkdale, where the Kennedy Coliseum was located, who expressed their profound alarm that such an event would be held within their borders. At an emergency meeting, they raised concerns about how to maintain law and order, control traffic, deal with garbage and sanitation, and protect public health and safety.

The people of Parkdale were not unfamiliar with intrusions on their peaceful existence. Each year, Old Home Week and the Provincial Exhibition were held on the Coliseum grounds. The raucous, risqué and rowdy midway featuring the Bill Lynch Shows had already proved too much for many people. A rock concert was clearly out of the question. The people of Parkdale did not want concert-going perverts pissing on their manicured lawns.

Junction '71 was denounced from pulpits across the province. A group of sixteen "prominent clergy" (as they piously portrayed themselves), representing the Island's major religious denominations, issued a public warning about the ever-present dangers of drugs, escapism and immorality, and the blasphemy of holding the event on the Easter weekend, which for many represented a time for family, fellowship and prayer. The group of leading Protestant and Roman Catholic clergymen expressed their "dread" about "mass drug trafficking and increase in drug addiction." Support for the ban also came from the Prince Edward Island Medical Society, which unctuously declared that the concert was "not in the best interests of the youth of the province." Summoning up all the outrage and indignation due their status, the ever-vigilant doctors warned that Prince Edward Island lacked the proper emergency medical facilities to deal with the anticipated outbreak of drug abuse and violence. Going one step further, the Medical Society issued what it termed conclusive evidence of the relationship between "acid rock" music and the legitimization of drug use. Emboldened by its position, the Society predicted that the holding of the concert would result in thousands of "speed freaks" roaming uncontrollably throughout the streets of Charlottetown.

The Royal Canadian Mounted Police, Prince Edward Island division, was already on the alert. Across Canada, the RCMP had been spying on, infiltrating, and interfering with similar events. It had already conducted a major examination of the relationship between lawlessness and rock festivals, concluding that they represented a major threat to law and order. The RCMP also regarded drugs as the top threat to Canadian society.* Superintendent Lou Pantry of the RCMP's "L" division on Prince Edward Island stated unequivocally in a report that rock concerts were "tantamount to drug orgies, conducive to drug pollution and misfortune to many innocent people." RCMP Corporal Brennan urged that all legal means and reasons be found to stop the concert.

The indignant howls of protest and outrage, whipped up by self-professed, zealous guardians of public morality, soon reached the doors of Province House where the Legislature was in session.

*   *   *

The second session of the fifty-second General Assembly of the Prince Edward Island Legislature had opened on February 18, 1971, and was dealing with a number of wide-ranging measures to implement the Campbell government's agenda.** Now, the furor

---

* *Prince Edward Island did not appear to fit the profile of alleged drug abuse in Canada, however; in 1970, only three charges were laid in the province for trafficking.*

** *The list of landmark pieces of legislation included the Prince Edward Island Labour Act, which would usher in a new era of labour-management relations; an Act to Establish a Building Code; an Act to Establish an Environmental Control Commission; a far-reaching Real*

---

developing across the province over the rock concert engulfed MLAs in its path. Nervous, angry constituents were contacting their representatives to express their concerns and demand that something be done, while indignant calls kept pouring into Campbell's office urging the government to take action. As the Legislative Assembly headed back to work on April 6 for what was expected to be the final week before adjournment, the public mood turned ugly. The Easter weekend lay ahead, with the rock concert scheduled for April 10 and 11. Gordon Bennett, the avuncular attorney general, was not immune to the hysteria, and instructed his officials to investigate a legal means of preventing the rock concert from taking place. When he declared that "drugs are unwelcome on PEI," Bennett reflected the prevailing mood of Island legislators.

On Tuesday morning, Bennett presented a proposal to Campbell. With no current legislation in place to give the government power to control such events as rock concerts, Bennett proposed new legislation to give it sweeping authority, specifically the power to prohibit any public gathering that failed to meet with its approval. Despite the draconian nature of this legislation, Bennett argued that given public antipathy about the impending event the political benefits associated with the new law far outweighed the risks. Campbell and Bennett then took the unprecedented step of contacting the Opposition, and invited the acting leader, Dr. George Dewar, and his caucus to lunch to discuss the bill before the afternoon session. The opposition MLAs, like the government MLAs, had all received hysterical calls from their constituents demanding that something – anything – be done. Although they did not like the provisions of the proposed bill, they liked the prospect of the rock concert even less. However, Dr. Dewar expressed major reservations about the sweeping powers of the legislation. He slyly suggested it would even give the government the power to prohibit the Conservatives from holding nominating conventions!

That afternoon, after Question Period, Attorney General Gordon Bennett rose in the Legislature and introduced Bill 55, An Act

---

Property Assessment Act that would streamline the antiquated system of property taxes across the province; and a new School Act that would initiate massive reforms to the educational system. By all accounts, this session was one of the most productive in recent times, coming as it did on the heels of the 1970 provincial election which gave Campbell a sweeping mandate.

---

to Provide for the Prohibition of Certain Public Gatherings. Section 1(b) of the act defined a public gathering as "any contest, game, dance, apparatus, amusement, display, device, exhibition, attraction, performance, presentation, program, festival, show or motion picture, operated either indoors or out of doors, which is or which may be attended by the public." Section 2(1) of the act gave the minister, with cabinet approval, the right "to prohibit any public gathering which in his opinion may contribute to the disruption of public order, or where in his opinion there are insufficient medical services, fire or police protection, sleeping facilities, or other essential services." Those contravening the act would be liable to a fine not exceeding $5,000, or one year in jail.

Speaking to the bill, Premier Campbell issued a thinly veiled threat to those who might erode the Island's pastoral image, and warned that, although he was not personally opposed to rock festivals, nevertheless the provincial government was determined to protect Island values. "Let it be clearly understood," he announced, "that PEI is not, and will not, become a drug haven as long as we have the means available to protect it."

Suspending normal rules, the government was able to hustle the bill through three readings in the Legislature in less than two hours. The only dissenting vote came from Dr. Dewar, who gave his opinion that the legislation was dangerous and would interfere with the right of assembly. The next day, just before the Legislature was adjourned, the act received Royal Assent. The government now possessed the authority it needed to put a halt to Junction '71.

*   *   *

Reaction to the Public Gatherings Act was swift, furious and unequivocal. Civil libertarians, the national media, and other opponents, immediately denounced it as repressive, unconstitutional and undemocratic. A hastily arranged demonstration took place outside Province House the day the act received Royal Assent. Parading under the banner "We Want Freedom," protestors derided the act, warning that a government could invoke it to head off strikes, anti-war protests, student demonstrations, or any other gathering deemed to be potentially disruptive to public order. Reshard Gool of UPEI's Department of Political Studies denounced the act as "the sort of legislation you might expect from a communist or fascist state."

The following Saturday, a protest demonstration was organized in Rochford Square in Charlottetown, opposite the Premier's Office. The demonstration was chaired by David Milne, Department of Political Studies at UPEI, and included a courageous denunciation of the act by Charlottetown Mayor Dorothy Corrigan. David MacDonald, MP for Egmont, drove down by car from Ottawa overnight to attend the demonstration. MacDonald, who just months before in October 1970, was the only MP to vote against the Trudeau government's War Measures Act, delivered a stirring and stinging rebuke to the Campbell government, calling both measures, federal and provincial, draconian attempts to stifle public dissent. Upwards of five hundred people attended the demonstration, which lasted an hour and a half, but as Allison MacKinnon wrote in the *Journal-Pioneer*, "the majority in attendance were interested or curious citizens who preferred to keep their hands in their pockets rather than expose them to the chill of the bitter April wind." The alleged presence of undercover RCMP officers taking pictures of protestors no doubt further contributed to the chill that hung over

Philip Mullally speaks to demonstrators in Rochford Square protesting the Public Gatherings Act. The act to prohibit certain public gatherings reflected what Time *magazine described as an "uptight little Island."*

the day and, indeed, the province. "It's the classic case of using a sledgehammer to kill a fly," said *The 4th Estate*, a leftist Halifax newspaper. Even the staid and straight-laced *Guardian* had to agree. "The solution to social threats of this nature won't come easy," it said in an editorial. "It will never be found in prohibitive legislation of the type the provincial government has hurried into being."

Opposition quickly spread across the country. In Ottawa, both the Conservatives and the NDP denounced the act as contrary to the Canadian Bill of Rights, while the Canadian Civil Liberties Association called for federal intervention. The national media speculated that Ottawa would use its powers to disallow the legislation. However, Justice Minister John Turner only said that he would let the courts decide on its constitutionality. Even those in Prince Edward Island who had urged the provincial government to invoke measures to halt the "Junction '71" legislation were taken aback by the extremity of the measures it had taken. The Right Reverend William Simpson, one of the group of clergymen opposed to the concert, described the Public Gatherings Act as "an over-reaction." "I don't think any of the clergy felt the government would go that far," he admitted sheepishly.

The atavistic Islanders who remained in adamant opposition to the rock concert resented the criticism directed at them and the government. Typical of the response was a letter to the editor of the *Guardian* stating that Islanders "do not intend to be ruled by outside political science professors and a minority of mixed-up youths whose principal objectives in life seem to be entertainment and demonstrations against authority." For its part, the provincial government offered only a feeble response. "We were looking ahead at June, July, August and September when the tourists are here in large numbers," said Bennett, "and rock festivals adjacent to our parks wouldn't be the answer." Campbell also pointed out that four out of five letters received by his office applauded this defence of the Island way of life.

The controversy over the legislation split Campbell's' inner circle wide open. Andy Wells, Campbell's principal secretary and trusted advisor, had argued vehemently against it, and clashed headlong with Bennett and other members of the cabinet. When the brouhaha died down, he went to Campbell and suggested that he take an extended leave of absence until the issue faded. He was appointed executive director of the Council of Maritime Premiers, and moved to Halifax.

Eventually, in the face of negative publicity and mounting opposition, the government quietly announced two weeks later that the Public Gatherings Act would be repealed.

No one is sure when the promoters of Junction '71 were advised that the Public Gatherings Act would shut down the event, but they hastily put plans in place to salvage what they could from the rubble. They scaled the event down to a "festival of life and music" and, facing certain financial disaster, slashed ticket prices to two dollars on a first-come, first-served basis. Cockburn, Edward Bear, and locals like Mike Mooney and Frank Turgeron showed up to entertain a dispirited audience of about two hundred people under the watchful eye of the police. The promoters also issued an open invitation to leading Islanders to attend a "youth forum" held as part of Junction '71 to learn more about the issues affecting young people. No one accepted the invitation.

The tempest subsided, but the damage was done. The Public Gatherings Act represented a last-ditch attempt to protect the traditional Island way of life from the "evils" and inevitable changes of the 1970s. Described by *Time* magazine as an "uptight little Island," Prince Edward Island would not easily give up its sacred shibboleths. Who won the battle over the Act is not clear, but both sides went away licking their wounds.

*   *   *

Junction '71 was not the first clash of cultures and generations to take place in Prince Edward Island, neither would it be the last. In response to Prime Minister Pierre Trudeau's challenge to young people to "see Canada," thousands of young people took to the roads in the late 1960s and early '70s. Youth hostels, some with financial help from the federal government, sprang up across the country to provide basic food and accommodation to the youthful transients.

A hostel in the form of a "tent city" was proposed for Prince Edward Island during the summer of 1971. The hostel would offer shelter in a tent, segregated sleeping quarters, cold showers and a meal for fifty cents a day. But Charlottetown City Council reacted vehemently; the city fathers did not want the hostel within city limits. In the eyes of Councillor Ivan Doherty, the young travellers were "undesirables." When a location was selected in East Royalty, safely beyond city limits, a group of thirty-six housewives erected a barricade of wooden posts and barbed wire around the site to prevent construction of the tent city in their neighbourhood. They criticized the provincial government for going ahead without their consent, and Charlottetown City Council for passing the buck. And they were not going to back down.

Authorities called in the RCMP to remove the protesting house-wives and tear down the barriers. While the protestors were kept at bay, the tent city was erected, and opened its "doors" to visiting young people from across North America and even beyond. No serious incidents were reported. On the evening of June 2, Premier Campbell, with his wife and children, stayed overnight at the hostel in a gesture of solidarity. While defending the Island's image as "clean, quiet, pastoral and unspoiled," Campbell was eager to demonstrate he was not opposed to either rock music or hippies.

CHAPTER NINE

"A New Level and Type of Public Involvement ..."

On June 28, 1973, as Prince Edward Island was celebrating its centennial year as a province of Canada, Premier Campbell attended the third in a series of public meetings to consider the establishment of a second national park to be located in the eastern Kings County area.* The meeting took place at the St. Columba Hall in Fairfield. As in the two previous meetings in Kingsboro and South Lake, Campbell presented a series of slides depicting the area as it was and what might happen if it were left to the ravages of private development. A national park, Campbell argued, would prevent the destruction of the natural landscape, and the negative consequences of overuse, overcrowding, lack of zoning, and especially poor planning.

The park that Campbell envisioned would embody a brand new concept in the development of Canadian national parks. It would incorporate features of both the natural and cultural landscapes, preserving the area's rare and special places as well as the way of life and livelihoods of the residents. It would represent a radical departure from the wilderness model on which most national parks in Canada were based. Campbell stated his belief that such a "wilderness" model was not appropriate for Prince Edward Island, and announced that he had reached an agreement with the federal government that would enable residents to continue to live in their communities, albeit with some restrictions. Campbell described the agreement to establish the East Point National Park, which reflected this new approach, as "making history."

The proposed park divided the community. Despite the assurances offered by Campbell and the legions of bureaucrats and planners who had worked on the proposal for close to a decade, local residents regarded the proposal with a combination of confusion,

---

* Coincidentally, Campbell's father, Thane, had been instrumental in the establishment of the first one, the Prince Edward Island National Park, in 1937.

mistrust and fear. Not surprisingly, people were concerned about the potential loss of their lands, their livelihoods, and their communities. They also resented the prospect of an invasion of visitors who would contribute only limited benefits, mostly to tourist operators. Still others chafed at any possible restrictions on the use or sale of their properties. Community sentiment was summed up at the earlier meeting in Kingsboro by area resident Tyrrell Pearson who voiced residents' concerns that, as people died or moved away, their land would eventually revert to parkland, and that a national park would destroy the social and economic fabric of the community. "We are one step nearer the time when there will be no community left at all," he warned.

The proposal to establish a second national park in Prince Edward Island was first raised in a federal-provincial shoreline study in 1964. Research concluded that the eastern Kings area offered a prime location for the kind of protection a national park would provide. The pastoral area was one of the most attractive in Prince Edward Island. Bounded by the rocky cliffs of the north shore and, on the south, by an ecologically rich system of sand dunes, ponds, and white sand beaches overlooking the Northumberland Strait, the area was characterized by rolling countryside featuring the brilliant greens of farms and forests and the glowing reds of fields and cliffs, while at its borders lapped the ever-changing sea. Settlers arrived in this area in the pioneer era and over time established a diversified and colourful cultural tradition. Much of the area was unique, unspoiled and undiscovered. Given its significant natural features and relatively undeveloped state, federal and provincial officials considered it a prime area for protection. In fact, in the 1966 provincial election (and more prominently in the ensuing by-election) the Shaw government included the establishment of this second national park as part of its election platform.

The eastern Kings area contained a number of small, closely-knit communities, where many of the people were related by family or marriage. The roughly one thousand residents earned their livelihood primarily in farming and fishing; the area was noted for its progressive potato farms and for a major harbour at North Lake that called itself the "Tuna Capital of the World." Some thirty-five commercial farmers and a number of part-time worked the land, while fishermen operated over one hundred boats out of North Lake harbour, where the fish-processing plant employed fifty seasonal workers. The area also boasted two motels, four tourist homes, and two provincial parks (Red Point and Campbell's Cove). It was an idyllic, relatively prosperous and self-sufficient community where residents of both major religious faiths worked together on local projects and conducted most of their business in the nearby town of Souris.

In the 1960s, however, this community was undergoing a subtle transformation, thanks to the increasing attention of outsiders. Estimates indicate that the greatest source of revenue from tourists came from the sale of land for cottage development. Already, somewhere between seventy-five and one hundred cottage subdivisions had been approved between Souris and North Lake, and "no trespassing" signs were going up at an alarming rate. Despite these concerns, the Campbell government continued to develop the proposal for the second national park based on the 1964 study. In November 1967, the proposal received approval in principle from the federal cabinet. Under the agreement, Prince Edward Island would be responsible for purchasing the lands and turning them over to Parks Canada. However, the provincial government was unable to come up with the necessary funds, and the project was put on hold.

Then in September 1969, with funding for the Comprehensive Development Plan in place, Premier Campbell wrote to Jean Chrétien, Minister of Northern Affairs and the minister responsible for Parks Canada, suggesting the resumption of discussions on the national park project. Since the location of the proposed park was consistent with the Plan's tourism objectives to encourage visitors to travel to the eastern and western ends of the province, Campbell proposed funds from the Plan be used for the province's share of the land acquisition costs. A meeting was subsequently scheduled between federal and provincial officials in Charlottetown in October at which officials immediately clashed on the concept for the park. Provincial officials, led by Deputy Minister of the Department of Development Hector Hortie, proposed a multi-use park, one which would preserve the pastoral charm of the area, its way of life, and the quality of the environment. Federal officials countered with the model that at that time guided the designation and development of national parks, which would have essentially phased out all other resource use – and most of the residents – except for tiny enclaves for the development and maintenance of North Lake and its fishing fleet.

Despite this broad disagreement over the concept, the provincial government proceeded with its discussions. On March 12, 1970, the *Guardian* headline announced a "Second National Park to be Established Here," taking in most of the area from North Lake to Basin Head. Tourism Minister Lorne Bonnell advised the Legislature that the federal government had agreed to cost-share acquisition of the lands, and explained that under the agreement all farms would stay in production. His assurances were backed up by Minister of Community Affairs Gilbert Clements, who added that no farmers would be forced from their land, and that other activities, such as Irish Moss harvesting, could continue undisturbed.

Residents of eastern Kings, fed only on rumours and speculation, greeted the announcement and assurances with alarm and scepticism. A number of petitions from those opposed to the park were presented to Campbell, raising concerns about the disruption to their communities, the imposition of restrictions, and the inevitable change to the area's social makeup. Already, a survey of land owners by the provincial government had identified major concerns. Of the eighty landowners contacted, a total of sixty-nine said they were not willing to sell their land for park purposes. Campbell's response reminded them that they would be entitled to full consultation before the project proceeded.

Negotiations and planning between the federal and provincial governments continued throughout 1970 and 1971, despite officials on the federal side continuing to insist that a "wilderness" policy with few exceptions should form the basis of the new park. Meanwhile, staff of the provincial Department of Development drew up proposals for the acquisition of certain strategic properties, some of which would require the relocation of residents. As negotiations proceeded, the provincial government took a number of steps to prevent land speculation from proceeding. In September 1971, Tourism Minister Lorne Bonnell announced that fourteen miles of shoreline in the East Point area had been designated for acquisition. He assured the public that no agricultural land would be involved, explaining that ninety percent of the properties to be acquired were either lands of uncertain ownership or already owned by the Crown.

The provincial government also moved to curb haphazard private development. The cabinet designated the whole of Lot 47 in eastern Prince Edward Island for protection under the Planning Act, which gave it control over the issuing of subdivision, building, and other permits. This move prompted further concern by residents, already very anxious about possible development restrictions and expropriation of properties. Rumours also abounded that certain lands had been excluded under the new restrictions, possibly through a number of under-the-table deals. The fate of farmland in the area bordering Basin Head belonging to provincial Agriculture Minister Dan MacDonald figured prominently in these rumours, although no substance to them was found.

Finally, on March 16, 1973, Campbell tabled a status report on the proposal in the Legislature. He stated that any agricultural lands purchased for the park could be leased back to farmers for their continued use; that activities such as forest and Irish Moss harvesting could continue; and that the community of North Lake would remain outside park boundaries. The proposal "should provide for maintenance of the cultural landscape," Campbell told the Legislature, adding that the final decision would have to come from the people themselves. He went on to provide further reassurances to the residents. "The government has turned thumbs down on the notion of expropriation," he announced. "One of the prime factors here is that although the acquisition of the land will be systematic and regular, it will be controlled, orderly and only in response to the wishes of the people in the area." A copy of the report was sent to all landowners in eastern Kings with a covering letter from Bruce Stewart, the area MLA.

Shortly after Campbell tabled the report, Urbain LeBlanc, managing director of the Rural Development Council, wrote to Bruce Stewart offering its services to help undertake public consultations with the people of eastern Kings. At this time, the RDC was under contract to the provincial government to carry out the public participation program of the Comprehensive Development Plan and had already been actively involved in a number of public consultations across the province. Stewart took LeBlanc's proposal to cabinet on March 21, and it agreed to invite the RDC to become formally involved in the process. Specifically, cabinet directed the RDC to provide information to residents on the various options contained in the status report, to help ensure the protection of their rights, and to document their opinions.

The RDC immediately assigned John Cain, one of its workers who had grown up in Kings County, to the project. Cain began work on March 22 and by June had personally contacted more than one hundred property owners to explain the options to them. Cain encountered the same kind of concerns and suspicions that had greeted the project from the beginning. Lingering resentment over the zoning regulations soon made itself apparent, particularly from landowners anxious to subdivide and sell off their property. Many were critical of transforming the area into a tourist destination. There was widespread fear about what would become of the land and the communities in the long term. Few saw any benefits for themselves, while others believed more importance was being attached to preserving the natural environment than the lifestyle of the people.

Cain soon reported to LeBlanc that people distrusted the government's intentions, and believed that this further consultation was mere "window dressing." The RDC itself was also suspect in the eyes of many people; they felt it was sent into the area to "sell" the proposal to residents. They believed, Cain reported, that even if residents remained in adamant opposition, the provincial government would go ahead with the project anyway.

The RDC scheduled a series of public meetings for late June in Kingsboro, South Lake and Fairfield to discuss the formation of a community group that would then negotiate the terms of agreement for the establishment of the park with the provincial government. The first two meetings were well attended. They opened with an explanation of the process by Cain, followed by a slide presentation by Campbell to show what would happen if private development, rather than a national park, were to determine the future of the area. Federal and provincial officials were on hand to answer any technical questions. During these meetings, Campbell reiterated the importance of preserving the landscape, and warned of the consequences of allowing it to fall into haphazard development. He explained that the government had targeted certain key properties for acquisition, while scenic easements would be applied to others. He confirmed that farming, fishing, forestry, and other activities would be maintained, and that families would retain ownership of their properties in perpetuity. The national park, he explained, would set a precedent by reflecting the special character of Prince Edward Island and its people.

Those attending the meetings were largely unconvinced. They remained suspicious and fearful; few left the first two meetings feeling positive about the establishment of a national park in their area. Following the presentations at the final meeting in Fairfield, a dispirited and disjointed discussion ensued about whether to vote on the establishment of a community group to continue negotiations with the government. Recognizing the mood, Campbell suddenly stood up and announced that it was his conclusion there was a lack of support in the community for the park. He tore up the agreement in front of the crowd, and declared that any further action on the proposal would have to come from the people themselves. To wild applause, Campbell assured them that his government would not impose a park against their wishes.

*   *   *

The East Point National Park issue symbolized a new era of public involvement in Prince Edward Island. The issue and the controversy that surrounded it signalled the beginning of the end of the traditional "boss-follower" style of politics. The old, shallow, hierarchical, paternalistic – and often venal and corrupt – approach was slowly giving way to a new civic culture, where citizens and governments interacted within a more formal, less partisan relationship. Involvement, not intimidation, was the watchword of the new political order. Against the background of the Island's traditional political culture, the initiatives that the government was proposing to involve the public were nothing short of revolutionary.

The new emphasis on public involvement played a central role in the implementation of the Development Plan. One of the basic tenets of development planning is that of public participation. As the Plan document stated, "It is the people of the province who will make the development goal a reality." The concept would be based on "a new level and type of public involvement in the shaping of society in the Province," and it would hinge on changing social attitudes and behaviours. "Effective public participation and involvement arises from the quality of leadership in non-governmental organizations," declared the document, "*aided by enlightened and broadened perspectives among the public at large*" (author's italics). This new concept would prove to be a heady challenge in a province where the most that was expected of citizens was to turn out to vote. In the past, if governments provided few services, they made few demands. Now, as the scope of government widened, the public was invited to engage in the process to help shape and define its future. The genie of "people power" was poised for release.

The Campbell government recognized the need to involve the public in the planning process. From the beginning, when he tabled the White Paper on Economic Planning and Development in the Legislature in 1967, Campbell warned that the Plan would not necessarily meet all the challenges, solve all the problems or achieve success unless the public got actively involved. "Such assurances," he said, "can only arise out of individual understanding of the needs, acceptance of responsibility for action, and full participation in the programs to come." But he was politically astute enough to recognize the difficulties of turning around attitudes and behaviours deeply rooted in the Island's rural and insular character. Even as the roles and responsibilities of government were being expanded, the old style of politics continued to flourish. The Island's anachronistic system of politics militated sharply against "a new level and type of public involvement in the shaping of society."

Electoral reform, improved education, greater social and economic mobility, and mass communications would gradually erode the older political system, but in the meantime the expectations now being placed on Islanders were unlike anything previously experienced. "One of our biggest jobs is to convince our population to participate in the effort," a frustrated Alex Campbell told the *Financial Post* in November 1967. "In order to succeed, we must enlist public appreciation of the problems we face and convince individuals that it is their effort which can make the difference. That means accepting new ideas, new methods and research."

Public participation as envisaged by the planners contrasted sharply with the largely deferential attitude of Islanders to the political system and its elite. In a society where government "looked after" people, those same people were now being given the opportunity to look after themselves. The goal – to help end the historic dependency of Islanders on government. As Campbell described it, "Whenever a group or an individual seeks a solution to a problem, their first – and all too often their only – answer is to toss the need in the lap of government." He and his planners were aiming to turn that historic dependence around and create new models for citizen involvement. "Government action alone does not create a strong community," he said. The Development Plan's proposal represented nothing short of a radical change in the political culture of the province.

In an article entitled "Invisible Causeways – Social Change and Citizen Participation on Prince Edward Island," published in 1970 by Maritime academics Jim Lotz and Thomas Haley, the authors acknowledged that Islanders would not accept the "wild dreams" of planners without question. "But it is well for the people of Prince Edward Island to understand the need for skilled and professional assistance," they admonished. "Harsh truths have to be told ... all the defensive attitudes in the world will not save the Island economy."

But as Campbell also told the *Financial Post* in July 1967, "someone has to direct the breakthrough. We intend to, and we hope the development program will open the door."

As an experiment in social engineering, the public participation program under the Development Plan was both exhilarating and terrifying. When it was all over, the province had changed its face forever.

*   *   *

The Prince Edward Island Rural Development Council originated in the mid-1960s as a small, loosely organized group of citizens who shared growing concerns about the decline of traditional Island rural communities. This group of earnest, self-proclaimed advocates, including both clergy and lay people, brought together an eclectic background of Christian social teaching, involvement in the co-operative movement, and an ingenuous belief in participatory democracy. They included people like United Church ministers David Barwise and David MacDonald, Roman Catholic priests Alan MacDonald and Gerald Steele, and lay people like Ken MacLean and others who were heavily engaged in the co-operative movement. They were united in a fundamental belief that the Island was losing control over its future, as evidenced by the struggle for economic and social change, high unemployment, and a major exodus from rural to urban communities and from the province itself.

In the winter of 1965, the RDC organized a seminar at St. Dunstan's University on "The Rural Economic Problem." Rev. Alan MacDonald, who taught sociology there, presented a paper on various themes including "dissatisfaction with the lassitude of rural life, low public participation and involvement, and the decline of the Island's rural communities and family farms." Out of this conference came the idea of "community schools," a program to be organized throughout the Island, in which the schools would be "aimed at community as well as personal development" and whose mission would include the promotion of the vitality and independence of Island communities.

The well-intentioned members of the RDC greeted the Campbell government's ambitious planning agenda with cautious hope. They were already attracted to the planning process, having earlier attended meetings with Rudi Dallenbach, a rural development specialist who worked with ARDA (Agricultural Rehabilitation and

Development Act). Ken MacLean and a number of other RDC members therefore watched with interest as several studies were undertaken to analyze the province's problems and opportunities. Following the election of the Liberal government, the RDC board invited Campbell to meet with them. During his speech to the group in Dalvay, Campbell reiterated the themes outlined in the White Paper on Economic Planning and Development, and pledged his strong support for the RDC's work in promoting public participation and involvement. He told them that a public participation program was an integral element of the Development Plan then being negotiated with the federal government.

Encouraged by Campbell's interest in promoting a dialogue between planners and the public, the RDC followed up with a letter to Del Gallagher, head of the Economic Improvement Corporation, recommending a possible mechanism to involve the public. "We suggest there is a certain urgency that immediate steps must be taken to involve the people of the province in a study and analysis of all major propositions set forth in the plan," they wrote. As the planning process continued, Gallagher made overtures to the RDC for more formal involvement. He indicated that "finishing touches" were being put on certain sections of the Plan, including the one dealing with "local involvement," and encouraged the RDC to consider what role it might play as the Plan unfolded.

Finally, in a letter to the RDC in May 1967, Gallagher officially invited it to consider delivering the public participation program. "It is not our wish to influence the direction of your day-to-day activities by means of attaching a number of specific considerations to any financial support which you might receive from us," he advised them. "I think we all agree that the effectiveness of your operations will be directly related to the voluntary nature of your group and the degree of independence which you can bring to both the advisory and operational functions which you may perform." The proposal created a dilemma for the RDC, one which Gallagher recognized and was willing to help resolve. "We are prepared to provide financial support for your program," he clarified, "and to do so unconditionally to the extent that this is possible."

Throughout these discussions, the RDC was caught up in a debate about the nature of its involvement. Some members of the organization wanted to keep it at arm's length from government and the planning process; others saw a need for a more formal role, with active involvement. The issue of whether or not to remain a grassroots organization free to criticize government, or become formally involved in delivering a government program, presented them with an ongoing dilemma.

As the Plan moved closer to realization, the RDC did agree to become formally involved in the community development and public participation programs. Although both the RDC and the EIC recognized that their interests and goals might sometimes clash, in October 1968 the RDC took the plunge and signed a contract. As Alan MacDonald pointed out, if it had not done so "the RDC would have been dead."

The contract gave the RDC the mandate "to aid individuals, groups of individuals and organizations in making adjustments towards their social and economic improvement. This will involve evaluating needs and potentials, both in the social and economic sectors, and bringing to bear all available resources to service those needs." The program would be carried out by community development workers with the job of "[making] the population aware of the opportunities and provisions of the Comprehensive Development Plan" and providing feedback.

From the outset, the precise role of the RDC was vague, which left it open to interpretation. Against the backdrop of the Island's traditional political structures, it represented a marked departure from the way people did business with government, and the public did not clearly understand its role. Many believed the RDC was more interested in advancing its own agenda than it was in facilitating community concerns. People also raised questions about the RDC's relationship to government, especially if conflicting views were to arise. Jim MacNeill, editor and publisher of the *Eastern Graphic*, pointedly asked, "Can Rural Development Council be Independent of EIC?" MacNeill also expressed deeper concerns which resonated with the public. Giving his opinion that the RDC was "great on theory but short on the practical end," the feisty MacNeill accused the organization of being top heavy with ministers, priests and university professors. He bluntly stated that the RDC was "out of touch" with the realities of ordinary Islanders.

It is unclear whether either the government or the RDC had a clear picture of what "public participation" meant and what form it should take. Even Campbell admitted that this was uncharted territory. When he met with the RDC just before the agreement was signed, Campbell told its members that its role would remain flexible for the next fifteen years. He explained that, although the need for community development was clear, circumstances would change over time and, as a result, he expected the RDC would "grow with the job." So the question remained unresolved: Was the RDC to take the government's message to the people, or the people's message to the government? What was its role in facilitating community development and public participation? These questions were destined to cause confusion and conflict within the RDC, between the RDC and the government, and ultimately, with the public – who collectively wondered who was speaking for whom anyhow.

The extreme elements of this self-selected, often myopic hierarchy with self-induced hallucinations of grandeur, eager to impose their arguably misguided vision and version of the Island as it ought to be, proceeded confidently, secure in the conviction that it was they – and only they – who spoke for Islanders. That they might lack the unqualified support of an unsuspecting, unenlightened, even unsympathetic public never occurred to them.

* * *

By 1973, the Rural Development Council was operating with a staff of twenty-one full-time employees and an annual budget of $350,000. They were young, well-educated, articulate people, gaining valuable experience in community development. They had intervened in a number of high-profile issues, including school consolidation; the organization of marketing boards; support for Irish Moss and oyster harvesters; tenant and landlord disputes; and an application for a rate increase by Island Telephone (which, it was argued, discriminated against rural Islanders). They had also provided organizational support for a broad array of special-interest and community groups. The East Point National Park was one such project.

Despite its widespread activity, the RDC was racked by internal dissent, personality clashes, and conflicts over its role and its relationship to government. Although a number of key resignations occurred over conflicts about its role, still that role was never fully clarified. An evaluation of the RDC carried out as part of a review of Development Plan programs in 1974 found a number of structural and operational weaknesses. The evaluation stated that, organizationally, the board was weak and the general membership inactive. The evaluation was even more critical of the RDC's performance. It pointed out that the organization lacked an overall community development strategy, spent too much time "putting out fires," and had frequently failed to initiate and maintain public interest in the concept of community development. Community schools, intended to promote discussion on local development issues, had become little more than "social groups."

Nevertheless, the evaluation concluded with a recommendation that the RDC be given a new five-year contract on the assumption that many of its growing pains were now behind it.

While some within and outside the RDC called for its contract with the government to be terminated so that it could regain its independent voice for disenfranchised Islanders, others felt that with financial support it could still do an effective job of representing the people. The RDC was faced with a difficult straddling act.

*   *   *

Fissures appeared very early in the relationship between the RDC and the Campbell government. When Campbell eliminated the Economic Improvement Corporation and rolled its activities into government with himself as minister, many within the RDC worried that this would signal the end of the independence they believed was essential to the development process. Immediately following the signing of the Development Plan with the federal government, the RDC wrote a sharply worded letter to Campbell voicing its concerns about possible political interference in the Plan's implementation. It urged that "the implementation of the Comprehensive Development Plan be carried forward through a development agency free from partisan political influence." Failing this, it demanded that government consult with the RDC on the hiring of the deputy minister of development; representation on the federal-provincial Joint Advisory Board established to oversee administration of the Plan; and free and open votes on the various projects in the coming session of the Legislative Assembly. One member of the RDC board echoed the concern that the entire Plan would become politically tainted. "Where does dedication to a principle end and the process of political expediency begin?" he asked. "There is a danger in this area and we have to be concerned about this fact of life."

As an elected politician, Campbell faced similar questions. An incident took place shortly before the agreement was reached with the RDC that revealed the difficulties inherent in reconciling the exigencies of practical politics with the non-partisan nature of community development. On September 6, 1968, Campbell met in his office with Bob Blakely, who was formulating the public participation strategy with the EIC, to discuss ways of informing the public about the Plan. Campbell told Blakely that, as premier, he wanted to be directly involved in the information stages, and suggested to Blakely that if the RDC held public meetings across the province he would like to outline the various provisions of the Plan on behalf of the government. Blakely responded that, given the sensitivities of the RDC to any overt political involvement, it was very unlikely they would invite Campbell to such meetings. "This aroused his ire," Blakely later reported to Del Gallagher, "but we had spoken of the political capital in the program and how this must be accommodated to a non-partisan overall image."

Campbell pointed out that he and his cabinet had a responsibility as elected politicians to become involved in public information. He went even further, advising Blakely that he also wanted to review a list of names being considered for positions with the RDC to "ostensibly check them out for political hatchet men and other types of undesirables," Blakely recalled. Campbell also suggested that a number of Conservatives could be hired in order to demonstrate that the Plan was non-partisan. Blakely reported to Gallagher that the Premier "seemed to agree that rural development officers to be effective must operate outside of government" but added that he doubted Campbell would "be willing to relinquish control over these people."

"It was not entirely a pleasant affair for either the Premier or myself," recalled Blakely. "There was considerable very straight talk about political capital versus the necessary non-partisan nature of the Plan." There would be more such "very straight talk" to come.

*   *   *

Members of the Legislative Assembly in Prince Edward Island, like those in other representative democracies, have a duty and responsibility to reflect the views and deal with the needs of their constituents, as well as hold the government accountable. With the Legislature in session for only a few weeks of the year, the MLAs' duties as lawmakers took a back seat to their duties to the constituency. "All politics is local," noted U.S. Senator Tip O'Neill. That was and is especially so in Prince Edward Island; the constituency is where "the rubber hits the road." With short legislative sessions, the lowest salaries in the country, and few real governing responsibilities, Prince Edward Island MLAs may be the last bastion of the political amateur in Canada.

In earlier times, government backbench MLAs exercised considerable power within their constituencies. They decided which roads would be improved and who would be hired (or fired), and dispensed other forms of patronage. MLAs on both sides of the Legislature attended wakes, weddings, concerts, fairs and community gatherings. Added to all this, they were expected to be readily available to deal with any constituent problem, real or imagined, large or small, any time of the day or night. The backbenchers who came in with the new Campbell government faced a new political world. The Civil Service Act introduced by the Shaw government reduced the number of patronage positions the MLAs controlled as the transformation of government into a bureaucracy left fewer decisions to politicians. At the same time, the power of the cabinet (the executive branch of government) made itself increasingly felt as it dominated and directed government policies and priorities. The Campbell government was the first in the province in which being a premier or a minister meant working full-time, now that their responsibilities were significantly elevated above those of the backbenches.

Furthermore, the dictates of rational economic planning carried out by the staff of the Economic Improvement Corporation of necessity pushed aside the preferences and prejudices of local MLAs. For example, decisions on road construction would have to be justified on the basis of need, not on the political persuasion of the residents involved. Where MLAs had based their actions on local needs and circumstances, now planners, bureaucrats, and policymakers were guided by different imperatives – and the Island government was being transformed in the process. Meanwhile, MLAs continued to move within a slower, more traditional orbit. It was not an easy time to be a Member of the Legislative Assembly.

The injection into local communities of a cadre of young, ambitious, and aggressive community development workers prepared to challenge the status quo threatened to undermine even further the changing relationship between MLAs and their constituents. It was not long before local skirmishes occurred. One high-profile battle ensued with the school board representing eastern Prince County. The RDC, increasingly critical of many of the decisions made by the new board, actually went to court on the question of the citizenship (and hence the right to serve) of one of its members. It was a nasty, petty spat, especially at a time of growing controversy over school consolidation.

Peter Prebble, an RDC field worker, was at the centre of some of these disputes. Along with a number of other people, Prebble was beginning to take a much more activist position in his community development activities. Compounding the problem was the RDC itself, which was gaining a reputation as an advocate for grassroots citizens battling an insensitive school board and an aloof provincial government. In the midst of one dispute with the Unit Two School Board in eastern Prince, Prebble dashed off a missive to Premier Campbell stating that he was representing the people of the school district and demanding that their concerns be addressed. "When were you elected?" came the testy response.

As the provincial government commenced negotiations on the second phase of the Development Plan, it extended the RDC's contract for an additional year beyond 1973, despite the troubled history of the first five years. That period had been marred by internal staff conflicts, continuing controversies, criticism by MLAs, and an inconclusive evaluation report. Therefore it appeared that the effort to establish "a new level and type of public involvement" was simply not working, despite help from the hoped-for "enlightened and broadened perspectives among the public at large." In fact, the provincial government was having second thoughts about its relationship with the RDC. This was reflected in the decision to renew the contract for just one year while it negotiated a new five-year agreement with the federal government (although some optimistically saw the one-year contract as an interim measure until Phase II of the Plan was started). At the federal-provincial Joint Advisory Board meeting in February 1975, Campbell announced that his government was reconsidering the RDC's role in Phase II of the Development Plan. It commissioned a report by Donald Nemetz, a professor in business administration at UPEI, to make recommendations on the role the RDC should play.

In March, Nemetz presented his report to Campbell and three of his cabinet ministers: Development Minister Dr. John Maloney, Treasurer Earle Hickey, and Tourism Minister Gilbert Clements. Nemetz stated his view that certain RDC activities placed it in an adversarial role with the government, and offered the suggestion that provincial government departments themselves could carry out much of the field work being done by the RDC. In his report, Nemetz wrote that "it would seem that the original idea of the RDC had merit and that there is a useful role for a non-governmental organization of that type, but not with government as the sole or even major source of funding." Earlier, Maloney, whose department was responsible for renewing the contract, had reached the private conclusion that the RDC was "doing us more harm than good."

Other officials were coming to the same conclusion. The acerbic David Catmur, a planner with the Department of Agriculture, considered the RDC's senior management inept and probably incompetent. The idea that the organization represented communities was at best only partly true and at worst "pretentious nonsense," he said. Campbell also heard from MLAs who were growing increasingly bitter about the role the RDC was playing in their constituencies. As they saw it, the RDC was usurping their traditional role through its promotion of Development Plan programs, its advocacy for government action on a range of issues, and its outspoken approach to certain issues, often at odds with government policy. As time went on and the RDC became more firmly entrenched in communities across the Island, MLAs regarded the community development workers as direct competitors for the hearts and minds of voters.

"The MLAs were the ones who were the most bitter about the role of the RDC, because it was the RDC that appeared [to] be out around the country delivering programs and speaking to organizations, speaking for the farm community," recalled Campbell. "And, you had then, a confrontation between what was traditionally perceived to be the role of the MLA, elected, and the role of the employees of an organization who had no constitutional responsibility, faced no elections, responsible to no one except their boss." Once again, Campbell found himself having to mediate between the traditional assumptions of the provincial political system and the emerging demands for more direct participation by citizens.

But Campbell harboured his own reservations. "The concept of the public being fully involved in the affairs affecting them is a concept to which I and my government are fully committed," he declared. "However, to suggest that we cannot have this public involvement without the RDC is just ridiculous." He was coming around to the view that in following the "process of public participation" government was under pressure from the RDC to deal with the immediate, day-to-day issues while more important long-range issues had to be pushed aside. In his view, discussions on questions of emerging concern such as energy supply and costs were being displaced by controversies over "rinks, sewage systems and ... the location or style of public buildings" – a clear reference to ongoing debates in some Island communities.* The Premier was willing to acknowledge the RDC's effectiveness in animating and informing the public, but he worried that, in the process, it was generating a level of expectation that the government could not easily meet. Despite these reservations, Campbell was quick to add that "None of this means that my enthusiasm for local community development has been dampened."

*   *   *

On May 13, 1975, Jean Mutch, president of the Rural Development Council, received a phone call at home, requesting her to meet with Dr. John Maloney, Minister of Development, in his office on the fifth floor of the Provincial Administrative Building in Charlottetown. Maloney bluntly informed Mutch that on May 8 the cabinet had decided not to renew the RDC's contract, but would give it six weeks to wind up all its activities related to the Development Plan. The board and staff of the RDC received the announcement with stunned surprise, and immediately mounted a vigorous campaign to overturn the decision. The day after her meeting with Maloney, Jean Mutch, board member Ken DesRoches, and general manger Harry O'Connell met with Campbell in his office to protest the termination of the contract. Campbell agreed to bring their objections to caucus that afternoon and to cabinet later in the week, but offered no assurance that the decision would be reversed.

The RDC also demanded a meeting with Gordon Fairfield, Maloney's deputy minister, in the belief that senior bureaucrats were lukewarm in their support and had influenced cabinet's decision to terminate the contract. Fairfield, however, refused to meet with them. But late in the Friday afternoon of May 16, Mutch and RDC staff members Pat Binns, Fred Eberman, Peter Prebble, and Alan Shaw, cornered Fairfield in his office. "We met him in the corridor, and he just ran from us, so we ran after him," recalled Mutch. "I've never

---

* *One of the buildings to which Campbell referred was the new Kings County Interpretative Centre at Pooles Corner, widely disparaged for its unique architectural style and extravagant displays. They also questioned how the Centre would succeed in redirecting tourists throughout the area.*

been so bold in all my life. We just wanted to talk with him – and this would have been, maybe 4:30 – so we thought, 'he has all evening, we will just keep him here.' And we did." Not even the appearance of Fairfield's wife later in the evening, wondering where her husband was, broke the standoff. The RDC was determined to fight the decision to the finish. At its board meeting on May 20, the RDC passed a resolution "that the Board emphatically rejects Cabinet's decision to terminate the public participation and community development programs, and staff, by ceasing funding, and asks the people of Prince Edward Island for their support to have this decision changed."

But the support did not materialize. The RDC took out newspaper ads, and wrote an open letter to Maloney, listing some one hundred projects in which it had been involved and the assistance it had given to numerous organizations. Still public response was limited. Past president Ian MacDonald admitted that "when the announcement came, the actual outcry was pretty small."

O'Connell went even further in expressing his disappointment. It was "sad," he felt, that the RDC had to try and stir public support, but it was also "sad" that the public had not responded. The RDC also launched a vigorous appeal to Don Jamieson, Trudeau's minister responsible for the Atlantic region. Jamieson simply informed them that the provincial government had acted within its rights, and there was nothing he could do. For his part, Campbell expected "all hell would break loose." He too was surprised by the evident lack of public support for the organization.

Despite these setbacks, the RDC refused to back down. It was buoyed by support from the media and from academics at UPEI. The *Guardian* editorial of May 17 gave its view that the "concept of public participation in government has received a severe setback." On the other hand, the *Eastern Graphic*, which had been critical of the RDC in the past, declared that termination of the contract was a "sign of success," given that the RDC had become too effective in mobilizing public opinion that was not always in agreement with public policy.

The RDC's failure to gain more support from the public and especially from government stemmed in part from its insistence that it, not government, spoke for the people. Campbell recalled that, after the RDC had been informed that the contract would be terminated, it "rejected our decision as if it were an equal or superior power to the elected government of this province." During their meeting with the Premier the day after they received the news, RDC officials told him that "the people of PEI cannot trust and communicate with their government." They said government needed the RDC as an "objective agency" to bridge the gap "so that people could better express their needs to government." According to Campbell, the RDC would have Islanders "accept the basic philosophy that government is not independent, not objective, not reflective of the will of the people, but rather some alien force to be dealt with through new systems of communications and through pressure groups." While he might have been willing at the outset to experiment with new models of public participation, he made it clear that "my colleagues and I have totally rejected this concept of democratic government."

The hurried presentation made by the RDC failed to convince Campbell to change his mind. In fact, it helped him to justify the wisdom of the decision. "All this combined to demonstrate what was already becoming clear to me," he recalled, "that the RDC would have us move to a new form of government which relegated MLAs, as biased persons, to the backwoods."

On May 22, the RDC took its case to the Liberal caucus, but received a cool reception. Dr. John Maloney later observed that caucus had been much less friendly towards the RDC than cabinet had been.

This whole RDC experience added to Campbell's growing understanding of the political pitfalls associated with the "new level and type of public involvement" that its partnership with the RDC had embodied. "We're faced with something of a contradiction in PEI," he told one reporter. "On the one hand, government wants local communities and organizations to assume even greater responsibility over the decisions that affect them. But the people, desiring change while retaining the Island's quality of life, have looked for action, not to their voluntary associations, but to the government." He added that the government's ability to deliver its programs would have been compromised if it was forced to act by consensus every step of the way. It was a difficult balance to achieve.

Ironically, the RDC received unexpected – and unintentional – support from an unlikely ally, the Legislative Assembly. During budget estimates, Opposition Leader Mel McQuaid introduced a motion calling for increased funding for the RDC, advising the Legislature that it was "the most important instrument in public participation that we have in the province today." Although the motion was defeated along straight party lines, the matter did not end there. Throughout the session, the Standing Committee on Agriculture, chaired by 3rd Prince Liberal MLA Edward "Eddie" Clark, had been drafting its report to the Legislature. It was a typical routine report, but when the final version was being considered in committee, only three of the Liberal MLAs were present. The opposition members, holding the majority, drafted a new section that contained a favourable reference to the RDC. Thanks to their majority vote, the new section made it into the report.

On May 30, three weeks after cabinet had decided to terminate the RDC contract, a red-faced Eddie Clark rose in the Legislature to table the report of the Standing Committee, including the last-minute recommendation: "In view of the tremendous service that the Rural Development Council has provided to the rural areas and particularly those associated with agriculture, and since this organization seems to be more and more useful and acceptable, the Committee recommends that its services be retained at the same level as last year, with a greater emphasis placed on field work activities." Although the recommendation was defeated by the government members, a sheepish Clark was obliged to vote with the Opposition in favour of his committee's report.

*   *   *

On June 30, with most of the Rural Development Council staff gone, Jean Mutch, Ian MacDonald and Ken DesRoches met with Campbell in a last-ditch effort to salvage the situation. They proposed that the government support the RDC to provide an ongoing public forum so that it could continue to raise issues. But the fight was over. In September, the RDC was unable to find enough board members to obtain a quorum.

CHAPTER TEN

"The Island is Not For Sale"

It came as a shock and a revelation to members of the Campbell government. On a chilly, overcast November afternoon in 1968, the cabinet listened to a presentation from officials with the Economic Geography Division of the federal Department of Energy, Mines and Resources. Supported by funding from the Canada Lands Inventory of the Department of Forestry and Rural Development, the division had completed a major socio-economic study on land ownership and use in Prince Edward Island. This was a massive project, involving thousands of personal interviews with landowners; interminable periods of time in the land registry offices attempting to piece together antiquated and incomplete property titles; mountains of maps, aerial photographs, and diagrams; and a voluminous collection of other data on every square mile of land on the Island.

The Economic Geography Division undertook the study as part of the analysis leading to the formulation of the Comprehensive Development Plan. Agriculture represented the economic engine of the Plan, and its success would depend on the protection of the province's limited land resources. It was also assumed that development of the industry would involve significant land adjustments and, in the parlance of the planners, the creation of larger, more economically viable units of production. In order to plan for the best use of the Island's limited land base, it was deemed essential to make a detailed survey of the existing pattern of land holdings in the province. The study would represent an unprecedented examination of the people and the land they inhabited.

On that November afternoon, the division's director, Charles Raymond, and his officials presented the results of their study to Campbell and his cabinet. Their report included some disturbing findings that most of their audience knew intuitively: that the number of farms had steeply declined, from over 12,000 in 1941 to about half that number by the mid-1960s; that the average age of farmers was over fifty; that over one third of farmers were part-time, marginal or nearing retirement; that the average size of farms was increasing, from just under 100 acres in 1941 to more than 150 acres by 1966;

that land holdings were fragmented over a number of properties; and that of the more than one million acres in production in 1931, less than half of that number were still being farmed. Ironically, the province that billed itself as "the million acre farm" was being transformed into a landscape pockmarked by deserted farmhouses, abandoned outbuildings, decaying barns, empty fields, and scrubby woodlots. And into this vacuum, unplanned and uncontrolled strip development and urban encroachment was insinuating itself.

Much of this the planners and politicians already knew. They were already devising strategies to "rationalize" land use in the province.

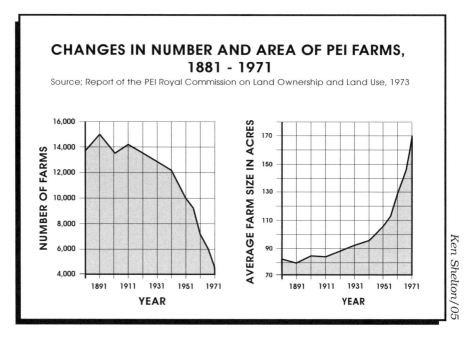

CHANGES IN NUMBER AND AREA OF PEI FARMS, 1881 - 1971

Source; Report of the PEI Royal Commission on Land Ownership and Land Use, 1973

Ken Shelton/05

Continuing a trend that persisted throughout the 1900s, farms in Prince Edward Island were fewer and larger, leading to concerns about the future of the family farm.

The Development Plan document, flying in the face of two centuries of struggle over land and the intrinsic value placed on it by Islanders, unabashedly stated that "the historical pattern of land ownership in Prince Edward is badly adapted to the needs of modern technology for agricultural, forestry and tourist development."

In 1969, the provincial government had established the Land Development Corporation (LDC) to assist in the process of land consolidation. The LDC's mandate allowed it to purchase tracts of land from retiring farmers and others who wished to sell, and transfer them to those who wished to expand. Its activities represented a key component in the plan to encourage the establishment of some 2,500 productive and profitable farms in the province. All others would be rationalized. In its first annual report to the Legislative Assembly, the LDC outlined its approach to the rationalization of land ownership and use. The tone was practical, straightforward, and hard-nosed: "Ideally, each plot of land in the province has a 'best' use, a use which will generate the optimum income to the occupant and to the province as a whole, within the total pattern of land use which will preserve the inherent pastoral beauty of the Island and maintain the best features of the present social structure."

The research carried out and presented by Charles Raymond and his staff undergirded much of the direction of land rationalization. But something else in the data they presented that November afternoon attracted immediate attention. On the brightly colour-coded maps pinned on the walls of the cabinet chambers, the audience could see a glaring patchwork of markings, particularly along the Island's coastline that stretched for more than four hundred miles. The markings served to illustrate that close to one quarter of the province's shoreline – upwards of one hundred miles, much of it prime beach frontage – was owned by non-residents. The maps further revealed that non-residents also owned somewhere between 70,000 to 100,000 acres of farm and forest land, much of which lay idle. In a province whose people had long struggled against absentee landowners, where the Land Question had attained mythic proportions, the implications were immediately apparent to Campbell. "The real shocker came when the land inventory came in through the Development Plan and we saw a map showing all the land owned by non-residents in a distinctive colour," recalled Campbell. "It really did shock us to see how much of our province was owned by non-residents."

The research on land ownership and use coincided with the growing attractiveness of the Island to those seeking escape from burgeoning urban sprawl throughout North America. Already, about

NON-RESIDENT LAND OWNERSHIP
on Prince Edward Island

Scale in Miles

Source: Report of the PEI Royal Commission on the Land Ownership and Land Use, 1973

Ken Shelton/05

eighty percent of North Americans lived in large cities; a rural refuge, especially one as breathtakingly attractive and inexpensive as Prince Edward Island, was attracting significant interest. "Why not buy the whole beach?" touted ads in New York papers, listing large blocks of land for sale in Prince Edward Island. Speculators in particular were discovering that, compared to many other areas in eastern Canada and the United States, land in Prince Edward Island could be purchased much more cheaply. The British Columbia-based Canada Land Fund, for example, was buying up huge parcels of land, including some offshore islands, for development and resale. In effect, the province was fast becoming a popular hunting ground for non-resident land speculators capable of outbidding and outhustling competitors for control of this finite and fragile resource.

The unprecedented rate of land sales to non-residents clashed head-on with the province's desire to protect and preserve its land resources for farming, forestry, and tourism development. But unlike other provinces with vast reserves of Crown land, over ninety-five percent of the Island's land was privately owned; private property rights were deeply entrenched and considered inviolable. Thus the Campbell government faced the prospect that if the rate of sales to non-residents continued – or, as expected, accelerated – within a few short years the Island's land resources would slip beyond its control. Some people even went so far as to project that if the acquisition of land by non-residents continued at the present rate, approximately fifteen percent of the Island would be held in the hands of non-residents by the year 2000. Neither Islanders nor their government relished such a prospect.

The growing tourism industry was also exerting a new kind of pressure on the Island landscape. As idyllic, pastoral Prince Edward Island emerged into the spotlight as a popular destination, residents feared that more land would slip out of their hands, while the Island's pristine image, collapsing under the sheer numbers of tourists, would succumb to the mediocrity and despoliation of an overpopulated tourist destination. Campbell recognized the dangers to land ownership and use posed by haphazard tourism growth. Now he faced yet

---

Opposite: *A detailed analysis of land ownership conducted in the late 1960s revealed that close to one-quarter of Prince Edward Island's shoreline was owned by non-residents. Non-residents also owned upwards of 100,000 acres of farm and forest land.*

Canada Land Fund

another major challenge – how much can the Island "do," he wondered, before it is no longer "the Island."

As Campbell later told a federal-provincial conference in May 1972, "We in Prince Edward Island have no intention of allowing our province, through attrition, neglect or oversight, to end up in the hands of non-residents who have little interests in the communities of our province, little concern for the preservation of our way of life, little involvement in our Island institutions, and who may simply view the province as a place either to spend a holiday or opt out of an urbanized society."

Still later, in a speech entitled "Prince Edward Island Is Not For Sale," presented to the Canadian Club of London, Ontario, in September 1974, he reiterated his position. "After all, what is a province, what are a province's people, what is a province's government, unless the people rooted and committed to the orderly growth and development of that province are in control of its destiny," he asked. Although he declared that he would welcome those who wished to purchase land and settle in the province, he added this caveat, "But we cannot allow our basic physical resources, the land, to slowly leak away into the hands of people who care nothing for our communities, our people and our fundamental institutions."

Sir Andrew Macphail once said that "one approaches the land question with some hesitation; it is so tiresome," but quickly added that "for over a century it overshadowed all others in the politics and history of the Island." Campbell was to find the Land Question overshadowing his government. His particular efforts to focus attention on the issue would represent a milestone in the Island's political history such as had not been seen since the landlord and tenant conflicts of the nineteenth century.

*   *   *

Opposite: The British Columbia-based Canada Land Fund offered prime P.E.I. waterfront properties for sale featuring what it called "the ultimate pleasure – possessing the best of nature's land on timeless islands." Its promotional literature described the developer as striving to achieve for its clients "places of peace and solitude, away from the sounds and tensions of the city, the maddening crowd, night latches and bolted doors ... to islands where health and happiness can take root. Where bigger is not better; slower may be faster and less may well mean more."

Prince Edward Island was conceived in corruption and cradled in conflict. Following the Treaty of Paris in 1763 when it became a British colony, the British government parcelled out the whole Island to its friends and supporters through a lottery. In return, the new landlords were expected to meet certain conditions, including the settlement of their properties and the payment of "quit rents" (funds to support the colony). Not surprisingly, most of the new proprietors failed to take their responsibilities seriously, which greatly retarded the Island's development. In the first number of years of settlement, the population barely exceeded one thousand people, and most of the land was basically unoccupied. By the 1840s, Lord Durham reported that Prince Edward Island's "past and present disorders are but the sad result of that fatal error which stifled its prosperity in the very cradle of its existence, by giving up the whole Island to a handful of distant proprietors."

As a result, Islanders always attached a special importance to land ownership, and when the land finally passed into the hands of the former tenants in the late nineteenth century, they jealously guarded the prerogatives they acquired from their former landlords – witness the persistence of the property vote. This vote, which gave property owners the right to elect two representatives to everyone else's one, reflected the determination of enfranchised property owners to reap the benefits of their hard-won status. Defending the property vote in the 1880s, MLA Donald Ferguson of Marshfield sniffed that those who could not acquire property worth at least $325 were hardly entitled to claim any special privilege.

The conflicts between tenants of the land and their mostly absent proprietors dominated every aspect of life in Prince Edward Island for more than a century after that ill-fated lottery. The Land Question, as it came to be called, was probably unequalled in both duration and bitterness in British North America. It was the root cause of political struggles and the subject of numerous inquiries. It even led to open rebellion. "Our country's freedom and farmers' rights," the slogan under which land reformer William Cooper led demands for reform in the 1830s, symbolized the underlying struggle. Inevitably, it left a profound and indelible impact on future generations. More than any other single factor, the land shaped the identity and character of the people of Prince Edward Island. The family farm represented the foundation of the rural economy and defined the nature of its communities. Hard work, frugality, and community were the cornerstones of the much-vaunted Island way of life. "A man who lives on his own land and owes no man anything develops all the dignity inherent in his nature," said Sir Andrew Macphail (although he was quick to confess that, having grown up on a family farm on the Island, his overriding goal was to escape it!)

Government control over land ownership was also deeply rooted. Although the provincial legislature passed an Act to Enable Aliens to Hold Real Estate in 1869 in order to attract possible American investment in the fisheries, the legislation restricted the amount of land which could be acquired to a maximum of two hundred acres. Thane Campbell's government relaxed that restriction in 1939, although a clause allowing ownership in excess of two hundred acres required cabinet approval. Even so, paranoia remained over non-resident ownership.

The growing number of land sales to non-residents, which started to gain momentum in the 1960s, was accompanied by a number of other disturbing trends. Dundas Farms, owned by the powerful Howard Webster family of Toronto, had purchased thousands of acres in central Kings County to raise cattle, buying up land of former family farms and transforming the community in the process. Vegetable processors such as Campbell & Burns in Central Bedeque and potato processor Seabrook Farms in New Annan were also looking to buy up thousands of acres to establish vertically integrated operations, while in the forest industry the Henderson Lumber Company was acquiring huge tracts to support its operations.

As the Campbell government became aware that its most important natural resource was slipping beyond its control, it also recognized that the land resource represented the foundation on which rested its ambitious plans to expand land-based activities under the Development Plan. As a result, in the winter of 1971 Campbell established a special committee of inquiry of the Legislature to look into the implications of land acquisition and land transfers to non-resident corporations and individuals. The committee tabled its report on April 2. While its members, which included backbenchers from both sides, recognized that the present acquisition rate of land by non-residents and corporations seriously jeopardized the Island's control over this vital resource, it was unwilling to recommend any steps to curb the trend. The committee, like the government, had to confront the intractable land policy issue, reconciling private property rights with the public good. During its deliberations, it heard from many people who flatly rejected any restriction on their right to sell to the highest bidder, resident or non-resident. "The Committee feels that the right of private owners to sell to the highest bidder should not be interfered with," it concluded.

If Island politicians were not prepared to introduce restrictions on what people could do with their own land, even if that meant the land would slip from the hands of Islanders, on the other hand they were not prepared to come up with an alternative. It was a Hobson's choice. But Campbell was not prepared to watch the province's vital land resources slip beyond its grasp. In April 1972, in an unprecedented move, his government introduced a far-reaching amendment to the Real Property Assessment Act. Under this amendment, drafted by Frank Sigsworth, henceforth no person not a resident of Prince Edward Island could acquire in excess of ten acres of land or five chains (337 feet) of shore frontage without permission from the provincial cabinet. In effect, the amendment clamped down on unrestricted land purchases by non-residents. Furthermore, for the first time in the province's history, it restricted the amount of land Islanders could sell to non-residents, thus depriving them of some of their precious property rights. The amendment, Section 3 and its subsections, subsequently passed through the Legislature and received Royal Assent.

It was a bold, politically risky move, but despite the immediate howls of protests from real estate agents, property owners, land speculators, and even ordinary citizens, it stuck. Although the legislation was more symbolic than real (cabinet approved the vast majority of applications) and although Islanders and non-residents used loopholes, political pressure, winks and nods, and other tactics to acquire land in the province, it sent a powerful signal to everyone concerned that the Campbell government was serious about maintaining control over non-resident ownership.

All the same, the legislation contained some major political pitfalls. For example, if cabinet turned down an application from an out-of-province buyer, the prospective seller's property transaction would collapse. Often out-of-province buyers paid premium prices that were not reflective of fair market value for the land in its present use, driving the cost far beyond what local residents could afford. As a result, the government could expect to face the ongoing dilemma of how to deal with a disappointed seller after it turned down a lucrative property transaction. To counter this problem, the government attempted to draft a protocol to compensate those whose land sale it refused to approve, but it was never fully satisfactory. Campbell later admitted that the provincial government would have had little choice but to negotiate the purchase and retain ownership of certain parcels of land it did not want to see pass into the hands of non-residents. These "ticklish situations" made it very sensitive about imposing restrictions above and beyond those it did put in place. At least the legislation provided government with some leverage against prospective developments. As a condition of purchase, for example, it could negotiate with developers over issues such as green spaces, beach access, and protection of significant environmental or aesthetic features.

The Campbell government was actually embarking on an historic constitutional path. The amendment to the Real Property Assessment Act rested on an uncertain legal premise – that a provincial jurisdiction in Canada could legislate on the fundamental issue of property rights. By restricting those rights, it was in effect challenging the perceived constitutional right of Canadians and others to hold property in any part of Canada, regardless of where they lived. Canadian citizenship, it was said, implied "being at home" in every province. An agreement reached in 1921 between Canada and the United States also provided for the protection of property and civil rights of American citizens by allowing them to purchase property in Canada.

It did not take long for someone to challenge the legislation. Two American citizens, Richard Morgan and Alan Jacobson, residents of New Jersey, made an offer to purchase a piece of property from Leo Blacquière, a resident of the Rustico area. When the application for approval reached cabinet, it was turned down. Morgan and Jacobson immediately appealed, and the case wound up in the Prince Edward Island Supreme Court. A judgment brought down by Chief Justice C. St. Clair Trainor on November 19, 1973, ruled in the government's favour. The court stated that because the legislation related to property and civil rights in the province it did not infringe on Parliament's exclusive authority to legislate on the rights of Canadians and non-citizens. The decision was then appealed to the Supreme Court of Canada, which sent off shock waves across the country. The federal government intervened on behalf of Morgan and Jacobson, while in a rare move all other Canadian provinces intervened on behalf of Prince Edward Island. The case for the two Americans was made by Alan Scales, with assistance from two out-of-province lawyers, and that for the provincial government by

Deputy Attorney-General Wendell MacKay and Canadian constitutional expert Maurice Fyfe.

The Supreme Court's precedent-setting decision was handed down on its behalf by Justice Bora Laskin on June 26, 1975. In his judgment, Laskin ruled that the legislation was within the power of the provincial government, as the terms of the British North America Act gave the provinces jurisdiction over property and civil rights. He further ruled that federal power could not be invoked to provide Canadians or non-citizens immunity from provincial legislation. Laskin wrote that "the province had made residence rather than alienage per se the touchstone of the limitation on the holding of land in the province," and that "federal power was not invaded by giving such preference in the holding of land, as s.3 provided in favour of residents." He rejected the appellant's argument that the legislation was suspect because it differentiated between classes of persons, and because of that was *ultra vires* beyond the jurisdiction of the provincial government. "I do not agree with this characterization, and I do not think it is supportable either in principle or under any case law," he wrote. "No one is prevented by Prince Edward Island legislation from entering the province or taking up residence there. Absentee ownership of land in a province is a matter of legitimate provincial concern and, in the case of Prince Edward Island, history adds force to this aspect of its authority over its territory."

The decision represented a major legal and political victory for Prince Edward Island, making it the first Canadian province to exercise the right to restrict property ownership.* Given the deep sentiments held by Islanders about land, this legal view that land could also serve a public good and should be protected and preserved represented a major breakthrough. It also sent out a signal that Campbell was serious about helping residents remain in control of the destiny of "the Island." In the words of Premier Campbell, Prince Edward Island was "Not For Sale."

* * *

---

* *The Canadian constitution, signed in 1982, would formally and explicitly recognize Prince Edward Island's right to restrict property sales to non-residents.*

While the provincial government had achieved the right to exercise some degree of control over land ownership, it had little if any control over land use. In a province with limited resources, economic survival meant making the best use of those resources. In the early, heady days of the Development Plan, everything mattered; exploiting the full potential of every resource was key to its strategy. As Campbell lightly suggested to a reporter with the *Ottawa Journal* in March 1969, just after the Plan was signed, "every person in every square inch of the province will come within application of the plan."

Following on the heels of the amendments to the Real Property Assessment Act, Campbell took another historically significant step to raise the profile of land issues in the province. He appointed a Royal Commission on Land Ownership and Land Use with the mandate to recommend land ownership and land use policies "designed to deal with effects of new demands and pressures on the land resources of Prince Edward Island." For the first time since 1860, land became the focus of a major public inquiry.*

The Royal Commission that Campbell appointed in 1972 was asked to develop policies to resolve the twentieth-century version of the Land Question. The task fell to Charles Raymond, the land use planner; James Wells (Andy's father), who had retired to the Island; and Pownal farmer Charles Jones. After holding thirteen days of hearings across the Island and receiving twenty-nine briefs, the Commission released its report on July 9, 1973. The report was based on a "firm belief in the integrity of Island landscape and community." It stated that, while landscape and community were not frozen in time, they should be respected and supported whenever possible. Referring to the various attributes of community, culture, and landscape that made the Island a "special place," the

---

* *The first land commission had been appointed in 1860 in an attempt to resolve the conflicts between tenants and proprietors. It recommended "two simple principles" to guide the future of land ownership and use in the province: that tenants be given the right to purchase the land on which they lived, and that both landlord and tenant be given a fair price. That commission gave its opinion that the recommendations, if accepted, would make Prince Edward Island "the Barbados of the St. Lawrence." In 1862, the Legislature passed two acts to put the recommendations into effect, but neither received Royal Assent. The result was renewed controversy at public gatherings, in the Legislature, and in the country-side where troops had to be called in from Nova Scotia to put down the insurrection.*

Commission noted that "it is those very qualities which make the Island increasingly special in a larger world where such qualities become increasingly rare."

The Commission made twenty-three recommendations that sought to balance the conflicting views presented during its hearings. One cornerstone of its recommendations was the principle of "minimum maintenance," based on the concept of stewardship. "How they use land matters" more than who owns it, the report stated. Although the Commission recommended ownership restrictions of two hundred acres for corporations, on the other hand it recommended that non-resident ownership restrictions be removed entirely after alternative land control measures had been put in place. The Commission further recommended that steps be taken to ensure continued access by farmers to good agricultural land. "Without these soils the Island economy would be in serious distress," it pointed out. Another recommendation proposed the development of a coastal land use plan that would protect the dwindling supply of accessible shoreline; the Commission noted that the growth rate of cottage subdivisions had reached alarming proportions.

Above all, the fundamental recommendation made by the Commission was far-reaching: that the government develop a land use plan for the province as a whole. "The economic rationale for balanced and related growth in agriculture, tourism and urban centres has a spatial or geographic dimension which required immediate definition in a general land use plan," it advised. The proposed plan should aim to designate lands for specific uses. For example, it argued that the subdivision of prime agricultural land should be curtailed. This zoning plan, the report indicated, would "authenticate what, in broad terms, is possible and desirable in the long term utilization of the Island's land resource," and would finally bring some order to the chaos that had characterized land use in Prince Edward Island for so long.

The 1973 report of the Royal Commission on Land Ownership and Land Use, hailed as the blueprint for guiding the development of the land and its communities into the future, represented a land-mark in the Island's troubled history of land use and ownership. And it touched off a storm of controversy. Farmers didn't like it because they feared the implications of minimum maintenance, which would attach certain conditions about their use of the land. Real-estate brokers didn't like it because it would interfere with market-ing in the private sector. Developers didn't like it because coastal zone restrictions would set rules on how they could carve up the shorefront. And Islanders in general didn't like it because they feared that zoning would intrude on their right to do whatever they wanted with their land.

The Royal Commission clearly outlined what the goals for land use and ownership ought to be. However, how to reach those goals was much less clear. While the Commission proposed a highly complex and sophisticated set of land use policies and regulations, the people apparently lacked the will to act on them. But Campbell had not anticipated such a degree of public opposition to the report. In an effort to contain potential political damage, he appointed Andy Wells as chair of a small committee of senior bureaucrats to recommend how the government should proceed.

In early January 1974, six months after the Commission had delivered its report, Andy Wells submitted his own report to Campbell. In it, he stated that the committee had been struck to examine the recommendations, but had concluded they were too radical for immediate implementation. In their place, the committee recommended the establishment of a land use commission, non-partisan and non-political, to develop land use guidelines and regulations and arbitrate disputes. In place of province-wide zoning, Wells and the committee recommended that zoning plans should be voluntary, because they believed that the proposed coastal land use plan and the provincial land use plan were politically unacceptable. As an alternative, where it was deemed that the public interest was at stake in land use decisions the committee recommended the implementation of "development rights," a form of compensation to those landowners who were refused permission to convert their property to other uses or to sell it outright.

In effect, the Commission's recommendations were put on hold. Obviously, Prince Edward Islanders were not yet willing to relinquish their cherished property rights. However, the recommendations continued to surface in subsequent years as the problems identified by the Commission mounted, leading to further conflicts and confusion. Instead, the Campbell government proceeded to implement the more politically prudent approach suggested by the Wells committee. Under the provincial Planning Act, the Minister of Community Affairs was given broad discretionary powers to issue or deny building permits, change land use conditions, and make other decisions on how land was used. The Land Use Commission, established as an independent, quasi-judicial body, was given far-reaching powers to reinterpret, reverse, or amend ministerial deci-sions and those made by municipal officials. It also took a lot of heat away from politicians on contentious issues related to land use con-flicts.

Among its noteworthy decisions, the Land Use Commission demonstrated its independence in 1977. The provincial government had applied for a building permit to construct a tourism information centre on prime agricultural land outside Summerside. The National Farmers Union appealed the permit, and the Commission upheld the appeal on the grounds that building a tourism information centre on good agricultural land was misuse, especially given the availability of alternate sites. This decision strengthened the reputation of the Commission as an independent body, although conflicts over land use continued to escalate.

Meanwhile, the government managed to take other modest steps to implement the recommendations of the Royal Commission. In the 1974 session of the Legislature, amendments to the Planning Act made provision so that property owners could voluntarily identify their land for non-development uses, while it extended favourable tax treatment for land maintained in agriculture. But it never seriously considered the purchase of development rights, which would compensate landowners who elected not to develop their properties.

Yet the Campbell government found it could only go so far. Land might indeed represent the Island's most important natural resource, but its ownership and use was destined to remain inviolate. Although some restrictions would apply, the tiny Island's limited land base would basically remain vulnerable to the capricious predations of developers, speculators, and others who placed private gain ahead of public good. In less than two decades after the Royal Commission report, more than 130,000 acres of Class 2 land – the best land available for farming – would be diverted to other uses, lost forever.

In January 1975, John McClellan, the first Executive Director of the Land Use Commission, lamented the lack of progress in reconciling private and public interests on matters relating to land. "How much are we prepared to sacrifice in terms of our personal freedoms and our ability to do what we please with our land in order to preserve what we have and develop in an orderly manner in the future?" he asked in an interview with the *Guardian*. Later, he reviewed the fate of the Royal Commission's groundbreaking work. "The 1972 Royal Commission made 23 recommendations," he recalled. "By my count, five were adopted by government, three were

partially adopted and 15 remain in limbo. Its major recommendations were not adopted. They included a generalized provincial land
use plan, a detailed coastal land use plan, and minimum
maintenance requirements for non-resident and corporate lands."
The guts of the Royal Commission's recommendations had been
eviscerated.

A virtual open-door policy for non-residents continued: no
monitoring or enforcement of land ownership levels; no policies in
place to protect agricultural land; cottage and residential subdivisions sprung up on prime farmland; no policies or regulations – not
even guidelines – to curb strip development; and nothing to prevent
or discourage speculation. In summary, any notion of comprehensive land use planning was anathema. Unfortunately, unplanned
and unfettered growth were destined to put major strains on
infrastructure, transportation policies, community development, and
especially on the land and landscape.

Even relatively sacrosanct matters such as protecting the Island's
finite and fragile natural areas were trampled upon. During his
tenure as environment minister in 1975, Gilbert Clements
established a Natural Areas Advisory Committee to formulate an
approach to the protection and preservation of the province's unique
and distinctive systems of dunes, wetlands, original forests, and other
rare ecological and environmental areas. But his immediate
successor terminated the committee. Later, in a 1977 report to
cabinet on natural areas, the Land Use Commission lamented "a
history of indecision, lack of coordination and absence of policy."
Such indecisiveness manifested negatively in numerous examples
across the Island. For example, in its efforts to purchase Oulton's
Island, the Land Development Corporation was stymied by the
Department of Finance, which had boosted the assessment value
beyond its reach. And just when the provincial government was in
the process of designating Point DesRoches as a natural area, a choice
parcel of the fragile site fell into the hands of a non-resident.

Through the Development Plan, the Campbell government did
manage to act ambitiously on a number of other fronts in an attempt
to transform the economy and the society of the province. But on the
vital issues affecting the land, it was destined to be stopped short.

* * *

The Campbell government would not be alone in confronting the Land Question. Over the following decades, its successors would grapple with the same issue. Close to two decades later, yet another commission, established to inquire into the thorny issues surrounding land in Prince Edward Island, reflected on the experiences of its predecessor. In its 1990 report (optimistically entitled *Everything Before Us*), the Royal Commission on the Land, chaired by Doug Boylan (Campbell's former cabinet clerk), observed that little had changed during the intervening years since the 1973 report. "We would be overstating the case to say there is no policy, no direction and no commitment," it said. "Yet, such exaggeration is not as inaccurate as might, on first reflection, seem."

This commission further denounced the failure of governments to act on matters relating to the land. "We submit that there is, in reality, no consistent, coherent set of land policies in place in the province, no vision for the future at the provincial level and no sense of direction in land issues on the part of the government," stated its report. "Not only have successive governments failed to provide policies that would enable answers to these questions but any attempt to do so has been marked by so many flip flops and exceptions that a confused public has lost confidence in most existing regulatory procedures." Islanders may have claimed that they wanted some rules about land use and ownership, but they were obviously not willing to accept the consequences of those rules. Nowhere was the clash of values and beliefs, convictions and aspirations, more evident than in the public debate about the land. In the absence of clear government direction and policy, private interests trumped the public good.

The 1990 report also offered some reflections on the experiences of the 1972 Royal Commission:

> In effect, the [1972] Commission was recommending that an individualistic land ethic – 'the land is mine to use as I choose' – be replaced by an ethic emphasizing land stewardship, 'I am a temporary custodian of the land, and must have regard for future generations.' Changing public perceptions and attitudes is never easy, and Islanders had been called upon to embrace a number of alternatives to their traditional lifestyles as a result of the Comprehensive Development Plan. There was a growing antipathy among many to the Development Plan with its school consolidation, farm rationalization and other changes.

For the Commission to expect that either government or the public would accept its recommendations was probably naive.

Naive or not, for the first time since the nineteenth century, the provincial government was attempting to protect the future of its most important natural resource. Once again, the Land Question haunted the Island.

CHAPTER ELEVEN

Reshaping Government

On coming to power in 1966, the Campbell government faced a dizzying array of decisions during its first cabinet meetings. Not only did it have to cope with the major issues of the day – dealing with the fallout from the previous administration; putting the provincial finances in order and preparing a budget; fulfilling its campaign promises; dealing with the federal government; managing the various government departments; initiating and amending laws and regulations; and responding to the demands of the electorate – it also faced a multitude of trivial matters.

The cabinet met weekly on the fifth floor of the Provincial Administrative Building in Charlottetown, across the hall from the Premier's Office. Each week, it found itself faced with fifty or more agenda items, some important, many trivial. These latter included such business as approving civil service transactions and travel; handing out welfare allowances; transferring funds between departmental accounts; and other routine transactions. Administrative arrangements for cabinet lacked efficiency: cabinet ministers received no detailed briefings; there was no staff assistance; and issues could be placed on the agenda at the last minute. In short, cabinet was ill-prepared for making the decisions it was faced with on a weekly basis. Mired as they were in detail, some ministers found it difficult to discern the direction the province should be taking.

To cope with the growing demands of its agenda, cabinet often met for two full days each week just to keep the machinery of government running; all too often, it made hasty and ill-advised decisions. The difficulties manifested around the cabinet table actually reflected a deeper problem: a government organizational structure and a public administrative style that were, at best, rudimentary. This was not a good situation for a government that had promised to be open, honest and accountable.

* * *

Over many years Islanders had fallen into a trap of increasing dependence on the provincial government. The close proximity of MLAs to voters, the small scale of Island constituencies, and the ever-present practice of patronage perpetuated that relationship. When Islanders wanted   something – anything – done, invariably they pointed their steps in the direction of their MLA's door. Of course, in a province where every vote counted the door was always open. Even deeper problems resulted from the parish-pump nature of Island politics. The MLAs narrowly viewed their job as obtaining benefits for their constituents, rather than looking after the broader interests of the Island as a whole. Getting, not doing, characterized the ambitions of most MLAs, even those who had been appointed to cabinet.

The Campbell government came to power at a time of escalating demand for public services. The post-war boom created new expectations of governments, which in its turn found its role broadened as it started to intervene more directly in the economic and social affairs of the province. In the past, government had played little part in the daily lives of people. Now, a symbiotic relationship had developed between the two. People were learning to demand more from their government and – within its limits – government was willingly to oblige. But the increased presence of government in the day-to-day affairs of the people also required more accountability. Citizens increasingly expected their government to provide efficient and effective public services through modern practices of public administration and management, so that it could effectively provide protection, regulation, support and service. A competent, neutral and independent public service was integral to the sound operation of government.

By the mid-sixties, however, an independent public service was still in its infancy in Prince Edward Island, which was the last province in Canada to introduce a Civil Service Act that provided for an independent civil service commission, a classification system, security of tenure and the merit principle.* The Shaw government introduced this long-awaited act in 1962 (to accusations from Liberals that it was intended to protect recent Tory appointees). Shaw, who had been a career civil servant before entering politics, of course recognized the need for greater stability and competence in the

---

* A Public Service Act was first introduced in 1937, but it had limited scope.

public service. Even then, the act covered only two-thirds of all government jobs; the remainder, mostly seasonal or temporary, would still be filled by patronage appointments.

The construction of the new Provincial Administrative Building on Rochford Street in Charlottetown best exemplified the modernization of the civil service. Until then, civil servants were located all over town, often in inadequate facilities. The new complex, constructed by Fuller Construction of Montreal (which had recently completed the Confederation Centre of the Arts), finally brought all the departments together in a state-of-the-art facility. In response to criticism over its size, the government pointed out that the complex would be able to accommodate increases in the number of civil servants for at least fifteen years. The building was so new when the Campbell government moved in that some of the furniture – acquired by the previous government through what the Liberals described as a "family compact" with close ties to the Shaw government – was still being delivered. Liberals also derided the new $15,000 courtyard fountain, designed by Charles Daudelin of Montreal. They dubbed the metallic structure rising above a pool of water "Rossiter's Roost," a reference to the alleged excesses of Shaw's Minister of Fisheries and Industry.

While the new provincial buildings might outwardly suggest the arrival of a new class of independent public servants, reform of the public service itself moved sluggishly forward. Prior to the passage of the Civil Service Act, the public service was under strict political control. The procedure for hiring, firing, promoting and paying public servants had no parallel in Canada; a change in government meant a wholesale change in personnel. In 1935, for example, the Liberals swept to power under Walter Lea, winning every seat, and promptly seized the spoils of office. Virtually all the incumbent Conservative appointees were fired in what was dubbed "Bloody Thursday," the day the Liberal cabinet issued dismissal notices.

Typical of the demands placed on a newly elected government for patronage appointments was a letter received by premier-elect Walter Lea asking for the reinstatement of a school supervisor, "a position that he held under the Liberal regime and lost under the Conservative party." The rationale was quite straightforward: "Since the provincial election just past has resulted in an overwhelming victory for our party, and since it is customary for certain government officials to lose their jobs, we the undersigned committeemen ... request that as soon as the Liberal party forms the government that Mr. ___ be reinstated ..." The Women's Liberal Club also submitted a list of names to Lea's cabinet in October 1935 recommending deserving female supporters for positions "in the gift of the Government." Governments found it hard to ignore such requests.

According to Dr. Frank MacKinnon in his pioneering book on the Prince Edward Island government, the early years of public administration were marked by limited functions that slowed its growth and by political patronage which prevented its efficiency.* As to reforms, he wrote, "Elaborate regulations with respect to appointment, promotion, and tenure were considered unnecessary, for the Government was never embarrassed by, nor did it need, a large number of applicants of ability and ambition."

All that began to change in the 1930s as ministers, often the only senior officials in their departments, came to rely more and more on experienced advice. Increasing responsibilities led to the need to improve the quality and status of civil servants. Perhaps chastened by the public uproar over "Bloody Thursday," in 1937 the Thane Campbell government introduced the Public Service Act, the first of its kind in the province. The act provided for security of tenure, although twenty-two more years would pass before a change of government put that provision to the test. Even with the new act, however, the cabinet or the responsible minister continued to make all appointments. The act also restricted appointments to Islanders only, which seriously limited recruitment of more qualified people (and raised the perennial question of who was an Islander). The "Islanders only" restriction delayed the introduction of administrative practices generally in place elsewhere. In consequence, these practices remained unknown, untried or unsuccessfully introduced in the Prince Edward Island government.

From the earliest days, patronage represented the principal method of conducting government business.** The "who gets what,

---

* The Government of Prince Edward Island, *published in 1951 by the University of Toronto Press.*

** *The prevalence of patronage was not confined to provincial politics. In his autobiography, former MP Heath Macquarrie recalled that, following his election in 1957 (which also saw the election of the new Conservative government in Ottawa), his time was almost totally taken up with demands for federal appointments and other forms of patronage.*

why, when and where" of patronage served as an invaluable tool for rewarding supporters, punishing dissidents, and attracting and maintaining political support. The political hierarchy ensured its survival through the practice of buying votes. As the Island entered the twentieth century, Liberal premier Donald Farquharson observed that "it is simply a matter now of who will buy the most votes, and the man who works the hardest and is prepared to use means fair or foul will get in."

On the other hand, the public's demand for the largesse of politicians knew no bounds. As the second ferry between Borden and Cape Tormentine came into service in the early 1930s, Premier Walter Lea declared in exasperation that the number of applications for jobs on the new ferry was "sufficient to man the British Navy." However, Island politicians were sometimes circumspect in dispensing patronage. Premier John H. Bell rebuffed his flamboyant cabinet minister, J.P. ("Big Jim Bill") MacIntyre, by refusing to put one of MacIntyre's supporters on the payroll at Falconwood Hospital, the mental institution in Charlottetown. "I may say that the Government does not like to interfere with the management of the asylum," he explained in a note to MacIntyre. "They leave it all to Dr. Goodwill [the superintendent]. He is very sensitive and if we interfered with his help he might resent it, or if anything went wrong, might blame us."

More pressing reasons for circumspection sometimes surfaced. Premier Bell, on being approached by one of his supporters looking to supply material for a provincial project being cost-shared with the federal government, wrote back that the provincial Public Works Department had to be "above board" when awarding tenders "because if the Federal Government got any suspicion of irregular or crooked work, then our chances of getting subsidy from that source would be imperilled." He added that even "the suggestion of opening of tenders and giving information to political friends would be fatal." Sometimes practical limits prevented the awarding of patronage. On another occasion, Premier Bell wrote to a colleague who was angling for one of his supporters to be appointed to a provincial government position. Bell replied that he would do what he could "but with an empty treasury and $250,000 behind for the current year, the chances for appointment for anybody are slim." People were often appointed according to the funds available or the duties involved.

The coming of the automobile opened up pork-barrelling on a grand scale. The demand for improved highways fuelled a flurry of roadbuilding in every corner of the province. Road work provided jobs for supporters and contracts for friends, and earned gratitude from constituents. As a result, Prince Edward Island eventually boasted the highest number of paved roads per square mile in all of Canada – roads paved by promises and patronage. Local MLAs held the most influence over decisions about highway construction contracts, but this did not always result in the most logical or coherent transportation network. The problems prompted the provincial auditor, in his report for 1966, to boldly suggest that politicians should not be so involved in these decisions. "The MLAs are involved in the selection of projects to be completed in their electoral district," the report noted. "Even though all projects qualify for selection because of the poor condition of most highways, this method of selection does not necessarily provide for the best allocation of resources on a provincial basis." The report, of course, was ignored. Visitors to the Island frequently commented on the fact that the pavement ended abruptly on many roads. With limited budgets, the government of the day tended to pass out highways projects piecemeal, so paving often stopped just beyond a supporter's gate.*

Inevitably, the long tradition of political patronage only served to compound the problems faced by a government trying to deliver programs and services to Islanders. In a small province like Prince Edward Island, with its limited tax base and conservative attitude towards government involvement (perceived as interference), the development of a competent and independent public service lagged behind other provinces. In consequence, the province suffered from a vastly inferior public service. Hampered by low salaries, minimal job requirements, and limited prospects, it attracted few qualified and talented people. Only when government responsibilities began to increase did the need for more skilled, professional, and technical assistance emerge. Even so, in many departments the senior official who made most of the decisions was a part-time minister.

As the province entered the second half of the twentieth century, the public service included just 336 permanent public servants (close to half of them in the Department of Health), and a number of part-time and seasonal employees such as road supervisors.

Even the Campbell administration was not immune from the practice. Referring to the many short stretches of roads being paved, Walter Shaw nicknamed Campbell the "Brylcream Man – a little dab will do you."

Unfortunately, the ubiquitous hand of political patronage, compounded by haphazard procedures and few benefits, had done little to encourage the development of a more mature public service. Mired in patronage, subject to the whims of politicians, and lacking public respect, the Prince Edward Island public service – unique in Canada – struggled along.

*　　*　　*

By the time the Campbell government came to power, the Civil Service Commission had been in place for just over three years. Thanks to hold-overs of some incumbents, security of tenure for less than qualified employees, and the fact that few positions required professional or technical qualifications, the general level of competence was rudimentary at best. These deficiencies became glaringly obvious as the Campbell government entered into negotiations over the Comprehensive Development Plan. The Plan explicitly recognized the pivotal role of the provincial government in the affairs of the province. As the new player in the province's economic and social development, the government would need the backing of a highly skilled, flexible, creative and competent public service to implement the Plan.

The signing of the Comprehensive Development Plan in early 1969 ushered in a new era of public administration. Still in its formative years, the civil service now faced the formidable challenge of implementing the Plan. Line departments found themselves saddled with the responsibility for implementing a plan that for the most part they had not devised, and which many neither understood nor accepted. The cabinet itself, for the first time in its history, was expected to devote full attention to its responsibilities, for which it would need significant staff support. And for its part, the provincial government as a whole faced the challenge of drastically changing the way it conducted the public's business. There was no way around it – a major overhaul involving all levels of government would have to take place.

At the time the Economic Improvement Corporation was established, Campbell recognized that the existing civil service staff lacked the capacity to manage the planning process, and welcomed the involvement of outside expertise. However, his long-term goal was to restructure and reorient the government, and provide it with the resources and the capacity necessary to successfully implement the Plan as well as improve the standard of other services. Even before the Plan was signed, he took some fundamental steps to reshape government. On December 31, 1968, he signed an agreement with a Chicago-based consulting firm, Public Administration Consultants, to commence the reform process. He asked its principal consultant, Donald Nemetz, to work on two areas: to develop a modern personnel system, and to strengthen the government's administrative structure and management system.

By this time, the government employed approximately 1,500 permanent civil servants, with another 1,000 or so seasonal or temporary employees. Nemetz soon identified serious deficiencies in the qualification standards and salaries of professional, technical, and administrative positions. He recommended a new system of classification and compensation, which the cabinet adopted in 1969. The government also stepped up its efforts to recruit and select qualified applicants, and instituted a broad range of programs to train and upgrade staff, including sending many back to school. Nemetz then addressed the other critical issue – the structure and operations of the provincial government itself. Although by far the smallest province in the federal state, the Prince Edward Island government roughly mirrored the structure of governments in other provinces. Maintaining close relationships with the federal government in crucial areas such as agriculture, fisheries, and transportation dictated the need to structure provincial operations in a certain fashion.

This requirement to maintain some semblance of a full-scale government in a small province, and to provide equivalent services to other jurisdictions, meant that Prince Edward Island was the most overgoverned province in Canada. With a lieutenant-governor, a judiciary, thirty-two MLAs, a premier and ten-member cabinet, four MPs, four senators, and countless officials at both the municipal and local levels, Frank MacKinnon dubbed it the "big engine, little body" syndrome. To make that engine work effectively and efficiently was a daunting prospect.

Not surprisingly, reforming an administrative structure that had slowly built up and ossified over the years proved more difficult than expected. In the first instance, Campbell hoped to more than halve the number of government departments (many with limited functions) from the present fifteen. But in the process he faced a thornier problem. Political economist John Stewart Mill wrote in his book, *Representative Government*, that the responsibilities of government were best provided, and the work best done, if all functions of a similar subject were assigned to single departments. This dictum had scant application to Prince Edward Island, where vested interests, demands from various sectors, and political compromises resulted in only a marginal drop in the number of departments during the early seventies.

Campbell achieved greater success in reforming the overall operations of government. He overhauled the complete operations of the cabinet; he established an Executive Council Secretariat to provide cabinet with staff support; he removed trivial matters from the agenda; and he gave ministers greater latitude in running their departments. In addition, he established a Treasury Board with five cabinet ministers and a professional staff to strengthen financial management. Eventually, a Planning Board, chaired by the premier, was established to help set priorities.

But internal and external conflicts beset the pace of reform. Programs under the Development Plan were still subject to federal government scrutiny and approval, and funds had to be individually earmarked to keep them segregated from regular provincial spending. For a long time, budget items were identified as "Plan" or "Non-Plan." All this delayed the development of provincial departments to reach a sufficient level of capacity and capability to plan and deliver their own programs. In the meantime, the Department of Development and the line departments struggled to sort out conflicting or overlapping responsibilities. It took close to a decade before the provincial government was able to fully integrate development programs with other initiatives. In the end, Prince Edward Island emerged with something approximating a modern public service.

*　　*　　*

Following the 1970 election, Campbell was ready to announce a new structure and style for the provincial government. For this he turned to John Eldon Green, a former federal civil servant who had been recruited to help strengthen the province's health and social services programs (an area left largely untouched by the Development Plan). Over a four-day period, Green put together a policy statement on government reorganization, drawing on the work of Nemetz and others. He delivered the report to Campbell at his cottage in Stanley Bridge; after a few minor changes, Campbell tabled the policy statement on government organization in the Legislature in the spring of 1970.

The statement outlined how government intended to work with Islanders over the coming years. "The Prince Edward Island citizen of 1970 receives and expects from his government services never contemplated by the citizen of 1950," remarked Campbell in the Legislature. He pointed out that in 1950 the provincial budget accounted for fourteen percent of the Island's gross provincial product, but by 1970 that had risen to thirty-two percent. He also explained that the range of services had changed over that time, while the traditional ways of delivering them had not. He stressed that administrative procedures must be greatly improved "if the legislative process is to continue to be responsive to the demands of the public." Campbell was challenging Islanders to take a more active role in setting policy direction. "I look, therefore, to the participation of the public, to the initiative and creative activity of each individual citizen, of all ages, in the fulfillment of our program," he announced. The willingness to involve the public in the decision-making process did not mean that government was abdicating its responsibilities, "but it is only when these demands reach the level of Executive Council that priorities can be determined."

The policy statement announced the establishment of new central agencies (such as the Treasury Board) to help government improve management and set priorities and directions; the reduction of the number of government departments to twelve; and the establishment of regional services centres to ensure service delivery to all areas of the province on an equitable basis. It also announced measures to strengthen the civil service, including staff training and development. Under the Campbell administration, the civil service mushroomed from 1,500 to more than 3,600 employees. At the same time, the provincial budget – augmented by a significant infusion of federal cash – ballooned from just over $50 million in 1966 to approximately $265 million in 1978. After counting in the number of casual and seasonal employees, the most overgoverned province in Canada boasted roughly one public servant for every thirty Islanders!

Within Campbell's policy statement lay a challenge for Islanders to take more control over their own affairs. "We believe that the people of this province have given their government a strong mandate to push forward with the program for the social and economic development of the province," Campbell declared when he tabled the policy statement. "This will require new initiatives on our part, decisive and timely action, and the creation of a means whereby the required partnership of the public and private sectors may be assured."

For Islanders and their government, accustomed as they were to patronage, paternalism, dependency and partisanship, the process of building a new partnership was fraught with difficulties. Over the next quarter of a century, successive governments would find themselves reorganizing, reforming and rationalizing their structure and operation in an attempt to create that partnership and get it right.

They are still working on it.

PARO

CHAPTER TWELVE

"Action Now ...
and For The Future"
- Liberal campaign slogan, 1974

On a brilliant July day in the summer of 1973, the Pie-Faced Kid, an Island farm boy turned desperado, infiltrated the tourism information booth in Borden. Before he was expelled, he had directed 582 carloads of tourists straight to the gravel pit in Hartsville. Before the day was over, he had cleared the beach in Cavendish by yelling "tidal wave" over a megaphone; taken a blowtorch to the figures at the wax museum; tinkered with the traffic lights on University Avenue in Charlottetown, backing cars up all the way to Cornwall; and in a final gesture of defiance released a thousand hornets between the second and third acts of *Anne of Green Gables* at the Confederation Centre. It was typical behaviour for the Pie-Faced Kid. He bore a terrible and implacable grudge against all tourists and foreigners. His resentment over what was happening to his beloved Island led him to traverse the countryside, committing random acts of wanton depredation. On that fateful day in July, he could contain himself no longer.

The Pie-Faced Kid was the creation of David Weale, a Prince Edward Island historian. In late 1972, just as the Island was preparing to celebrate its centenary as a Canadian province, Weale, in collaboration with fellow historian Harry Baglole, founded a semi-satirical organization called the Brothers and Sisters of Cornelius Howatt. Centennial celebrations had been planned to observe this milestone, and the nature of the promotional hype to mark the celebrations served as a catalyst for the formation of the group. The Pie-Faced Kid and his side-kick, Ho Hum, a disillusioned Hong Kong songwriter, gave expression to the concerns of Weale, Baglole and others about the message the province's Centennial Commission was sending out through the celebrations.

The Centennial Commission had chosen as its symbol a "Smiling Father of Confederation." The Brothers and Sisters believed that the Commission, and the centennial celebrations themselves, grossly distorted the Island's history. In a release entitled "Why Is This Man Smiling?" they warned, "The Island is now being hailed as the 'Cradle of Confederation' when the plucky little colony refused to join Canada in 1867, and did so only very reluctantly six years later. We seem to have conveniently forgotten much of our history – and the Centennial Commission is certainly doing very little to enlighten us." For its part, the group adopted a manure spreader as its symbol, with the slogan "Spread the Word."

Logo of the Brothers and Sisters of Cornelius Howatt, formed as a semi satirical group to protest the "egregious silliness" of the 1973 Centennial celebrations. Its founders also bemoaned the loss of the traditional Island way of life.

The issue over representation of the centennial celebrations was not the only one on the minds of the Brothers and Sisters of Cornelius Howatt in 1973. The group was named after one of the two Island legislators who had voted against Prince Edward Island joining Confederation, so its members wanted to ensure that the independent tradition of Howatt and others like him was kept alive. They were concerned not only about how the province's history was portrayed, but also about the erosion of the Island's autonomy in the face of pressures from the Development Plan, especially the impact of tourism, the problems of non-resident land ownership, and the threatened demise of rural communities.

The "egregious silliness of the Centennial celebrations," as Weale described it, served as the rallying point for those opposing the course of change on the Island. Despite their whimsical and humorous antics, the Brothers and Sisters of Cornelius Howatt seriously reminded Islanders about the spirit of self-determination.

Throughout the one year of its existence, the group's warnings about loss of identity and about wholesale changes to the Island's social fabric struck a resonant chord with many people. Through its satire, the group reflected deep concerns that, in the rush to modernize, the Island was at the same time abandoning its traditional way of life. "At the present time the Island is once again in the throes of a crisis of major proportions – one which is in many ways similar to, and in some ways a consequence of, that of a century ago," declared the Brothers and Sisters. "At the very root of this crisis is the fact that the traditional Island way of life – a way of life based primarily on agriculture and fishing, on the land and on the sea – is coming under greatly increased attack, and the distinctive rural flavour of our province is being threatened."

Members of the group also chafed about what they viewed as the degradation of the Island's cultural distinctiveness, thanks to the Development Plan. They regarded as futile all the efforts to "keep up" with the rest of Canada, thus producing a pale imitation of some place else. In a letter submitted to the *Journal-Pioneer*, member Alan Rankin called for a rejection of what he termed the "psychology of underdevelopment," the notion that the Island must be developed according to standards imposed from outside. Behind it all lay the feeling that Prince Edward Island's long tradition of self-reliance was in jeopardy from the pressure to compare its progress against national standards. The Brothers and Sisters clung to their conviction that the future should reflect Island values. "We have learned that economic prosperity is not the solution to all our human ills, and that the quality of life does not automatically rise and fall with the consumer index or the gross national product," noted Weale.

The loosely knit group organized a number of high-profile activities throughout 1973. On May 26, the centenary of the vote in the Legislature to join Confederation, they held a mock referendum, reminding Islanders that the people themselves were never given a chance to vote for or against joining Canada. They conducted the referendum by publishing mail-in ballots in local newspapers offering people a choice of voting for Home Rule or for colonial status under Great Britain. The polling booth – an outhouse – was set up on the grounds of Province House from where the results were released. On June 2, the organization announced an overwhelming victory for home rule. The result, it announced, was "indicative of a grave concern on the part of the Island people that the autonomy, independence and self-reliance of the Island community is being threatened."

Other activities reminded Islanders of the threats to their province. The group printed bumper stickers bearing the slogan "Save Our Soil" to publicize the issue of non-resident land ownership, and held public meetings across the province to further highlight this problem. Members of the organization even paddled by canoe to St. Peters Island (where a British Columbia-based company was in the process of acquiring fifty acres of land), planted a provincial flag and claimed the island "in the name of the people of Prince Edward Island to be held in perpetuity for the free use and enjoyment of present and future generations." They vigorously protested the plan to relinquish ownership of Province House (which was being restored as a national historic site) to the federal government, and they organized a wheelbarrow relay to protest the construction of a causeway to the mainland. This last action stemmed from the fact that, ten years earlier, a group of students at St. Dunstan's University had pushed a wheelbarrow-load of clay to Borden in a gesture of sup-

In protest over the registration of fifty acres of land on St. Peters Island by Canada Land Fund without Cabinet approval, the Brothers and Sisters of Cornelius Howatt sailed to the island in 1973, and planted a Prince Edward Island flag. Taking part (from left to right) were Alan Rankin, Irene Rogers, Wayne MacKinnon, David Weale and King Howatt.

port for the causeway. In an equally symbolic gesture, the Brothers and Sisters wheeled the clay back, canned it and sold it in front of Province House. The "Can the Causeway" campaign gained widespread media attention and raised enough money to cover the groups's $150 debt.

Although some people branded the Brothers and Sisters of Cornelius Howatt as a communist organization, and others failed to grasp its satirical messages, their antics did underline the serious debate emerging throughout the province over its loss of identity and community. Islanders were beginning to feel the impact of the Development Plan and many of them held to their resentment that the Plan had been devised, by and large, by outsiders with little appreciation for or understanding of their way of life.

In a speech to the Charlottetown Rotary Club in late May 1973, Premier Campbell made explicit reference to the criticisms raised by the Brothers and Sisters of Cornelius Howatt. In acknowledging the serious points underlying their levity, he admitted, "What they are saying to me ... is 'Watch out' ... Watch out and be careful that we don't view progress in modern terms as necessarily providing a better life for ourselves; watch out that we understand and respect our past; watch out that we recognize the value of a slower, more humane society." Campbell (who revealed he was a great-great-great-grandson of Cornelius Howatt, which made him, as he said, a "real brother") recognized the validity of these concerns. "I have considered and advocated for some time that we in Prince Edward Island must carefully examine change so that we are able to weed out those aspects of change which would be detrimental to our way of life, and, at the same time, take advantage of those aspects of change which will enhance and improve our quality of life," he told the meeting.

The speech, entitled "Between Two Cultures," also reflected Campbell's increasing understanding of the need to find an accommodation between the Island's past, present and future. "Balance, to my mind, is the key word," he said, and added, "I firmly believe ... Islanders, given all the facts and an opportunity to study and think about the issues, can collectively achieve that balance and, in the process, build a better society."

Some people interpreted Campbell's stance as an about-face, given that the Development Plan had presided over the assault on many of the Island's traditions and myths. In fact, the Rotary Club speech gave expression to his growing belief that rapid industrialization and modernization would not necessarily produce a better quality of life. In a later speech, this one to the Science Council of Canada in June 1975 at Brudenell, Campbell continued to advance that theme. "We should endeavour to reach a socially acceptable and useful balance between the societal trends of today and the less disruptive, more human attributes and values of yesterday," he said. "To challenge some of the Western tenets of so-called capitalism and democracy is not as dangerous as it would have been a few years ago, but it is still a difficult undertaking for a Canadian politician."

Whether the speech to the Rotary Club represented Campbell's maturing belief in the values of a conserver society or a well-timed response to growing discontent with the direction his government was taking, it did underline the very real political challenge of straddling two cultures. In a letter to the *Guardian*, University of Prince Edward Island political studies professor Reshard Gool termed the speech an "historic document." "I would hazard that in no other province – possibly not even at the federal level – has any politician made such an eloquent, concerned and perspicacious public statement," he wrote.

As promised at the beginning of 1973, the Brothers and Sisters of Cornelius Howatt self-destructed on New Year's Eve of that year, nailing its "last will and testament" to the doors of Province House. But a statement made at the launch of the group would prove prophetic. It expressed the hope that "long after the Centennial Commission has doled out its last dollar, Cornelius Howatt and friends will retain their deserved position in the continuing Island tradition." Over the years, in the Island's struggle to preserve its sense of identity and community, it gave birth to many incarnations of the Pie-Faced Kid that found new ways to enliven provincial politics through "random acts of wanton depredation."

*   *   *

The early years of the 1970s proved to be a defining period for the province and its people. Those years saw a resurgence of debate over the Island's identity, its prospects, and its autonomy. Not since the Confederation debates of a century earlier had such fundamental issues arisen, nor were people so engaged. A cacophony of conflicting viewpoints collided in the narrow confines of the political arena. Canadian journalist Harry Bruce later noted the new political consciousness emerging in the Prince Edward Island of that time.

"Despite whatever hick image of Prince Edward Island ignorant outsiders might hold, it has recently become perhaps the most complicated, sophisticated, lively and locally knowledgeable little political society in the country," he wrote.

From this ferment emerged some militant protests against the Campbell government. One of the strongest occurred in the summer of 1971 when, following a series of tractor demonstrations over the summer, the National Farmers Union staged a major rally on the evening of August 18, blocking the TransCanada Highway between Charlottetown and Borden. The rally took place after NFU representatives refused to meet with Minister of Agriculture Dan MacDonald to discuss their grievances. Instead, they demanded a meeting with Premier Campbell to resolve the issues forthwith. Ostensibly, these demands included reduced farm truck registration fees, a tax exemption on fuel, and low-interest loans. Most importantly, the NFU feared the demise of the family farm. It demanded an end to corporate farming and vertical integration within the industry, which gave too much power to processors. The protests were set off by that year's disastrous farm cash receipts, compounded by frustration that the government was ignoring the interests of farmers in its "headlong rush to develop" other sectors of the Island's economy.

Campbell and his agriculture minister, Dan MacDonald (far right), were drawn into controversy by the National Farmers Union for the agricultural policies under the Development Plan. At far left is NFU district director Urban Laughlin.

After refusing to meet with MacDonald, members of the NFU stepped up their protest the next day. A number of them blocked the access road to the Borden ferry terminal with their tractors, at which the RCMP was called in and arrested three of the demonstrators: Jimmy Mayne, Hubert Stewart and Wayne Sharpe. They were taken into custody, charged, and later released. On the morning of August 20, Premier Campbell went on radio to denounce the NFU and its demonstrations. "The role of government today," he said, "is to protect the whole public against the excessive demands of special interest groups." Campbell's refusal to accede to the NFU's demands only stiffened its resolve. Particularly galling to some members was the reference to the NFU as "a special interest group." Prince Edward Island farmers did not see themselves in that light.

In reaction to the broadcast, two hundred NFU members led by national president Roy Atkinson from Saskatchewan drove their tractors back to Borden and blocked the ferry terminal again. Attorney-General Gordon Bennett promptly called in the RCMP and ordered them to clear the highway. At seven o'clock that evening, fifteen patrol cars and a number of school buses carrying 150 police officers moved into Borden, well backed up by a number of road graders from the Department of Highways. The demonstrators left, but returned the next day. Once again the RCMP moved in. This time they arrested Atkinson and stormed the newsroom at CFCY Radio, where they seized tapes of an interview Atkinson had given at the station. Atkinson was charged with conspiracy, but the charges were subsequently dropped.

Underlying the NFU protests ran a current of unease over the direction in which the agriculture industry seemed to be heading. In 1969, a Federal Task Force on Agriculture produced a landmark report that called for increased "industrialization" of agriculture. The NFU regarded the report as a frontal assault on the future of the family farm, on farming as a way of life, and on the very fabric of rural Canada. The problems in agriculture were endemic. For example, Seabrook Farms, a potato processor located in New Annan, had declared bankruptcy earlier in 1971, owing money to farmers. As it was, many other farmers barely broke even that year because of disastrous potato prices. So the downward spiral of the family farm continued, accelerated by the agricultural programs under the Development Plan. Between 1966 and 1971, the Island lost a farmer a day; the number of farms had dropped from 6,357 in 1966 to 4,543 by 1971; and the farming population dropped from one-third of the province's total to less than twenty percent. Of the remaining farms, one-third were marginal at best, earning gross incomes of less than $2,500.

Even the Department of Agriculture acknowledged the serious crisis faced by farmers. Its 1971-72 annual report noted that the agricultural economy "has undergone a very trying economic depression." By the early seventies, the agriculture industry – the "economic engine" of the Development Plan – had run into serious difficulty. It was not supposed to be that way. The original aim of the Plan's agriculture program was to double the net value added by the industry in a period of five to seven years, to be accomplished by farm consolidation. As a result of this measure, the government forecast improvements in production practices, increased mechanization, greater specialization, and more aggressive marketing strategies that would place agriculture as a leading growth industry in the provincial economy. Through a significantly expanded extension staff, the Department of Agriculture offered many new programs to help farmers adjust to the new agricultural economy.

The NFU demonstration underlined the serious tensions building in the province over these changes. While the NFU worried about the future of the family farm and the place of agriculture in the Island's economy, other people shared similar concerns about the threats to other aspects of Island life once considered sacrosanct. The nostalgic rhetoric upholding the Island's traditional way of life was fading in the face of the cool, unrelenting logic of transformation. To these people, the demise of the "Island way of life" was not being reversed but accelerated, not cursed but celebrated.

The future of the family farm had become synonymous with the future of the Island itself. Criticisms of government agricultural policy stung Campbell more deeply perhaps than any other single issue. Government policy was driving the loss of family farms, it was charged. In reality, the family farm of 1900 had already disappeared, just as the family farm of 1950 had faced extinction. Throughout those years, farmers had been forced to make changes in their operations through expansion, mechanization, specialization, and higher financial capitalization. The Development Plan only facilitated that process. But rational explanations of the need for change proved to be no match for the emotional rhetoric which feared it. Despite the inevitability of change, the Campbell government became fixated on saving the family farm.

The early seventies witnessed the emergence of lively and divisive debate over the future direction of the province. Although governments had always faced criticism, never before had such an outpouring of protest gushed from such a wide range of people. It is a cruel irony of politics that when confronted with change – even for the better – people cling to the familiar and curse those who try to help. The surge in public outcry caught many in government by surprise, even though Campbell himself had been actively encouraging the public to get involved. "I was calling for public participation," Campbell recalled, "but it was coming and it made its presence felt."

This increase in public engagement marked one of the most important changes that occurred in Island society during the Campbell administration. The citizens were finally learning to throw aside their traditional deferential attitudes and obsequious behaviours, and were demanding to be heard. Tractor demonstrations, strikes, protests, and a cacophony of public comment became commonplace. Politics in Prince Edward Island was no longer a purely spectator sport.

*   *   *

Islanders looked askance at the new Kitten Club at the Brudenell Resort. An Ontario company, Kitten Lounges, obtained a lease to operate the dining and bar services at the new resort in Roseneath. Perhaps inspired by the Playboy Bunnies, the Kitten Club featured hostesses in cat suits complete with ears, whiskers and tails. This style of hostess stood out in stark contrast to the bucolic image of the "Land of Anne." It was a tangible sign that a new tourism industry was taking hold.

An Ontario company called Kitten Lounges was given a lease by the provincial government to operate the dining and bar services at the new Brudenell Resort. Its hostesses were dressed in cat suits, replete with ears, whiskers and tails. Some people felt it did not reflect the image the Island was trying to present.

Although visitors had been coming to the Island to enjoy the countryside and the cool sea breezes for many years, the development of tourism as a real industry had never been given serious consideration. The first department of tourism was not established until 1960 under the Shaw government, providing some impetus for new tourism operations to spring up to accommodate and entertain the growing numbers of visitors, aided by the development of organized marketing campaigns. The Development Plan, however, went further than just marketing the province. Under the Plan, the government took its place as a major investor in the tourism industry to help guide and shape its direction. Tourism objectives now included a more even distribution of tourists throughout the Island; investment in accommodations and recreational facilities (such as resorts in Brudenell and, later, Mill River); and improved financial and marketing support for the private sector. The government also attempted to prevent unsightly development, and instituted signage regulations to preserve the beauty of the Island's landscape and communities.

With the impetus provided by the Shaw government in the sixties, the tourism industry underwent rapid changes during that decade. The enthusiastic amateurs of earlier times gave way to second-rate hucksters who developed theme parks, wildlife parks, go-cart tracks, miniature railways, playgrounds, mini-golf courses, castles, canteens, craft outlets, wax museums, historic replicas, and other attractions and facilities designed to amaze, amuse and impoverish tourists. An article published in the *Star Weekly* in November 1971 entitled "Tourist Traps, Billboards and a Plaster Kangeroo" offered a vivid warning that the Island's unspoiled landscape and rural innocence faced the threat of rape and prostitution. Even the aesthetics of the Island's development were called into question. Angry at the replacement of old fish shacks at the North Rustico harbour by nondescript structures clad in metal siding, Island artist Marc Gallant phoned Campbell at his cottage in Stanley Bridge one Saturday night to protest the desecration of the charm and unique architecture so long part of the community.

Ann Simon, a tourism industry analyst from Massachusetts, gave a public lecture in Charlottetown in November 1973 in which she warned about the impact of unbridled tourism development. Pointing to what befell regions such as Cape Cod, she suggested that too much tourism development was akin to being "a little bit pregnant." Provincial tourism planners were also concerned about the industry's ad hoc growth and haphazard development, poorly supported with inadequate services and facilities. Henceforth, according to the tourism development strategy, the Island's best features – from its pastoral charm to its cultural attractions – were to be managed as "resources."

The notion that Islanders themselves were considered "resources" in the "cultural landscape" rankled a few. As part of the 1973 season's tourism marketing strategy, the Department of Environment and Tourism introduced a "Sidewalk Ambassador" program designed to enlist the support of Islanders to make the province more appealing and hospitable to tourists. The "Sidewalk Ambassadors" concept was supported by a brochure outlining ways the public could help.* One piece of advice encouraged Islanders to "speak slowly and distinctly (but don't 'shout') when assisting a foreign visitor." According to a member of the Brothers and Sisters of Cornelius Howatt, the program "was so degrading, it was worthy of a Third World dictatorship trying to cow the natives into changing their behaviour."

Although tourism promised new growth and jobs, some people regarded the industry as an intrusion into their lifestyle. They pointed out that tourism exacerbated seasonal employment, and worried that the inherent dignity of those employed in worthy pursuits such as agriculture and the fishery would be turned into "a pandering people – a province of flunkies and attendants." Another bone of contention, that tourism would contribute to land use conflicts, was exemplified by the case of a farmer who wanted to construct a piggery near the Mill River Resort but who was denied an application for a building permit. He won his appeal to the Land Use Commission, but the issue heightened concerns that the continued growth of tourism would result in further restrictions on farmers. Even the decision to locate a swimming pool at the Mill River Resort led to consternation among local residents. The community had been lobbying for a swimming pool at a local school, so the Mill River project was perceived to be in competition with the one proposed for the school.

In response to growing concerns about the effect tourism would have on the Island, the Campbell government commissioned an

---

* *It was suggested the brochure also be posted for information in churches and synagogues. Although the Island had lots of churches, no synagogues were found.*

economic consulting group, Abt Associates of Cambridge, Massachusetts, to conduct an impact study. The report attempted to identify an acceptable level of tourism, and a framework for the management of future growth. The report noted that over seventy-five percent of Islanders wanted to keep tourism growth under three percent annually, far short of the envisaged rate of ten percent. People were also voicing fears about the consequences of unbridled tourism growth on the landscape. Campbell, who had vacationed in Bermuda, was impressed with the controlled development and quality of the tourism industry on that island, and became concerned that Prince Edward Island likewise be saved from degenerating into a tasteless wasteland.

Other initiatives besides tourism met with only a lukewarm reception from those concerned about protecting the "Island way of life." The government believed that major efforts should be undertaken to diversify the economy and create new jobs, especially for those being displaced from the traditional industries. Under one of Campbell's most accomplished and visionary ministers, Dr. John Maloney, the provincial government embarked on an aggressive program to attract new manufacturing and other industrial enterprises to the Island. The centrepiece of Maloney's efforts was the West Royalty Industrial Park, which contained the necessary infrastructure to accommodate a range of businesses. Maloney and his officials went prospecting across North America and Europe for footloose businesses, offering them incentives to relocate to Prince Edward Island. The industrial park soon became home to a wide range of companies manufacturing skis, jeans, magnesium wheels, metal products, chemicals, eyeglasses, and many other products not indigenous to the Island.

By 1979, no fewer than twenty-three companies had established themselves in the West Royalty Industrial Park, and more had been attracted to other communities across the province. However, industrial diversification on that scale was a risky strategy, so there were bound to be failures. True to form, critics assailed the government's industry development program from all sides. They felt it detracted support from traditional businesses and industrial sectors, and resented the financial assistance offered to business people who had no previous connection to the Island. In the election campaign of 1974, the Conservatives promised to abolish or drastically revamp the industrial development program.

PARO

The West Royalty Industrial Park represented the provincial government's efforts to diversify the economy and create employment.

Once more, Islanders found themselves in a state of vacillation, yearning for but distrusting modernization, just as they celebrated yet loathed certain aspects of the "Island way of life." Campbell described this contradiction as a "Jekyll and Hyde schizophrenic complex." On the one hand, Islanders valued a "quiet, rustic and rural community;" on the other, they desired "cars, paved roads, services, T.V. – all the advantages of urban developed areas." Nowhere was this inherent conflict more visible than in the often acrimonious debates about school consolidation.

*   *   *

The Prince Edward Island school system had remained basically unchanged since 1852, when the Liberal government of George Coles, the first premier following the inception of responsible government, introduced the Free Education Act. Recognizing that access to education was crucial for the development of the colony in its early years, Coles placed it at the top of his government's agenda.

This one-room school in Brooklyn was one of more than 400 around the Island which were closed in the wake of consolidation.

Despite the importance attached to education, educational standards remained drastically uneven across the Island. Some 475 school districts had been organized, their boundaries defined by what was considered a reasonable walking distances, or along ethnic, religious or linguistic lines.* Although some outstanding success stories survived from that early period, for the most part the system suffered from poorly trained teachers, sporadic attendance, high dropout rates, a minimal curriculum, and primitive facilities. Administration was left in the hands of local trustees, many of who were indifferent to their responsibilities. The system was inefficient at best, and operating on a shaky financial structure. Expenditures per student were the lowest in Canada, less than half the national average.

* By 1966, a total of 412 schools administered by 403 school boards were operating in the province, as well as fifteen regional high schools established by the Alex Matheson government and continued under the Shaw government. In addition, eight smaller consolidated schools served the elementary level in areas where districts had pooled their resources.

The education system was rudimentary. In 1889, school inspector John Arbuckle observed that "in many cases it is the survival of the cheapest rather than the fittest." In particular, the one-room schools themselves lacked many basic amenities, which prompted school inspector L.W. Shaw in the 1920s to endorse Arbuckle's view with the comment that "many farmers would hesitate to winter their stock in some of the school buildings I have visited." But while the one-room schools may have come to occupy a mythological place in the hearts of Islanders, beneath the veneer of their romantic image lurked a harsher reality. Typical of these schools was the one in Glengarry in western Prince County. Campbell visited the school one day and noted that cardboard boxes had been nailed to the walls to provide insulation.

Nonetheless, the school system played an integral part in local communities. The government provided basic expenses for teachers' salaries and set minimal standards, but the communities hired the teachers, supplemented their salaries, maintained the buildings, and oversaw the teacher's practices. In effect, the school became an extension of the home, reflecting community norms, values and traditions.

The Campbell government recognized the relationship between education and economic growth, and soon made education the centerpiece of the Development Plan. In 1970, shortly after the Plan was signed, an Educational Planning Unit was established within the Department of Education. It included teachers, trustees, parents, and educational administrators from several sources: the department, the University of Prince Edward Island, and Holland College. The Educational Planning Unit acknowledged that the nineteenth-century network of little one-room schoolhouses could not possibly respond to the administrative, financial and pedagogical demands of a modern educational system, or keep pace with the requirements of a growing economy.

Thus began a radical overhaul of the entire educational system. In the early '70s, the existing 403 school boards were abolished and replaced by five regional administrative units. At the same time, the government took over financing the entire cost of education to ensure a more even standard across the province, and announced a massive program of school consolidation to replace the one-room schools. Further, the government introduced new measures to improve teacher qualifications and expand the curriculum.

The upgrading of the educational system, together with school consolidation, clearly reflected Campbell's belief that education was critical to the success of the modernization thrust under the Development Plan. However, the inclusion of education – a provincial jurisdiction – was fiercely resisted by federal negotiators, and became a *sine qua non* for the provincial government. Donovan Russell, chair of the Educational Planning Unit, expressed his views of the importance attached to education in 1970. "[It] was viewed, perhaps for the first time in the Province, as a powerful engine for development, and an investment which would yield high dividends," he remarked. "The stage was set for more than just an evolutionary reform of the school system. Conditions were right for education in Prince Edward Island to leap from the nineteenth century to the cutting edge."

It was a risky political move for the Campbell government. The educational reforms it planned to introduce would end more than a century of local control. More than four hundred "school boards" and the local trustees who ruled them would be pushed aside to make way for a new model and approach to education. In effect, the government was declaring the one-room country schoolhouse – the centre of the community – redundant.

This set the stage for a confrontation with local communities. Not only were they losing control over their children's education, but now they had to send their children to be educated outside the community. A new educational system – modern, urban and centralized – was about to displace the traditional, rural, communitarian system. On the one hand, parents and concerned citizens recognized the need to improve education to better equip students for the world beyond, and were ambivalent about criticizing reforms; on the other hand, they wanted to maintain local control. By making consolidation an integral part of educational reform, the planners created a dilemma for their critics. Rejecting consolidation meant rejecting reform. Embracing consolidation meant giving up control. The idea that a model more appropriate to the Island might be possible did not occur to them.

The clash of values soon manifested itself in protests against loss of control and loss of schools. At the root of these protests was the fear of loss of the community itself. The traditional school system played a key role in the transmission of a community's collective values and outlook. At stake was a new vision of Island life and society. Many people felt that the loss of the local school would drive the very nerve centre out of small rural communities. While large schools brought resources together, they foresaw communities torn apart. After all, they had already witnessed the loss of farms, stores, services, and residents. Closure of the local school would remove yet another pillar on which their well-being rested. "The net effect of school reorganization is to destroy what future rural areas have," lamented economist Jim MacNiven, formerly of the Atlantic Provinces Economic Council, who conducted an evaluation of the educational program. "The children are trained to leave by the structure of the school, if not by the curriculum. The end result ... is that the rural areas generally become extensions of urban areas."

People soon organized protests on the issue of school consolidation. Concerned Citizens for Education, an ad hoc group critical of the plan for school consolidation, emphasized the importance of preserving the best features of small, local schools and adapting new educational technologies and practices to them. They argued for a more compatible approach that would maintain what they perceived as distinctive and valuable in rural communities. They challenged the premise that "bigger is better."

Despite this opposition, the school boards faced a general public by now more or less persuaded of the need for reform (or who had simply given up the fight) and they became willing accomplices of the educational planners; in fact, they became key instruments in the drive to consolidation. Backed by a pro-consolidation government and lured by financial incentives, they undertook to complete the move towards consolidation in their respective school units. In the process, they faced pockets of continuing opposition. The bitter fights dragged on as community after community came under the threat of school closures. As protests mounted by parents and concerned citizens increased, the provincial Home and School Association requested the government to call a moratorium on further consolidations.

The Campbell government found itself fighting for consolidation on another front as well. Schools in Charlottetown and Summerside were facing an increase in enrollment and were in danger of becoming overcrowded as families migrated to urban areas. In reaction, angry parents demanded that these schools be expanded in order to cope with the problem, only to be told that school construction priorities had been directed to the establishment of consolidated schools in rural areas. To smooth the waters, Campbell personally appeared before an irate group of parents at Colonel Grey High School in Charlottetown to defend the government's education plans.

The decision to establish a new, centrally located high school in west Prince County also provoked controversy among the major communities in the area, each seeking the school in its proximity. Education Minister Gordon Bennett dithered and vacillated over the location, in turn alienating citizens in O'Leary, Alberton and Tignish. When the litany of complaints reached the cabinet table, a red-faced Bennett left the room; twenty minutes later his secretary appeared with his letter of resignation. Campbell dispatched Bruce Stewart and Elmer Blanchard to Bennett's summer home in Stanhope; they convinced him to return to cabinet. The fact is that, in the 1970s, the minister of education held the most unenviable job in the provincial government.

The battle lines were drawn over the future of education: bigger versus better; rural versus urban; community versus educators. Compromises, however, proved difficult. For instance, in February 1977, the Unit II School Board voted to remove grades seven and eight from Borden area schools and transfer them to Summerside, which would have resulted in the closure of three small schools. A bitter controversy between parents, citizens, and the school board ensued for more than a year, but the board did not back down. Not only Education Minister Bennett Campbell, but Premier Campbell himself, intervened in an effort to bring both sides closer together. Eventually, it was agreed to leave the two grades in Borden, so only two of the three smaller schools closed down. It was typical of the battles carried out across the province during this period. Yet, by the time the forces opposing consolidation had coalesced, it was too late for compromises. With rare exceptions (in places like St. Teresa and Grand Tracadie) the small schools were uprooted from their communities and disappeared. The one-room schools were gone.

School consolidation illustrated the complete transformation of an education system that had been in place since the nineteenth century – one of the clearest demonstrations of the Development Plan's goal to modernize every facet of Island life. Piece by piece, the last vestiges of the old order were being dismantled. The now empty one-room schools stood as silent witnesses to a way of life that was no more.

*   *   *

Politics is the art of the possible. As Campbell and the Liberals headed into the 1974 election campaign, they put behind the polemical rants and the philosophical debates of the early, heady days of the Development Plan. The uncompromising logic and internal consistency of planners and plans was giving way to the language and largesse of politicians and politics.

In its conception, the Development Plan was breathtakingly rational, its synchronicity designed to move the province forward in lock-step fashion, the pieces fitting together in a coherent new shape and order. But eventually, it all came unravelled. The Plan, which held such hope and promise, ultimately faded away under the glare of political expediency, cynicism, and common sense. It soon became an elaborate mechanism to obtain federal funds. But at least it had stimulated some effort to turn around the long-stagnant economy.

Successful politicians know themselves and their times. "Bread and butter issues are more important to Islanders than a general debate on whether the Development Plan has been good or bad," Campbell told a news conference when he announced the election for April 29. The announcement came one hour after the Legislature had been dissolved on the afternoon of April 3. In toning down the rhetoric over the merits of the Development Plan, Campbell was preparing to run the campaign with greater emphasis on his government's record of the past four years.

Just the day before, Provincial Treasurer Earle Hickey had announced the government's fifth surplus budget in a row, indicative of the province's improved financial position. Total estimated expenditures amounted to $150 million, with a surplus close to $500,000. The provincial debt now stood at $74 million, which was actually less than it was five years before. The massive infusion of federal cash through the Development Plan had helped the government to introduce many new programs and services. It was a good-news budget, with cuts in property taxes as well as a sales tax exemption on clothing, footwear, and other essentials – all aimed at reducing the alarming increase in the cost of living resulting from higher inflation and, more worrisome, rising energy costs. Campbell summarized the thrust of the budget as dealing with living costs and continued economic development.

Throughout its second term, the government had been kept busy countering criticisms over a wide range of development issues, from agriculture to industrial development to school consolidation. These years had also sharpened Campbell's political instincts and his self-confidence, imbuing his leadership with a much more pragmatic tone.

In 1970, he campaigned on a platform to improve the standard of living while preserving the quality of life for Islanders, and had learned that reconciling those two goals was a difficult balancing act.

In 1972, for example, after having faced a barrage of criticism from the National Farmers Union and other agricultural leaders over the direction of the agriculture industry, Campbell himself took over the agriculture portfolio and made the unprecedented step of devoting the entire Speech from the Throne to farming.* The government used the Throne Speech to demonstrate its commitment to the family farm, the most sacrosanct institution in Island life, announcing a new family farm program that included capital grants and support for new farmers. Campbell declared that the Throne Speech, with its singular emphasis, was "intended to do everything in its power to stem the tide which is eroding away the family farm."

* * *

This refrain ran like a thread throughout the government's second term. The pre-election budget document of 1974 described the family farm program as "the foundation of the Island way of life." In agriculture, as in other issues, the Campbell government stressed the importance of the Development Plan as a way of supporting that way of life. The Plan, Campbell suggested later, was "a very flexible way of addressing economic opportunities."

The 1974 campaign illustrated just how flexible. Early in the campaign, the Liberals took out a full-page ad in Island newspapers under the heading "Our Record," which trumpeted its achievements since coming to office – "a record," claimed the Liberals, "of progress, development and prosperity unequalled in Island history." The list was impressive: tax cuts for property owners and consumers; supplements to family allowances; $5 million for family farms; support for commodity boards; a new grain elevator in Kensington; low-interest loans for farmers; new holding, handling, storage, and haulout facilities for fishermen; market development initiatives for the primary industries; new government agencies devoted to land use, women's issues, and the environment; forgivable loans for small businesses; support for job training; support for the construction of

---

* Daniel J. MacDonald, the previous agriculture minister, had resigned to seek a federal seat in the Cardigan riding. He won, and went on to become Canada's Minister of Veterans Affairs.

The 1974 Liberal campaign slogan -"Action now ... and for the future."
(Cartoon by Robert Tuck)

R.C.Tuck/PARO

nearly 1,500 new homes and 4,679 home improvement projects; the construction of 273 co-op houses and 286 new senior citizens houses; improvements in transportation, with twenty-five percent of the province's roads paved in the last eight years; a fifty-percent increase in grants to municipalities; five new elected school boards; the full costs of education transferred to the provincial government under the Foundation Program; a comprehensive medicare program, including the first dental care program in Canada; and the first full-time department of labour. "The Liberal government is proud of the action we have taken to promote the good way of life which is the treasured possession of all Islanders," an ad predictably declared, adding that Campbell's government stood for action now and for the future.

The platform, however, received an unplanned addition. Following the passage of the ill-fated Public Gatherings Act in 1971, Jack MacAndrew, artistic director of the Confederation Centre of the Arts, became very critical of the way the Campbell government bungled the issue. He had worked on the 1970 Liberal campaign, but distanced himself from the Liberals after 1971. With the help of a number of other people, he established the first civil liberties organization in the province's history. But as the 1974 campaign entered the planning stage, the Liberals invited him back to help and he agreed. One of MacAndrew's first tasks was to take the list of Liberal campaign promises and shape them into a cohesive platform. As he worked on the "we will" list given to him by the campaign team, he quietly added one of his own. At the next meeting, Campbell reviewed the draft platform and noticed MacAndrew's addition – the establishment of the province's first Human Rights Commission. Campbell smiled and nodded his agreement; the commitment became part of the Liberal election platform.

The government had faced a number of serious issues leading up to the 1974 election, some of which it had badly mishandled. These issues related to the family farm; school consolidation; disputes with organizations such as the National Farmers Union and the Rural Development Council; the move to industrialization; land use policies; and other major changes that made it seem to Islanders as though all the familiar landmarks were being summarily torn down and replaced. The government also faced its first whiff of scandal. A well-known Liberal entrepreneur, Harry MacLauchlan, had faced criticism over his purchase and subsequent quick resale to Parks Canada of a tourist resort in Brackley Beach. Although the affair did not touch Campbell personally, it did provoke controversy.

A poll taken by Ben Crow in 1972 showed Campbell at the lowest ebb of his popularity since becoming premier. Therefore, at the urging of his advisors before the start of the 1974 election campaign, Campbell brought Andy Wells back from the Council of Maritime Premiers (where he had gone following his disagreement over the brouhaha associated with the Public Gatherings Act). Wells helped refocus the government's energies and cleaned up some of the political fallout from the past two years. For his part, Campbell took to the road in a motor home, and throughout April criss-crossed the sixteen electoral districts in a whirlwind tour, constantly on the move, pressing the flesh, meeting as many Islanders as he could visiting wharves, farms, factories, businesses, homes, coffee shops, street corners, impromptu gatherings, rallies – anywhere people were gathered, all the while dispensing his not inconsiderable charm.

In this election Campbell faced a new opposition leader. In November 1971, after failing to win his own seat in the 1970 election, George Key had resigned as Conservative leader. This time Campbell faced Mel McQuaid, a Souris lawyer and former MP. McQuaid did all he could to cast suspicion on the Liberal record. During the campaign, he made use of leaked evaluation reports on the Development Plan, alleging that it was falling well short of the ambitious targets set at the outset, and challenged the government to table the reports before the election date. Campbell brushed the criticisms aside, insisting that the reports had to be read in context. "The Tories aren't a very exciting party, but it's good to have them there for the sake of comparison," Campbell mischievously told the *Guardian*. In turn, one of the newspaper's editorials lightly questioned why, in light of Campbell's momentum, the Liberals bothered to campaign at all.

In fact, the election campaign might not have happened that time at all. From his place in the Legislature, Dr. John Maloney, who was a skilled physician, was making concerned notes about external signs of McQuaid's health. Naturally, the Liberals were not keen to call an election if McQuaid were likely to be taken ill. On the day appointed to call the election, the Liberals anxiously waited to see if McQuaid would turn up at the Legislature. He did, and John Brehaut, waiting with the Liberal ads outside the *Journal-Pioneer* office in Summerside, received a phone call giving him the go-ahead to place the ads.

As expected, on April 29 the Campbell Liberals won an overwhelming victory, winning twenty-six of the thirty-two seats – only the second government in the province's history (and the first in the twentieth century) – to win three elections in a row. All of Campbell's ministers were re-elected, and were joined by newcomers such as Catherine Callbeck and George Henderson. The *Guardian* concluded that "the opposition did not make sufficient impression on the electorate in general which opted to stay with the party in power rather than risk whatever shake-up a different administration might make with the comprehensive development plan." Nonetheless, the New Democratic Party under leader Aquinas Ryan made its strongest showing ever. It fielded twenty candidates, Ryan himself capturing close to twenty percent of the popular vote. The NDP had attracted a number of disaffected voters who felt the Campbell government had badly mishandled development policies. The surprising strength of the NDP unsettled the Liberals. Publicly, Campbell dismissed suggestions that the NDP, and to some extent the Conservatives, had capitalized on discontent with the government and the more controversial aspects of the Development Plan. On the Tuesday following the election, he declared that the opposition parties had honed in too much on the specific complaints of minority groups.

The campaign gave Campbell a chance to talk personally to Islanders about their future and to listen to their concerns. He remained philosophical about many of the controversies that had swirled about the Development Plan over the past four years. "No progress is possible anywhere without stresses and strains and now that we are more aware of them I think you can expect some surprises and changes," he announced. Little did Islanders realize what "surprises and changes" were in store for them during Campbell's next term in office.

*   *   *

Campbell's third cabinet (1974-78). (From left): *Dr. John Maloney, George Proud, Bruce Stewart, Dr. Bud Ings, Campbell, George Henderson, Arthur MacDonald, Bennett Campbell, Catherine Callbeck, Gilbert Clements.*

The Pie-faced Kid, the satirical creation of the Brothers and Sisters of Cornelius Howatt, was not the only one concerned about what was happening to the identity of his beloved Island in the 1970s. Speaking during the Throne Speech debate in the Legislature on the eve of the 1970 provincial election, in what may go down as an important footnote in Island history, Premier Campbell announced the establishment of the Prince Edward Island Heritage Foundation. "One of the great contributions that we as Legislators and we as Islanders can make towards the celebration of our 1973 anniversary," he suggested, referring to upcoming plans for the centennial celebrations, "will be to identify more clearly the history and the historic items of significance within our province." Travelling throughout the Island, he said, "I have met on so many occasions, and I have witnessed the very deep and abiding interest which Prince Edward Islanders have in their Province and in the history and the traditions and the cultures which are Prince Edward Island, which comprise the fabric of our cultural life here in Prince Edward Island today." The Foundation would bring together all the groups, organizations and individuals who dealt with matters of historical significance to the Island.

In proposing the establishment of the Heritage Foundation to spearhead the commemoration of the Island's heritage and culture, Campbell wanted the centennial year celebrations to leave behind a legacy. The Centennial Commission had been promised $400,000 from the federal government for commemorative projects, and was busy deciding how these funds should be spent. Meanwhile, Campbell's tourism minister, Lorne Bonnell, proposed that the centennial funds be used for local community projects such as halls, rinks and other facilities. Although such politically popular projects had sprung up in great abundance during the 1967 Canadian centennial celebrations, Campbell was resolved not to repeat that type of project. He invited Jack MacAndrew and Fred Hyndman, a local insurance broker, to meet with him at his office and asked them to make a proposal to the Centennial Commission to establish a heritage endowment fund. After hearing both proposals, the Commission decided to establish the fund. The Heritage Foundation was now in business.

The funds earmarked for the centennial celebrations provided for the refurbishment of Beaconsfield, the Foundation's new headquarters in Charlottetown, and the restoration of three historic sites commemorating the Island's agricultural, fisheries and shipbuilding past at Orwell Corner, Basin Head and Green Park respectively. No previous government had so richly recognized and provided for the preservation of the Island's past.

The cynics pointed out a certain irony in the announcement, that the government that was about to dismantle so much of the Island's traditions was now its champion. Others suggested, even more cynically, that Campbell perceived the province's history as just another resource to be managed. Others, more sanguine, acknowledged the need for the province to maintain its roots with the past as it moved forward into the future.

A more profound explanation for Campbell's interest in preserving the province's heritage and culture emerged in 1973 as Islanders sought to assert their identity. Alex Campbell and the Pie-faced Kid were actually brothers-in-arms.

To Restore the Lands, Protect the Seas, And Inform the Earth's Stewards

an ark for prince edward island

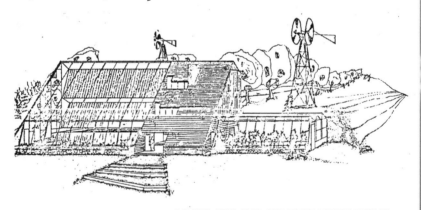

A FAMILY–SIZED FOOD, ENERGY AND HOUSING COMPLEX, INCLUDING INTEGRATED SOLAR, WINDMILL, GREENHOUSE, FISH CULTURE AND LIVING COMPONENTS

CHAPTER THIRTEEN

"Small is ... practical"

On a warm, sunny afternoon in September 1976, a large crowd gathered at Spry Point, a picturesque piece of land jutting out into Boughton Bay on the Island's east coast. Visitors, guests, and media from all over the world – Europe, Africa, the United States, the rest of Canada, and all across Prince Edward Island – had travelled to be here on this day. They were attracted by the official opening of the Ark, a futuristic bio-shelter designed to produce food, energy, and an ecosystem containing examples of all the great kingdoms of life on the planet. According to one account, the Ark was one of the most innovative buildings in North America.

As the crowd watched in anticipation, a helicopter swooped down and landed in an adjacent field. Beneath the whirling blades, a diminutive figure emerged to be greeted by a young girl carrying a bouquet of flowers. Welcomed to the podium, Prime Minister Pierre Trudeau prepared to officially open this much-heralded project.

In his speech, Trudeau emphasized what an important moment this was in the history of the country, and that there was no more natural a place than Prince Edward Island for it to happen. "More than a hundred years ago the idea of Confederation was developed here and now I like to think that this Island which has shown hospitality to this political idea which created Canada is now providing hospitality to a new commitment, a commitment that the environmentalists refer to – and I think it's a beautiful phrase – as 'living lightly on the earth,'" he said.

The Ark was the brainchild of John Todd, who founded the Cape Cod-based New Alchemy Institute. Todd, a Canadian-born scientist and ecologist, described his work as "taking knowledge from many disciplines to achieve more ecological understanding of how to live in the world." Inspired by the work of visionaries such as Buckminster Fuller, Lewis Mumford and Rachel Carson, and influenced by movements as diverse as Buddhism and feminism, Todd and the members of the New Alchemy Institute (an eclectic group of scientists, hippies and architects) were intent on no less a challenge than reinventing civilization and breaking out of what they described as the "bondage of corporate money mindset."

During the Ark's official opening, Todd spoke eloquently of his hopes. "Here where the sea and the land and the wind and the sky come together there is a sense of place and there is a sense of the past," he declared. "There is a sense of what we have and our own limits. Perhaps it's through the sense of place and past that we can begin to design and create for the 21st century." The official opening of the Ark was a joyous, hopeful, promise-laden occasion. Although some of the media questioned Trudeau's use of an energy-guzzling helicopter to travel to the event, it did not dampen the enthusiasm of those who partied well into the night. For them it represented an exciting new beginning to society's understanding of how to live in harmony with the planet. The Ark became a symbol for those who believed it represented a practical alternative for a more sustainable future. While the earth was capable of producing in great abundance, they feared it could also be destroyed. Apparently Trudeau thought the same. During his speech, he quoted Indian chief Seattle who warned that "whatever befalls the earth will befall the sons of the earth."

The opening of the Ark in September 1976 attracted international attention. In front (left to right): *Premier Campbell, John Todd (founder of the New Alchemy Institute), Nancy Jack Todd and Prime Minister Trudeau.*

*   *   *

The Ark owed its existence to a fortuitous mix of timing, changing public awareness, and the need for political action related to the increasing energy crisis. Both federal and provincial governments were scrambling to find solutions to the rising costs of energy and the forecast depletion of non-renewable energy supplies. In both these areas, Prince Edward Island was especially vulnerable.

Then in early 1974, Andy Wells met John Todd at a conference in Ottawa. The two became friends and they began discussing a project to put some of Todd's theories to the test. The February 1974 issue of the *Canadian Magazine* reported that Todd "has his eye on PEI for another New Alchemy project – if he can drum up some grant money." In November, Todd prepared some preliminary plans for what he called a bio-shelter, which would serve as both a working home and a laboratory for an integrated research program including agriculture, aquaculture and renewable energy.

The project Todd had in mind was radical. He believed that the world's economy was on the verge of collapse, which would result in an imminent and massive transformation in society. He outlined his proposal in a twelve-page paper entitled "Weathering Collapsing Global Economic Systems: A Blueprint for PEI." In this paper, he expressed his belief that the industrial world was teetering on a razor's edge. "Because Prince Edward Island is land-based, non-industrial, has tillable soils and more or less owns her own lands, she is perhaps the most fortunate of all regions in the west, particularly as she does not have a large industrial population to care for," he wrote.

In the early 1970s, the Island's bucolic setting and traditional way of life had strong appeal for many people who sought a simpler life. The province became a mecca for those – draft dodgers, hippies, environmentalists and back-to-the-landers – who wanted to escape the excesses of modern society, including industrialization and militarism, materialism and imperialism, pollution and nuclear threats, and other societal ills. It was a time of intensified concern about a dying planet, when even good growth had its limits and many were "dreaming in green." A climate of apocalypse and rebirth permeated the planet; putting down roots in Prince Edward Island, these most recent residents discussed and attempted to practice a new way of living in the world. They were also attracted by the small scale of Island society, a place where people could live at a humanly manageable level, where living closer to a democratic ideal might be possible, and where even the Premier had embraced the idea that "small is beautiful."

In 1975, with Wells' assistance, the federal Department of Urban Affairs granted $354,000 to the New Alchemy Institute to construct a demonstration project encompassing the working home and research laboratory contained in its initial proposal. The provincial government contributed Crown-owned land at Spry Point, and construction soon began under the direction of two young, creative architects, Yale graduate David Bergmark and Massachusetts Institute of Technology-trained Ole Hammarlund. The Ark was designed to be self-sufficient and demonstrate how the food, shelter and power needs of urban and rural families could be supplied in a single structure. When the complex was completed (just hours before the official opening), David Bergmark and his partner, Nancy Willis, moved in with their two children and pet dog. Their new home came complete not only with running water, electricity, and the latest appliances, but also grape vines, fig trees, and other assorted

The Ark was described as one of the most innovative buildings in North America. The New Alchemy Institute named it a "bio-shelter." It was designed to produce food and energy, and act as a working home and laboratory for an integrated research program, including agriculture, aquaculture, and renewable energy.

plants and vegetables; a 2,500-square-foot commercial greenhouse; 3,500-gallon fish tanks to grow thousands of fish indoors; 36 solar collectors; three tanks under the living room floor containing 60,000 gallons of water to store enough heat to keep the place warm for a month; a windmill facing the ocean to generate electricity; and extensive plots of land to evaluate organic agricultural practices. During a tour of the facility that glorious September afternoon of 1976, Trudeau confided to Willis that this was the kind of place in which he and his wife, Margaret, would like to live.

Environmentalists around the world watched intently as the project unfolded. As it progressed, it attracted media interest as diverse as the *Globe and Mail* and the *Financial Post* national newspapers; a Swedish televison network; *Science, Harrowsmith,* and *Chatelaine* magazines; and the *New York Times.* Even film crews came from around the world. Up to six hundred visitors a week came to see the Ark, some out of sheer curiosity, others genuinely interested to view what was called "reverential ecology." (Inevitably, Bergmark and Willis were sometimes awoken in their bedroom in the early morning by less-than-reverential visitors anxious for a glimpse of what it was like to live in an Ark.)

For a time in the 1970s as the project matured, the Ark came to represent a beacon for those who believed in a better world. *Saturday Night* magazine quoted Arthur Cordell, co-director of the International Conserver Society project, who was deeply impressed with the Ark's pioneering approach. "As the Ark is to PEI, so PEI can be to Canada, so Canada can be to the rest of the world," he enthused. Canada's smallest province was emerging as a world leader in the movement to "live lightly on the earth." Thanks to the Ark and other energy initiatives, Prince Edward Island came to be referred to as an "international eco-centre." Amory Lovins, the world-renowned scientist and alternate energy advocate, visited the Island in 1976 to speak to members of the Legislature during a special four-day hearing on energy issues, and applauded the leadership the province was taking on energy and related issues. "You really are in the lead within Canada and I think compared to nearly all countries," he declared. "Your experiment here is clearly attracting much interest in the rest of Canada and the rest of the world. I have been in many countries recently where people stood up and asked 'What is happening in Prince Edward Island, how is that going? We are very interested in it; we want to learn from it.' I think your influence on this continent can be much greater than you realize."

The Ark was not perhaps the best example of Prince Edward Island's bold experiment to reshape society, but it was the most tangible and enduring one. For a time, it represented Premier Campbell's vision not of a new society but a new direction for society. Confronted with the most serious energy crisis in the history of the province, Campbell took the unprecedented step of turning not to Ottawa for help but to the Island's innate capacity for survival on its own. Pursuing alternate energy strategies would "return to the Island much of the resourcefulness and wisdom of our pioneer ancestors," he pointed out. Rather than ask what Canada could do for Prince Edward Island, Campbell was suggesting what Prince Edward Island could do by showing Canada and the rest of the world a new path towards sustainability and stewardship. In a society that mostly took energy for granted, politicians often lacked the courage and vision to explore ways of cultivating a new ethic. In those heady days, Prince Edward Island was well on the way to becoming the world leader in conservation and renewable energy.

Optimism filled the air from the opening ceremony on that large September afternoon in 1976, but it would not last long. Right from the start, the Ark was beset with problems. It could never hope to achieve the grandiose expectations of its founders. For instance, the technologies utilized in the windmills and solar panels were still in their infancy so these systems never worked as they should (according to one observer, they were "more bleeding than leading"). And with inadequate funding for its ambitious research program, the Ark was in financial jeopardy from the day it opened. Neither did it quite overcome the inherent skepticism of Islanders, some of whom wanted to close down the road and shut off the power to Spry Point for the winter to see how long it could survive on its own. The perception held by local residents that a bunch of American hippies were living on government dollars didn't help the cause either, despite the best efforts of those associated with the project to share their research findings with the public. Islanders may have been proud that the Ark was attracting so much attention to their province, but they were not willing to stand by its side.

The project suffered from internal strains as well. Once the Ark was established, confusion reigned about what to do next. Underlying tensions developed between its dual roles as a demonstration project and as a serious research facility. Within a year, its original residents moved out, seeking escape from the thousands of visitors who regularly showed up to get a glimpse of the way of the future. And there were deeper, more pervasive issues. Federal and provincial governments, then and later, never took the Ark's environmental agenda seriously enough. They lacked commitment to the ideals that had spawned the project, and distanced themselves from it. The situation was exacerbated by energy officials in the provincial government who were indifferent, short-sighted, and totally incompetent to deal with the energy challenges of the day.

On July 30, 1981, the Ark project died. By then, one of the most pressing issues that had led to its creation – high energy prices – had evaporated as oil markets stabilized and people went back to their old ways. The truth was that the Ark was less connected to the realities of life in Prince Edward Island than it was to global environmental concerns. Even some of its more loyal supporters began drifting away. The provincial government announced that the land and buildings, valued at $175,000, would be sold. The fish tanks were drained, the organic test plots abandoned, the gates padlocked. The experiment in alternate living was over. Today, the Ark remains in spirit only – part myth, part legend – a testament to the failed hopes and dreams of a gentler world.

*   *   *

Prince Edward Island's foray into the field of alternate energy began thousands of miles and political light-years away. In October 1973, eleven Middle Eastern nations, members of the Organization of Petroleum Exporting Countries (OPEC), placed an embargo on oil exports to the United States, Canada, and other nations that had sided with Israel during the 1967 Six-Day War. Since OPEC controlled fifty-five percent of the world's oil output, this move drove the world market price of crude oil to new and unimagined heights. The cost of oil immediately rose by seventy percent; by December it had climbed by over one hundred and thirty percent, and later by more than two hundred percent. Crude oil, which was selling on world markets for approximately $2 a barrel, was now commanding over $20 a barrel. The economy of the western industrialized world, based on cheap energy, faced chaos and ruin.

All governments across Canada were spurred into action, scrambling to deal with the fear and panic created by the energy crisis.* Prince Edward Island was especially vulnerable to an energy crisis of this magnitude. It possessed no energy-generating capacity of its own, and Islanders – earning among the lowest per capita incomes in Canada – were already paying the highest energy costs in the country. Meanwhile, bureaucrats in the federal Department of Energy, Mines and Resources, used only to dealing with conventional issues of exploration, and supply and demand, were completely unprepared for this latest unexpected issue. All of a sudden, officials found themselves paying more than lip service to alternate and renewable energy. They launched a spate of new programs to help conserve energy. In Prince Edward Island, the government established a new agency called Enersave to help businesses and homeowners adopt energy conservation measures.**

*   *   *

Throughout the 1960s, people in the ecology movement asserted that humans needed to rethink their relationship with nature. Now, the energy crisis made this approach not only reasonable but necessary, and renewable and alternate energy quickly became fashionable. "Squandering energy is not a privilege of our way of life," said Trudeau to an apprehensive nation, "but a threat to it." Suddenly, energy conservation was everybody's business. The energy crisis coincided with a period in which many were beginning to seriously question the impacts of industrialization and modernization throughout the western world. Factories spewing pollution were contributing to environmental contamination, and the headlong rush to

---

* *Later, the federal government instituted a number of controversial measures to bring domestic prices below world levels. These included subsidies; the establishment of a new national energy company, Petro-Canada; and a divisive new national energy policy that pitted oil-producing provinces against those dependent on imports. This policy was especially despised in western Canada, where politicians expressed the hope that the "eastern bastards would freeze in the dark."*

** *The name originally proposed was Project Conserve, but this was quickly dropped when it was pointed out that the initials matched those of the opposition Progressive Conservative Party.*

Andy Wells, Campbell's closest political advisor, provided a philosophical streak that nicely matched Campbell's political pragmatism.

consumerism revealed now more than ever the emptiness and ugliness of a material world. People could build machines but they lacked a philosophy to use those machines humanely. A ruthless economic structure extracted huge personal costs, with a concomitant loss of dignity and meaning in people's lives. Rapid progress, according to social philosopher Lewis Mumford, was alienating man from nature, and ultimately from himself and the rest of society. In the relentless pursuit of progress, man "has lacked all direct contact with the sun and the sky and other living creatures, including his own," he stated.

The energy crisis, along with growing disillusionment over the supposed benefits of progress and modernization, had a deep impact on the Campbell government, inspired by the thinking of Andy Wells. Described as the Machiavelli to Campbell, the prince, Wells found in the Premier a receptive audience for his ideas and was soon putting his thoughts into Campbell's speeches. Wells was Campbell's most trusted and loyal advisor, who exhibited a philosophical streak that nicely complemented Campbell's political pragmatism. It was an ideal match. For his part, Campbell said of Wells that he could "put a striped blue suit on an airy-fairy subject."

Wells had arranged for the cabinet to watch a film by the Club of Rome based on its landmark study, *Limits to Growth*, which foresaw a world running out of resources. According to Wells, the events of the early 1970s forced a re-examination of many of the assumptions that had influenced the formulation of the Development Plan. A fundamental rethinking of alternatives had to take place: no growth versus rapid growth; decentralization versus centralization; self-sufficiency versus integration into a global economy. In short, the Development Plan was being turned on its head. By the time Campbell entered his third term of office in 1974, he had started to talk about the virtues of a conserver society. "My interest was stimulated by things which had come along in the early '70s," he recalled. "It was a direction that intrigued me." The original objectives and expectations of the Development Plan had to be reshaped, often in surprising ways. "In politics, if you're not running on you're going to get weary," said Campbell. He was now running on – and ahead.

In 1974, as the country was still reeling from the shock in energy prices, Campbell surprised his fellow premiers during a national energy conference by calling for an end to the subsidization of energy costs. Although Prince Edward Island was not a major player in the field of energy and had the most to gain by a subsidy, Campbell argued instead for conservation, explaining that lower costs would do little to discourage consumption. He repeated this argument the following year during the annual premiers' conference, and added a pitch for the development of alternate energy sources (prompting Alberta premier Peter Lougheed to exclaim, "Great speech, Alex, wrong forum!") In that same spirit, the Campbell government chose not to purchase a portion of the nuclear power plant in Point Lepreau, New Brunswick, even though construction of an underwater cable across the Northumberland Strait would have delivered much cheaper and more reliable power to the Island.

As the fallout from the energy crisis intensified, Campbell, Wells and others began to examine practical ways of turning the Island onto the path towards self-sufficiency. Following the 1974 election, he was invited to speak on "The Uses of Smallness" to a conference hosted by the Institute of Man and Science in Rensselaer, New York. This invitation came from a Massachusetts Institute of Technology engineering professor, Frank Davidson, whom he had previously met while investigating sources of funding for the construction of the causeway. Davidson had been involved in putting together the financial package for the English Channel tunnel and was willing to help arrange financing for a privately constructed Prince Edward Island causeway. At the conference, Campbell was impressed with the extensive range of scientific research being conducted on alternate and renewable energy. He began thinking that Prince Edward Island was ideally suited to research of this nature, so he invited Davidson and a group of New York City-based consultants whom he had met at the

PARO

A landmark meeting in 1974 laid the foundation for the provincial government's foray into renewable energy. Among Islanders attending the meeting were (back left) Andy Wells, Lynn Douglas (third from left, whom Wells later married), Anco Hamming (fourth from left), Campbell (centre), and (to his left) Dr. Ian MacQuarrie; Dr. Regis Duffy; Dr. John Maloney, Minister of Development; David Catmur, Department of Agriculture, and (front, third from right) Dr. Tom Connor, Deputy Minister of Development. The group also includes alternate energy consultants Campbell met at a conference in Rensselaer, New York, on "The Uses of Smallness."

conference to come to the Island and evaluate its potential as a laboratory for practical and applied research. During a two-day workshop in Charlottetown, attended by government, academic and private-sector representatives (such as Anco Hamming from the Federation of Agriculture, UPEI biology professor Ian MacQuarrie, and businessman Regis Duffy), the idea of an organization to carry out applied research was born.

In January 1975, Campbell announced the establishment of the Institute of Man and Resources, a non-profit organization incorporated by an act of the provincial legislature to research and demonstrate conservation and alternate energy technologies. To underline the intended non-partisan nature of the Institute, the act was sponsored jointly by Campbell and Opposition leader Mel McQuaid. The mandate of the Institute of Man and Resources was no less ambitious than to address solutions to alleviate the planet's growing energy and resource problems, and showcase Prince Edward Island to the rest of the world as an example of what could be accomplished. As Campbell said in introducing the legislation, the Institute would "exercise a coordinating and leadership role in the execution of demonstration projects, in the dissemination of information locally, nationally, internationally, in the assembly of knowledge and the testing and evaluation of alternate energy and food production systems."

With a start-up grant of $100,000 from the provincial government, the Institute embarked on a far-reaching, innovative program to analyze, invent, adapt and apply "socially desirable and ecologically sustainable" energy, food and crop production, and living and shelter systems. In the course of its brief life, it became "one of the most carefully planned and well-structured efforts at energy and self-sufficiency in existence anywhere in the Western world," according to Canadian historian Alan MacEachern. If the Institute of Man and Resources could not change the world, it would at least attempt to show it how to do things differently.

As Campbell told the annual meeting of the Science Council of Canada later that year in Brudenell, "We shall endeavour to reach a socially acceptable and useful balance between the societal trends of today and the less disruptive, more human attitudes and values of yesterday." Once again, Campbell found himself fully engaged in the effort to strike that elusive balance.

*   *   *

It is perhaps not surprising that the leader of Canada's smallest province, concerned about the consequences of a headlong rush towards modernization, would embrace a "small is beautiful" philosophy. Only recently, in 1973, that philosophy had been articulated by eminent British economist and Rhodes scholar E.F. Schumacher in his watershed book of the same name. In *Small is Beautiful*, Schumacher questioned the basic assumptions of modern economics, and advanced his own concepts of "ecological economics" – economics as if people mattered.

Schumacher believed that large-scale technology and production resulted in a fundamentally dysfunctional civilization, with stultifying workplaces, a poisoned planet with depleted non-renewable resources, and an essentially soulless society. Work, he proposed, could be transformed by "intermediate technologies" more suited to a human scale; he also believed it was possible to fulfill society's material needs by means of less expensive and simpler equipment instead of costly, computerized, labour-saving machines. He called for a return to smaller, more localized production and consumption, believing that "good work was essential for proper human development" and that "production from local resources for local needs is the most rational way of economic life."

Following Schumacher's death in 1977, his work was continued by George McRobie, a fellow British economist and a founder of the Intermediate Technology Development Group, who became one of the world's most distinguished proponents of sustainable development. His book, *Small is Possible*, built on the thinking of Schumacher and others. McRobie held a special affinity for small islands. "Island communities are strongly inclined to insist that their cultural integrity is not sacrificed to economics," he wrote. "They recognize that economics should serve the culture, the lifestyle, and the values which make life worth living, and not destroy or dominate them."

Meanwhile, others such as Buckminster Fuller (dubbed "the planet's friendly genius") were concerned with "finding ways of doing more with less to the end that all people everywhere can have more and more," as he wrote. Wells was highly influenced by the theories and principles advanced by Schumacher, McRobie and their contemporaries. He and Campbell had long discussions about how to apply those principles and theories to Prince Edward Island. Thus Campbell became an enthusiastic proponent of "small is beautiful" as a guiding principle for the sustainable development of the

Island's economy and its people. As he told journalist Harry Bruce in the spring of 1976 as the Ark was being constructed, "I am one who believes that small is not only beautiful but in the long run more practical."

Campbell's apparent conversion from developer to conserver found its roots in a growing recognition that Prince Edward Island ought to be charting its own course based on increased self-sufficiency, rather than attempting to integrate more closely its economy with the rest of North America. In a speech to a Technology for People Conference at the University of New Brunswick in May 1977, Campbell acknowledged that "in our efforts to promote growth and development modeled after the traditional central Canadian model, we have struck at the very roots of our economic and social base."

Several practical reasons also stimulated Campbell's conversion to championing the idea that small was beautiful. Some of these stemmed from experience in implementing regional development strategies. By now, many economists were coming to the conclusion that regions which abandoned indigenous resources and endeavoured to adopt a social and economic model foreign to their nature were creating a house of cards. In a speech to a Liberal Party policy convention in Memramcook, New Brunswick, in 1977, Campbell chastised the defeatist attitudes which too often pervaded both politicians and public throughout the region. "Our common rallying points are poverty and a regional inferiority complex, self-destructive negative attitudes and too often, a belief that everything from away is better or that Ottawa has all the answers, all the power and all the money," he said. "We have sold out to the centralist and the subsidy."

Campbell was soon presenting his ideas across the country. In a speech to the Rotary Club of Montreal in June 1976, he outlined the choice between a highly centralized, capital-intensive development strategy or one based on diversification. It was one of his clearest statements about the kind of society he envisioned for the future. "What I am presenting to you then, is a suggestion not for a new society, but for a new direction for our society," he explained, "one that emphasizes self-reliance and involvement of our citizens rather than encouraging them to be passive consumers. It accentuates decentralization of capital and decision-making, rather than intensive control. I envision a highly diversified society. I believe this is in keeping not only with our traditional values but also with our modern aspirations for a pluralistic society."

Campbell was also interested in protecting the unique attributes of the Island itself. Struck by the phenomenon of tourists flocking to its countryside, he recognized the Island as a special place to which they drove, as he described it, "for thousands of miles under almost unbearable traffic conditions in order to live a little closer to their fellow man ... [in] a frenzied effort to escape from their ordinary lives." Protection of the Island landscape and Campbell's commitment to living in harmony with the natural world went hand in hand. In a speech to the Summerside Chamber of Commerce in January 1977, in which he outlined his government's energy strategy, Campbell said, "We have striven to [develop renewable energy sources] within a framework that preserves and protects the landscape and other aspects of the physical environment that is part of every Islander."

Campbell had further concerns about the increased centralization of Canadian society, and the consequences that carried for rural areas and marginal societies. At a First Minister's Conference on the Economy in February 1978, at which the premiers were presented with forecasts indicating that the majority of Canadians would eventually live in just three major metropolitan areas, Campbell argued that the country needed a new vision. "I propose that we, as leaders of government, conceive of a new vision," he told his fellow premiers, "one that revitalizes the smaller towns and cities of this nation where people live and grow both economically and spiritually. I see these communities made up of industrious, self-reliant, conserving people, employing high technology to manufacture useful goods."

Behind it all was Campbell's conviction that Prince Edward Island needed to take more control over its own future. In the Throne Speech debate in the Legislature during the spring session of 1977, he acknowledged the difficulty of the Island becoming more self-sufficient unless Canadian industry decentralized and found ways of producing goods on a smaller scale. He warned that Prince Edward Island was becoming a province of merchants, selling goods produced elsewhere, and competing for business with other provinces in what he described as "an industrial rat race."

The national economy, he bluntly acknowledged in the months leading up to the 1978 election campaign, was not organized to serve the best interests of Prince Edward Island or the Atlantic provinces. It was a familiar refrain that politicians in the region had been chanting for decades, but this time there was a difference. Campbell was proposing a fundamental restructuring of the Island's relationship with the rest of Canada, one that would involve giving the Island a degree of self-sufficiency it had never before experienced.

The restructuring would begin with energy, the most pressing issue then facing the province. The current centralized and heavily capitalized sources of energy would gradually be replaced by locally controlled, small-scale, renewable resources. In his speech to the Rotary Club of Montreal, following the formation of the Institute of Man and Resources, Campbell explained that "because energy is such a crucial component of modern life, the path we choose could influence the type of society we have." The work of the Institute of Man and Resources demonstrated Campbell's belief that small was indeed practical.

*   *   *

By 1978, the Institute of Man and Resources boasted a professional, technical and administrative staff of twenty-three people operating on an annual budget of $1.2 million. It was actively involved in the development and application of wood, wind, solar, and low-level hydraulic energy. Its energy conservation projects were aimed at reducing demand on finite resources. Its achievements were impressive, including a spin-off enterprise manufacturing, testing and demonstrating wood-burning equipment; the construction of several homes to demonstrate energy conservation techniques; and a district heating study exploring ways to recycle energy from the waste-burning facility on the Charlottetown waterfront. In addition, a dam on the Dunk River in Breadalbane was restored to demonstrate the potential of small-scale hydro-electric power generation, and funding had been secured from the Department of Energy, Mines and Resources to establish the Atlantic Wind Test Site in North Cape on land donated by the provincial government.

The Institute received thousands of requests annually from Islanders and from people around the world for information on energy conservation and alternate energy sources. Major companies such as Gulf Oil, Imperial Oil, the Royal Bank, Canada Packers, Labatt Breweries, Xerox Canada and IBM backed its projects, while its work was attracting the attention of the United Nations Energy Program, the National Research Council of Canada, the Canadian Wildlife Federation, the Biomass Energy Institute, the Solar Energy Society of Canada, and the Canadian Science Council.

Atlantic Wind Test Site

The Atlantic Wind Test Site's 300-degree exposure to the windswept Gulf of St. Lawrence made it an ideal location for testing wind energy equipment. This was to be the most enduring of the alternate energy projects initiated by the Institute of Man and Resources.

In 1976, the Institute organized a four-day legislative session called "Energy Days," which the Canadian Broadcasting Corporation televised live. Energy Days brought the world's foremost experts together to discuss with members of the Legislative Assembly the best options to meet Prince Edward Island's future energy requirements. One of the participants was Amory Lovins, whose groundbreaking work on energy issues had been published earlier that year in the authoritative international journal *Foreign Affairs.** As Lovins told the Legislature, current approaches to energy generation and use were akin to "cutting butter with a chainsaw." He endorsed Prince

* The Wall Street Journal *later named Lovins as "one of 28 people in the world most likely to change the course of business," while* Newsweek *magazine dubbed him "one of the Western world's most influential energy thinkers."*

Edward Island's efforts to follow what he described as a "soft energy path" – renewable, diverse, and easy to understand.

Prince Edward Island seemed poised on the leading edge of efforts to turn away from massive, capital-intensive, non-renewable energy systems. During Energy Days, speaker after speaker – including Lovins and George McRobie – lauded Prince Edward Island's progressive attitude to alternate energy, envisioning the Island as the perfect place for the application of the "small is beautiful" philosophy. At one point in the heady four-day discussion, Premier Campbell interjected to express his doubts that tiny Prince Edward Island was likely to change the world, to which Lovins replied, "Why not?"

Why not, indeed? It was a time when people dared to dream. Officials of the Institute of Man and Resources were confidently predicting that, once the pressing issues of energy had been dealt with, it would pursue the other parts of its mandate: to blaze new trails in food and crop production, and in living and shelter systems. In 1978, looking back at the impressive list of the Institute's accomplishments, Andy Wells recalled that the previous few years had been "hectic at times, difficult and frustrating on occasion, but always stimulating and rewarding." In early 1976, he had been appointed to head the Institute. Prior to the formal establishment of the organization in October 1975, Campbell had personally attempted to recruit some high-profile candidates, including Maurice Strong of the United Nations Energy Program, for the top position. Strong and others whom Campbell approached, such as former Islander Dr. Gordon MacEachern (an agricultural economist at McGill University's Macdonald College) and Donald Chant (head of the Canadian environmental organization, Pollution Probe), declined his invitation to join a fledgling organization with an uncertain future.

Wells was an obvious choice. The Institute was the product of his thinking and his long-standing interest in renewable energy and sustainable development. Leaving his position in the Premier's Office, he threw himself wholeheartedly into the challenge of charting new directions for the Island. He soon recruited a highly qualified staff committed to the Institute's goals and ideals, including Stewart Bennie, Dr. Kirk Brown, and Malcolm Lodge (who spearheaded the work at the Wind Test Site in North Cape). In the fall of 1976, the Campbell government negotiated a three-year agreement on renewable energy development with the federal Department of Energy, Mines and Resources, which granted $3 million to the Institute. Campbell had submitted the agreement proposal to the federal government in light of heightened public interest in the subject following the establishment of the Institute. In a letter to Energy Minister Alistair Gillespie, Campbell wrote, "We are unprepared to deal with the overwhelming national interest in the subject." The eventual agreement put Prince Edward Island at the forefront of applied energy research and development in Canada.

Campbell spoke confidently and enthusiastically about the province's prospects with regard to becoming energy self-sufficient and transforming the Island way of life. In October 1976, he told the *Guardian*, "Here we can stop the spread of centralization, remove many of the social and political factors leading to individual and regional alienation, lessen our dependence on faceless and uncaring bureaucrats and bureaucracies, and once again provide some real understanding and meaning to our place and role in society." Not everyone shared that view. In an accompanying editorial, the *Guardian* gave expression to many reservations about the changes Campbell was advocating, some of which emanated from his own MLAs. "This sounds like an ideal situation – almost Utopian – but one must wonder how alternate energy sources when they become practical enough to meet society's requirements can bring that situation about," it stated. "Will new energy resources lead to decentralization, a reduction in social problems, less regional alienation and smaller bureaucracies? ... [L]ets not have the politicians pull the plug on society's present technological apparatus before new methods are guaranteed – winter nights get awful dark and cold."

Despite the flurry of interest and activity following the establishment of the Institute of Man and Resources and the Ark, the euphoria evaporated as interest in alternate energy peaked. Oil consumption, which had been in decline after the energy crisis of 1973, started to climb back up again by 1977. The habits of a society traditionally reliant on fossil fuels were not easy to change, even though Islanders were paying twice the national average for electricity (up to three time for commercial and industrial uses). The installation of a cable across the Northumberland Strait, which now brought sixty percent of the province's energy requirements from New Brunswick, buttressed the public attitude. Lulled by the assurance of constant supply and inured to the costs, Islanders quickly lost interest in alternate energy. They shut down their wood stoves, relit their oil furnaces, and wondered what all the fuss had been about. The Institute could no longer exist in this atmosphere; the world that gave it life now brought about its demise.

The closure of the Institute of Man and Resources was presaged by the Ark. The New Alchemy Institute had received funding from the federal Department of Urban Affairs to build the Ark, and additional funding from Energy, Mines and Resources under a three-year agreement for operational and research program costs. However, expenditures proved to be twice as much as expected, so the project found itself on shaky financial ground from the beginning.

Other problems soon surfaced. Overwhelmed by insatiable public curiousity, the staff at the Ark felt obliged to limit the number of visitors; when they placed restrictions on visiting hours, and closed the front gates to deter the uninvited, a public relations fiasco developed. The project also suffered major cost-overruns on the windmill and solar panels, and the technologies never worked as intended. The Ark itself was drawing electricity from the grid at six times the rate of the average Island home, prompting the Ark's manager, Ken MacKay, to explain in its defence, "We're researching self-sufficiency without claiming to be self-sufficient!"

Neither did it help that Islanders regarded the research with skepticism. Although John Todd held a number of meetings at the community centre in nearby Little Pond to share the research results, he faced an audience that was unprepared to deal with challenging questions about the status quo, such as the drive to adopt the latest appliances, and the use of pesticides in agriculture. Especially in a community where many households still relied on a wood stove for their main heat source, the highly sophisticated technologies put in place at the Ark seemed excessive. Even one of the original architects was having second thoughts. Islanders, with their simpler technologies "were so far behind, they were way ahead," observed David Bergmark. "I was a little embarrassed we were building this thing." The cultural gap between unconvinced Islanders and crusading ecologists was proving difficult to bridge.

Confusion also reigned about the Ark's role in the government's overall alternate energy strategy. It was unclear from the funding agreement for the Ark to whom it was accountable – the Department of Energy, Mines and Resources or the Institute of Man and Resources. Meanwhile, as early as June 1977 (less than a year after the Ark opened), Wells was beginning to worry that the problems related to the Ark might damage the Institute's reputation. By January 1978, Energy, Mines and Resources officials were confronting Todd with serious questions about overspending at the Ark. By

March 1978, in view of the mounting financial problems, the New Alchemy Institute made an agreement with the Institute of Man and Resources for it to manage the Ark, while the New Alchemy Institute would act as consultants. It was not a harmonious match. John Todd started to complain that he was being pushed aside, while Andy Wells grew resentful of the drain on resources required to keep the Ark afloat.

Neither the Ark nor the Institute of Man and Resources survived long after 1978. The federal government failed to renew core funding for the Institute, and the subsequent provincial Conservative government under Angus MacLean lacked interest in funding alternate energy and building on Wells's ideas. The world energy crisis was over now. People went back to their old ways.

*   *   *

An article in the Canadian Magazine *entitled "The Gardener of the Gulf" described Campbell as the "jolly green giant."*

An article entitled "The Gardener of the Gulf" by journalist Harry Bruce, published in the April 1975 edition of the *Canadian Magazine*, ran with a cartoon depicting Alex Campbell as a "jolly green giant." Bruce examined Campbell's commitment to local, sustainable development; alternate energy; the environment; and his embracing of the "small is beautiful" philosophy.

According to Bruce, Campbell's message represented a call to Islanders to resist the North American propensity for "resource guzzling materialism," and a denunciation of "growth-at-any-cost planned obsolescence and the mad machinery of an industrial society that sacrifices reflection, spiritual health and the forever elusive 'quality of life' to more speed, more things and always, more general despair."

Campbell's third term in office essentially focused on two issues: the quality of life of Islanders, and the need to sustain their society in the light of diminishing non-renewable resources. Rapid industrialization, he repeatedly pointed out, does not necessarily produce a better quality of life. Once again, Campbell was attempting to achieve a balance between two conflicting cultures. "It is a question of choosing between 'modern growth' and 'traditional stagnation,'" he explained. "It is a question of finding the right path of development, the Middle Way, between materialist heedlessness and traditionalist immobility, in short, of finding the 'Right Livelihood.'"* The pursuit of the "right livelihood," according to Harry Bruce, earned Campbell a special niche in Canadian politics. "For he is the *other* philosopher king of Canadian public life," concluded Bruce, "or, rather, the unsung philosopher princeling."

Philosopher king or princeling, Campbell was also the consummate politician. On April 6, 1977, he became the longest-serving premier in the history of Prince Edward Island. By that date he had served for ten years, eight months and four days, beating the record of W.W. Sullivan, who served during the 1880s. And as spring dawned across the Island in 1978, he broke a second record, becoming the first Prince Edward Island premier ever elected to a fourth term of office.

---

* *The concept of "right livelihood" is an ancient one, embodying the principle that each person should follow an honest occupation which fully respects other people and the natural world. It implies responsibility for the consequences of actions and taking only a fair share of the earth's resources.*

PARO

"Building Now, For The Future"

- Liberal campaign slogan, 1978

The 1978 election produced bittersweet results. Alex Campbell's government was, indeed, re-elected for a record fourth term in office, but that mandate rested on a precarious two-seat margin, with seventeen seats to the Conservatives' fifteen. Twelve years earlier, the Campbell Liberals had been elected with the same slight majority, but in the two subsequent elections they had roared to power, winning an unprecedented percentage of the popular vote and the overwhelming support of Islanders. Now, that confidence was shaken. Campbell felt the results of the 1978 election as a bitter personal disappointment. Left with virtually no legislative majority, reluctant to rely on the vote of the Speaker to save the government, and unwilling to be held hostage by disgruntled MLAs, petulant cabinet ministers or a capricious public, his political zeal took a mortal blow. If the government had not been defeated, neither could it claim a clear victory. The results, Campbell optimistically suggested, showed that Islanders were not intent on rushing out to effect change nor were they willing to hand the government a clear mandate to do so.

The Liberals had harboured no illusions heading into the spring election of 1978. In late January and early February, Liberal pollster Ben Crow conducted his sixth study of political attitudes since the party had come to power. The poll showed that Campbell's overall level of acceptance among voters was at least as high as it had been in the previous peak year of 1970, and significantly higher than the nadir year of 1972. Image profiles revealed that he was perceived as a strong, aggressive leader, intelligent, imaginative and resourceful, who had a good rapport with people. He received lower marks, however, for planning versus taking action, his image in this respect still suffering from the days of the Development Plan.

To compound matters, Campbell now faced a new, formidable foe in Opposition Leader Angus MacLean, a widely respected politician who had served twenty-five years in the House of Commons. He had resigned from Parliament to seek the leadership of the

Conservative Party in Prince Edward Island, and subsequently won a by-election in 4th Queens in November 1976. The ubiquitous but enigmatic MacLean, running under a pledge to strengthen rural communities, struck a resonant note with Islanders growing weary of change. According to Island historian Dr. Edward MacDonald, "The campaign contrasted a careworn leader atop an ageing platform with a party that had taken Islanders' inchoate resentment, anxiety, and guilty aversion to change, and shaped it into a seductive policy that seemed to look both ways at once."

Respondents to the poll thought Campbell had a more compelling personality than MacLean, but rated MacLean higher in terms of being more down-to-earth and practical. MacLean also won higher ratings for preserving the traditional values inherent in the Island's way of life, and for his perceived rapport with people. Although some people considered him at age sixty-four too old for premier, the picture detected by Ben Crow indicated the probability of a closer battle with MacLean than Campbell had faced with previous opposition leaders. "All things considered," Crow advised the Liberal strategists, "Mr. MacLean is a formidable contestant for the premiership in the upcoming election." Since the poll showed Campbell and MacLean virtually tied on overall acceptance by voters, once again the Liberals strategically placed their leader front and centre throughout the campaign. Checking his numbers, Crow noted, "Even though he has been Premier for three terms of office, electors consider him to be still bright and fresh as opposed to getting stale."

But the polling numbers revealed another ominous warning: Liberal support had declined from the fifty-four percent it had received in the 1974 election to forty-nine percent. The five-point difference was picked up by the Conservatives, who now stood at forty-five percent, while popular support for the NDP remained unchanged at six percent. As a result, from the outset the Campbell campaign team recognized it was in for a tough fight, one that would pit Campbell, still young and vigorous – the "apostle of change," against the grandfatherly MacLean, the "steward of tradition." Ultimately, the result would be determined by which of the two men Islanders believed could best reflect their sacred if ineffable and euphemistically defined Island values and aspirations.

The Campbell government entered the campaign banking on its record of progress and its plans for the future. The Speech from the Throne on March 2 proclaimed a freeze on taxes; the creation of some two thousand jobs in small industries; the establishment of a new energy corporation; and ongoing support for the development of the primary industries. "The Liberal government led by Premier Campbell will do everything in its power to preserve and strengthen our unique Island way of life," proclaimed a campaign advertisement.

*   *   *

As a portent of what might be expected from the Opposition during the campaign, MacLean dismissed as a "deathbed repentance" the government's glowing review of its accomplishments and its avowed intent to preserve and strengthen the Island way of life. But there was no denying that the province had experienced phenomenal growth in the mid-seventies. The Gross Provincial Product had increased by a whopping fifty-seven percent since 1973, the labour force by eighteen percent, and personal incomes by an astounding sixty-three percent. Added to this, provincial finances were sound. "The Liberal government is an action government," asserted the party's ads. "We get things done." And it promised Islanders that progress would continue. "The rewards of our earlier labours are now within our grasp," Campbell told a boisterous crowd of two thousand supporters during the campaign kickoff in Summerside on March 31. "The future is in our hands."

Alex Campbell was the Liberal Party's greatest asset. The stature of Prince Edward Island in the eyes of the rest of Canada had also risen by leaps and bounds since Campbell became premier. A new sense of pride pervaded the Island, which, like the rest of the Maritimes, had always been regarded as a backward "have not" province holding few prospects. By the 1970s, that had all changed. Prince Edward Islanders had gained a new pride and respect for their province, both for its past and for its prospects. Campbell himself had earned a respected position on the national stage. During a country-wide speaking tour in 1973 as the Island celebrated its centenary, he attracted much favourable attention to Prince Edward Island. Islanders wanted their leaders to be respected at the national level – and Campbell gave them a reason to be proud of themselves and their home. He first made his presence felt nationally at the Confederation for Tomorrow Conference in Toronto in November 1967, which brought the prime minister and provincial premiers together to discuss constitutional reform. Following the conference, Canadian journalist Peter Newman wrote that "Premier Alex Campbell emerged as the young statesman of the conference. Here was a man

Canadian Intergovernmental Conference Secretariat

Campbell was credited with rising above the parochial concerns of his province and made his presence felt on the national stage. Here at the First Ministers' meeting in 1971, front row (l-r): Gerald Regan, Nova Scotia; William G. Davis, Ontario; Prime Minister Pierre Trudeau; Robert Bourassa, Quebec; Richard B. Hatfield, New Brunswick. Standing (l-r): Edward Schreyer, Manitoba; William A.C. Bennett, British Columbia; Alexander B. Campbell, Prince Edward Island; W. Ross Thatcher, Saskatchewan; Harry E. Strom, Alberta; Joseph R. Smallwood, Newfoundland.

who ... rose above the parochial concerns of his province to show that his vision was wide enough to make him an important new father of Canada's reconfederation."* By 1978, the Campbell government could legitimately take credit for many of its accomplishments, and it headed into the campaign united solidly behind its popular leader.

Campbell was a consummate campaigner, energized by the

* Campbell also spearheaded a new era of co-operation in the Maritimes, together with premiers Gerald Regan in Nova Scotia and Richard Hatfield in New Brunswick. Although the three provinces saw themselves as

people he met. He loved campaigning, and radiated a relaxed, open and friendly style everywhere he went. Since becoming leader, he had taken the art of campaigning to new levels and mastered its nuances. Often the last person to leave a meeting, he made everyone feel important, and was genuinely interested in the people he met. He established a rapport with Islanders that few have matched. He was also mindful of the necessity of paying attention to detail. At least twice a month, in his office on a Friday morning, he would meet with Bill Morrison, the party's executive director, to catch up on the latest news and gossip from across the province. They would discuss trouble spots, potential candidates, and local concerns. When matters needed attention, Campbell would dispatch the appropriate minister to deal with the situation. He also made it a point to keep in close touch with party workers. He and his cabinet were always available to attend party functions or meetings of the party executive, and he made it a point to attend every one of the party's nominating conventions.**

Party workers carefully crafted their campaign plans. About six months prior to the anticipated election date, Campbell's closest advisors (including Bill Morrison, Andy Wells, Mike Schurman, Sid Green and Jack MacAndrew) met each week to gauge the pulse of the electorate. Between elections, this group also served as an informal sounding board for Campbell. Sometimes they were joined by others such as Ned Belliveau, who had handled the party's advertising since 1966, and as the campaign kick-off approached, Campbell himself attended more frequently. They met in an apartment tucked

---

having a shared regional interest, in practice the political environment was much different. As have-not provinces, each jealously guarded whatever political advantage it had in Ottawa; unilateral relations generally supplanted regional co-operation. However, following the completion of a ground-breaking study on Maritime Union in the late 1960s, Regan, Hatfield and Campbell established the Council of Maritime Premiers to undertake joint initiatives in a number of areas. Although the Council and the proposed co-operative initiatives never fulfilled original expectations, it was an important first step in more aggressively asserting a regional consciousness.

** Campbell also held great respect for the role of the political party as a whole, seeking and inviting its input. The year after the 1974 election (by which time he had been leader for ten years), he asked the party to organize a leadership review, at which he was solidly endorsed.

Campbell with Nova Scotia Premier Gerald Regan (right) and New Brunswick Premier Richard Hatfield. Together, they established the Council of Maritime Premiers to promote greater regional co-operation.

PARO

e Guardian

"Covers Prince Edward Island Like The Dew"

CHARLOTTETOWN, PRINCE EDWARD ISLAND, TUESDAY, FEBRUARY 8, 1977

WEATHER

Cloudy clearing this morning with highs near minus four. Outlook for Wednesday; sunny.

20 CENTS 14 P

Premiers Okay Maritime Union

In a secret meeting late last night the three Maritime premiers agreed to unite Prince Edward Island, Nova Scotia, and New Brunswick into a single province to be known as Maritima, the Guardian has learned.

In a surprise move Premiers Campbell, Regan and Hatfield put aside past differences and decided to create one province out of what has been since Confederation a tripartite governed area comprising the land between Quebec and the Atlantic coast.

Reliable sources say Premier Alex Campbell of Prince Edward Island will be the first premier of Maritima.

Official notification of the move was sent by telegram to Prime Minister Pierre Trudeau late last night. He is reported to have shrugged.

Notification also went to Queen Elizabeth II in the wee hours of the morning. She received personal notification of the move in recognition of the 25th anniversary of her Majesty's accession to the British throne, sources say.

Former Premier Richard Hatfield of New Brunswick has agreed to take on the position of

troversy at recent meetings of the now defunct council of Maritime Premiers.

Intergovernmental Affairs Minister Richard Hatfield is reported to have said recent discussions be held in Iran, Iraq, Saudi Arabia, and Kuwait led to an offer of 63 camels, which will be sent to Charlottetown to form the nucleus of a Maritime herd of dromedaries.

"It is obvious," the minister said, "that our recent difficult and, I might say, boring discussions with the Minister of Transportation have led me to look for new solutions to the age old problem of getting — as it were — from one place to another."

"Since it takes so long using the traditional forms of transportation — like airplanes — to move around the area, we might as well do it properly. Camels, who can live for 30 days without water, should do the trick," he said.

In the spirit of the newfound cooperation Premier-Elect Campbell has offered Prince Edward Island's only buffalo herd as an adjunct to the veterinary college.

"We are not sure what will happen when the camels meet the buffalo," the

Reaction: Confusion

A Guardian telephone survey last night found mixed and confused reaction to the announcement that the Maritime provinces will combine to form a single province to be called Maritima.

A country court judge in Cape Breton expressed displeasure at the move. "Gaharas would have been a more logical site for the capital especially in view of all the efforts we have made to develop this part of Cape Breton. After all, you can't even buy Salamagrundi in P.E.I."

A Progressive Conservative MP who requested anonymity expressed great alarm that the P.E.I. ferries may lose their subsidies since they would no longer operate between provinces.

The Rev. Dr. F.W.P. Bolger complained that the "Cradle of Confederation has produced a monster."

Beverly Duggan showed little enthusiasm for the concept. "Now we'll have all them foreigners from away coming over here takin' our land since

I've been a member maritime union for 2 and nobody ever told th about it before.

Whales

Beache

MAYPORT, Fla. (AP least 41 dead pilot whal counted Monday at Fort Inlet, where a herd of th mals returned to the be spite human efforts t them back to sea.

About 20 divers plung the water in an effort off 40 to 50 whales b come ashore against th tide, said Lieut. Glenn of the Florida Marine P

Keefer said as many whales may have die Sunday on the shore and bar 200 yards out in the the mouth of the St

During a meeting of the Council of Maritime Premiers in Charlottetown in 1977, Campbell had a fake version of the Guardian delivered to the hotel rooms of premiers Regan and Hatfield proclaiming approval of a political union of the three Maritime provinces.

PARO

Campbell on the campaign trail. He became the consummate campaigner.

away on the second floor of Schurman's building supply centre on Longworth Avenue in Charlottetown where, with a standing order of Chinese food from the Canton Café, they discussed strategy well into the evening. The discussions were frank and open. Over the years, Campbell had acquired a reputation as a good listener. He listened respectfully to all opinions and sought advice on troublesome issues. He would sit contemplatively rubbing his chin, or pace restlessly back and forth across the room. Nothing was sacred. At one point, after Campbell had gained some weight, Wells exclaimed that he looked like "a fucking baby seal" and told him to go on a diet. He did.

The campaign team became masterful at organization, keeping their plans under wraps until the campaign had been announced. They reserved radio and newspaper spaces in the name of a trusted Liberal business, and carefully concealed posters and literature (even in the Cutcliffe Funeral Home receiving vault!). Not even the caucus knew the details until the last minute. Even Ben Crow, the Liberal pollster, kept his counsel. In the run-up to the starting gate of one campaign, he booked into the Charlottetown Hotel under the ambiguous name of Dale Evans.

When the election campaign was finally underway, Campbell threw himself wholeheartedly into campaigning across the Island, meeting with people, talking and listening, reinvigorated by the long days and late nights. He especially enjoyed meeting children and young people. "I always felt exhilarated by their zeal and optimism," he said.

In 1978, as had been the practice since 1966, Liberal party workers organized "Campbell Days" featuring their popular leader in events and activities in every single district. To cover the gruelling schedule, Campbell travelled by van, constantly on the move. Campaigning under the slogan "Building now, for the future," the Liberals confidently looked forward to repeating the sweep they had made in the previous two elections. This time, however, the organizers recognized in Angus MacLean the strongest opposition leader Campbell had ever faced.

The two leaders' paths actually crossed at the Red Rooster Restaurant in Crapaud on April 4, when both were campaigning in the same district. John Jeffrey, then a reporter with the *Guardian,* wrote of the encounter, "Angus MacLean's campaign style is completely opposite the out-going, almost free-wheeling manner of Premier Campbell," but noted that MacLean, on the other hand, "never loses his calm composure and has the habit of standing back as though constantly speculating upon the events going on around him."

MacLean harboured a deep affinity for Prince Edward Island. His farm in Lewes included blueberry production and a carefully managed, diverse woodlot. Plodding and deliberate, he seemed out of touch with the demands of political campaigns for glitz and glamour. "He looks agonized on public occasions," observed the *Globe and Mail.* "He is the man who has stepped off the bus at the wrong stop – bewildered, vaguely embarrassed, uncertain where he is or how he got there, groping for words which might explain his predicament ... On the platform he has all the charisma of another Prince Edward Island product, the potato." MacLean took it all in his easy, unhurried stride. As he jokingly recalled in his autobiography, "It was quite a contrast to come back to the Island and find myself depicted by some of the local media as a country clown – an absolute hayseed ... I had not realized I was such a bumpkin."

The Conservatives' overall campaign theme – a Rural Renaissance – vowed to "preserve and enhance the beauty of our landscape, our communities and the character of our people." Individual themes – heavily influenced by David Weale, Harry Baglole and Alan Rankin – were expressed not through specific promises but in terms of what they called "principles." It was a risky strategy in a province where people expected promises to be tangible. The Conservative principles were based on the importance of individual enterprise, "appropriate" development, and revitalization of the rural economy. "The Island is a special place," trumpeted Principle #10, for example. The themes were broadly outlined at the Conservative Party's kick-off rally in Summerside on March 31. "The PC party is committed neither to bigness or smallness," MacLean told a crowd of six hundred. "We are committed rather to a sensible and responsible approach, when decisions are determined, not by any preconceived notion of size, but by the determination to develop this Island in a way which is sensitive to its history, its resources and its people." Little wonder that some Islanders felt the policy seemed to look both ways at once. It was whatever they wanted it to be.

Following MacLean's explicit directive, the Conservative campaign largely avoided attacking the government, but soon centred on two targets: the controversy over school consolidation, and the future of the family farm. Both were integral to the "rural renaissance." At a campaign rally in O'Leary on April 19, MacLean took aim at the Liberals' agricultural record. "They began by informing Island farmers that their farms were too small and inefficient, and that the numbers of them had to be reduced dramatically," he charged. "Now they are presenting themselves as the guardians of the small family farms." In 4th Prince, Conservative candidate Rev. William MacDougall zeroed in on the controversy surrounding school consolidation in the Borden area. "People are concerned about losing their children from communities to big factories, as one person put it," he declared. "When children are taken out of a community, it takes the soul out of the community." This sort of charge reared it head often during the campaign.

MacLean accused the Liberals of flip-flopping on their commitment to the Island way of life. "Whereas they began with a callous disregard for the Island's way of life and the Island way of doing things," he remarked, "now they have begun to speak glowingly of our heritage and our traditions." The campaign eventually degenerated into a series of accusations and counter-accusations about who were the "real Islanders." The Conservatives publicly contrasted campaign styles, accusing the Liberals of running a "slick" election (the Liberals were once again using the services of Wilshar Advertising, now run by Bill Belliveau, Ned Belliveau's son). Bill Morrison, the Liberal Party's executive director, defended their campaign style, pointing out that if one wanted to get a good haircut one went to a proficient barber. In turn, the Liberal campaign team spoke dismissively of the amateurish look of the Conservative advertisements, and countered with accusations that the MacLean campaign organization was receiving outside advice from Gary Lynch of CHUM Radio in Toronto. Conservatives, with an air of injured innocence, denied the accusation, insisting their campaign was not using advertising and public relations flacks. "Our campaign is made by Islanders, for Islanders and we believe an Island-made product is good enough, is superior even for Island uses than something that is imported," boasted MacLean.

Most Islanders ignored the inter-party sniping. However, the rhetoric about a rural renaissance appeared to resonate with voters. MacLean told supporters at a rally in Bedeque in the early days of the campaign that he was encouraged by the responses he was receiving. "There seems to be a sense of change," he said. "People seem to be saying no government should be in power for 16 years. Enough is enough." It was a sentiment difficult to dispute. Compounding the difficulties for the provincial Liberals was the growing unpopularity of the federal Liberals under Prime Minister Pierre Trudeau. The Trudeau government had been in power for ten years, and many Canadians were growing restive for change.

The baggage of being in office for more than a decade was catching up to the Campbell government. The Development Plan had failed to live up to its expectations, and by the mid-seventies it ceased to represent a vehicle for long-term change. The idealism of the planners was trumped by the pragmatism of the politicians; the Plan now served as little more than a mechanism for accessing federal dollars. The energy crisis had abated – "small is beautiful" now seemed hollow. And, for the first time, the Liberals were accused of being arrogant and aloof. Unfortunately, during a campaign meeting in Montague, Liberal Party president Joe Ghiz, who was chairing the event, had cut off a questioner in the audience, which did nothing to alleviate the criticism.

Campbell worked with renewed effort in the last days of the campaign, but the effort seemed forced and formulaic compared to the freshness, vitality and excitement exuded in previous campaigns. Mike Schurman, Campbell's long-time campaign manager, was not involved in 1978. Instead, Joe Ghiz had joined the team, but his flamboyance and self-assuredness were no match for Schurman's canny discipline.* This time around, some of the team sensed a lack of the spark that ignites people into a mood of exuberance, and provides that elusive, essential ingredient – momentum. Even the *Guardian* sensed something was amiss. "Whatever happened to the fun and excitement associated with provincial elections of the past?" it mused in an editorial early on in the campaign. "The last election was staid to say the least and, so far, the 1978 version is about as exciting as a ragpickers' reunion."

On April 22, the Saturday evening before the election, the Liberals wound up their campaign at a massive rally at the Simmons Sports Arena in Charlottetown. As usual, Campbell fired up the faithful. "We all have a mission," he told the cheering crowd. "We all share a vision – a vision of what our province can be and a mission to turn that vision into reality."

A record 74,857 Islanders were eligible to vote on April 24. A typically high 86.3 percent of them turned out to cast their ballots. After the votes had been counted, the Liberals were re-elected, although reduced to the slimmest possible majority, its popular vote dropping to just under fifty percent. The government that started out with a bare two-seat majority twelve years earlier found itself back in that same position.

But times were changing. The 1978 election signalled a subtle shift in the composition of the people returned to the Legislature. A number of prominent members of Campbell's former cabinet did not run this time, including Earle Hickey, Bruce Stewart and Catherine Callbeck. Gordon Bennett had resigned earlier due to his appointment as Lieutenant-Governor. Gilbert Clements, one of Campbell's most effective and ambitious members, was narrowly defeated by 24 votes, while Clements' running mate, Charles Fraser, was defeated by newcomer Pat Binns. Other backbenchers, including Addie MacDonald, Waldron Lavers, Levi McNally and former Speaker Cecil

---

* *Other members included Andy Wells, who took a leave of absence from the Institute of Man and Resources to handle the day-to-day details; John Brehaut, assistant to Veterans Affairs Minister Dan MacDonald; Bill Morrison and Percy Downe from the Liberal party office; Merlin Clark, a Charlottetown automobile dealer who had taken over fundraising duties from Sid Green; and Len Bradley, Campbell's principal secretary. All but Bradley had been involved in previous campaigns.*

Miller, went down to defeat. Even Campbell's own running mate, Wally MacGillivray, was unable to retain the seat formerly held by Hickey. "The people of Prince Edward Island spoke. That's what happened," said Campbell tersely in response to reporters' questions about the results and what it meant for the future of his government. "I am still digesting the election results and I have not yet begun to contemplate the answer to that question." MacLean put his own interpretation on the results, saying of the government that "it's just a matter of whether it's going in one fell swoop or in installments." The following year, his interpretation proved prophetic.

The election over, Campbell picked his new cabinet and announced that the Legislature would reconvene on June 6. Then he headed into a desultory, listless summer.

*   *   *

PARO

This was Campbell's last cabinet. Front row (left to right): *George Proud, Edward Clark, George Henderson, Lieutenant-Governor Gordon Bennett, Campbell, Dr. Bud Ings. Back row,* (left to right): *Arthur MacDonald, Bennett Campbell, Jim Fay, Robert Campbell, Dr. John Maloney.*

On September 11, Alex Campbell resigned. "It was the most difficult decision of my political career," he said. "I loved what I was doing."

During the months following the 1978 election, Campbell agonized over his political future, keeping his options closely guarded. By then, he had spent more than half his adult life in politics. "I enjoyed every day I was in politics," he said, although he acknowledged that as premier he "was very much a captive of the job." He had entered politics when his oldest son, Blair, was just three years old. By now, his three children were well on their way to being grown and Campbell had missed most of their childhood. The pressures of bringing up a family were also exacerbated by the lack of financial security that came hand in hand with a political career.

Had he stayed, he would have worked hard to regain the support and confidence of Islanders, but the demands of office were beginning to show. He suffered serious disc problems in his back and had long been troubled with severe migraine headaches. He was a heavy smoker, and that began wearing on his health. In a wide-ranging, two-hour interview with Lorne Yeo of the *Guardian* following his resignation, Yeo noted Campbell smoked a total of sixteen cigarettes. The stress of long hours and unremitting demands on his time were also beginning to have an impact on his health. Above all, Campbell wondered if he still had the "political legs" to carry on.

On the day Campbell announced his resignation, he called his wife, Marilyn, just before the news conference. She was finally able to tell the children their father was leaving public life. "It's good to get him back," she delightedly told reporters. When asked about their plans, she simply said, "I do know we've got a lot of vegetables and I'm going to start making pickles." For the first time in their lives, Campbell and his wife took a good long holiday. They relaxed on a beach in Florida for a month where Campbell, whose schedule had always been tightly mapped out, considered what he was going to do next.

For Campbell, the inveterate politician, the transition to a life without politics proved difficult. Inevitably, he missed politics, and later recalled that it took him two years to make the adjustment to private life. During that time, he continued to snap to attention whenever the telephone rang or the news came on. Finally, on December 1st – his forty-fifth birthday – Campbell was appointed to the Supreme Court of Prince Edward Island. His political career was over.

EPILOGUE

In his delightful collection of Prince Edward Island sayings, David Weale offers one that suggests why the soil on this Island is so red – because Islanders bite their tongues so much. Reticence indeed may be part of the reason, but a more profound and sinister explanation lies beneath the surface. This fair and beautiful land, imbued with such majesty and mystery, has been mortally wounded and is slowly bleeding to death. Its blood has seeped into the soil, and the rivers run red as it is washed away into the sea.

For close to three hundred years, this island has suffered invasion, attack, abuse and neglect. It has been violated, robbed, defiled and destroyed. Its once-proud forests have been decimated, its fertile soil degraded, and its life-giving underground streams, older than civilization itself, despoiled. This vulnerable fragment of the universe, little more than a sandbar rising up from the Gulf of St. Lawrence, is being drained of its very life and soul.

For Prince Edward Island's fate has always rested in the hands of strangers. They have betrayed it over and over again. From time to time, it has struggled back, searching for its own purpose, voice and identity, only to give up the fight again in the face of indifference, ignorance, apathy and ennui. Now, it has lost control over its future. It is on life support, force-fed to satisfy the rapacious greed of those who continue to bastardize, brutalize and vandalize its remains. While the countryside bleeds to death, the towns and cities, bloated and sprawling shamelessly over the landscape, wreck everything in their path. The Island's culture has morphed into another commodity to be bought, sold and traded away.

The guardians of this finite, fragile place have abdicated their responsibilities. Too many of them are engaged in a feeding frenzy over what is left of the spoils. The people stand by and watch the Island being victimized, offering little protest. Or perhaps they are just too polite, too reticent.

An island has nowhere to run, no place to hide. How soon will the time come when this island is not be "the Island" anymore?

It could have been so different ...

BIBLIOGRAPHY

Baglole, Harry, and David Weale, eds. *Cornelius Howatt: Superstar!* Summerside: Williams and Crue, 1974.

Bruce, Harry. "The Gardener of the Gulf." *Canadian Magazine.* April 1970.

Canada. Department of Regional Economic Expansion. *Development Plan for Prince Edward Island.* Ottawa, 1970.

Canadian Annual Review. Toronto: University of Toronto Press. 1965-1979.

Clark, Marlene. "The Franchise in Prince Edward Island and its Relation to Island Politics and Other Political Institutions." 1968. Unpublished master's thesis, Dalhousie University.

—. "Island Politics." In F.W.P. Bolger, ed., *Canada's Smallest Province.* Charlottetown: Prince Edward Island Centennial Commission, 1973.

Driscoll, F.L. "The Island and the Dominion." In F.W.P. Bolger, ed., *Canada's Smallest Province.* Charlottetown: Prince Edward Island Centennial Commission, 1973.

MacDonald, Edward. *If You're Stronghearted.* Charlottetown: Prince Edward Island Museum and Heritage Foundation, 2000.

MacEachern, Alan. *An Environmental Fable.* Charlottetown: Island Studies Press, 2003.

MacKinnon, Frank. *The Government of Prince Edward Island.* Toronto: University of Toronto Press, 1951.

—. *Church Politics and Education in Canada: the PEI Experience.* Calgary: Detselig Enterprises, 1995.

MacKinnon, Wayne. "The Politics of Planning: A Case Study of the Prince Edward Island Development Plan." 1972. Unpublished master's thesis, Dalhousie University.

—. *The Life of the Party*. Summerside: Williams and Crue, 1973.

—. "Dependency and Development in Prince Edward Island." In Godfrey Baldacchino and Robert Greenwood, eds., *Competing Strategies of Socio-Economic Development for Small Islands*. Charlottetown: Institute of Island Studies, 1998.

Marquis, Greg. "Uptight Little Island: The Junction '71 Affair." *The Island Magazine*. Fall/Winter 2002.

Mathias, Philip. *Forced Growth*. Toronto: James Lewis and Samuel, 1971.

McKenna, Mary Olga. "Higher Education in Transition." In Verner Smitheram, David Milne and Satadal Dasgupta, eds., *The Garden Transformed*. Charlottetown: Ragweed Press, 1982.

McNiven, J.D. *Evaluation of the Public Participation Program Embodied in the Prince Edward Island Development Plan*. Halifax: Institute of Public Affairs, Dalhousie University, 1974.

Milne, David. "Politics in a Beleaguered Garden." In Verner Smitheram, David Milne and Satadal Dasgupta, eds., *The Garden Transformed*. Charlottetown: Ragweed Press, 1982

Nemetz, Donald. "Managing Development." In Verner Smitheram, David Milne and Satadal Dasgupta, eds., *The Garden Transformed*. Charlottetown: Ragweed Press, 1982.

O'Connor, Ryan. "The Brothers and Sisters of Cornelius Howatt: Protest, 'Progress,' and the Island Way of Life." 2002. Unpublished paper. Islands of the World conference, University of Prince Edward Island.

O'Grady, Michael. *From Grassroots to Grim Reapings: A History of the Prince Edward Island Rural Development Council.* Charlottetown: Institute of Island Studies, 1997.

Prince Edward Island. *White Paper on Economic Planning and Development.* Charlottetown, 1967.

—. *White Paper on Post-Secondary Education.* Charlottetown, 1968.

—. Commission of Inquiry into Matters Pertaining to Bathurst Marine Limited and Gulf Garden Foods Limited. Report. Charlottetown, 1969.

—. *Policy Statement on Government Reorganization.* Charlottetown, 1970.

—. Royal Commission on Land Ownership and Land Use. Report. Charlottetown, 1973.

Schumacher, E.F. *Small is Beautiful.* London: Abacus, 1973.

Smitheram, Verner. "Development and the Debate Over School Consolidation." In Verner Smitheram, David Milne and Satadal Dasgupta, eds., *The Garden Transformed.* Charlottetown: Ragweed Press, 1982.

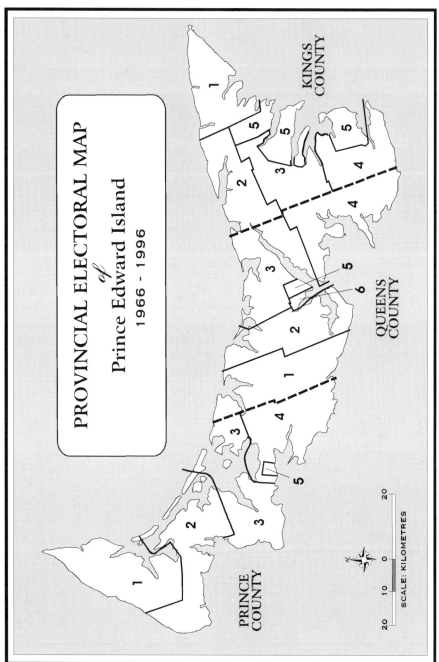

PROVINCIAL ELECTORAL MAP
of
Prince Edward Island
1966 - 1996

PRINCE COUNTY

QUEENS COUNTY

KINGS COUNTY

SCALE: KILOMETRES

Ken Shelton/05

APPENDIX

Official Provincial General and By-Election Results*

GENERAL ELECTION, May 30, 1966 and
DEFERRED ELECTION – 1st Kings, July 11, 1966

PARTY STANDINGS
Liberals, 17
Progressive Conservatives, 15

COUNCILLOR		ASSEMBLYMAN	
1st Kings			
Daniel J.MacDonald (L)	1228 (e)	Bruce L. Stewart (L)	1201 (e)
Peter J. MacAulay (PC)	1021	Keith MacKenzie (PC)	1043
2nd Kings			
Frank Sigsworth (L)	651	Don Anderson (L)	688
Leo F. Rossiter (PC)	889 (e)	James W. Dingwell (PC)	851 (e)
3rd Kings			
Louis W. Roper (L)	663	D.A.C. MacDonald (L)	686
Preston MacLure (PC)	912 (e)	Thomas A. Curran (PC)	888 (e)
4th Kings			
William K. Clark (L)	1093 (e)	Mark L. Bonnell (L)	1195 (e)
Willard MacLean (PC)	817	Robert J. Dorgan (PC)	709
5th Kings			
George J. Ferguson (L)	693 (e)	Arthur J. MacDonald (L)	688
Harry McConnell	688	Joseph C. Sinnott (PC)	689 (e)
1st Queens			
Lorne R. Moase (L)	1209	Ella Jean Canfield (L)	1184
Walter R. Shaw (PC)	1292 (e	Frank S. Myers (PC)	1306 (e)
2nd Queens			
Horace B. Willis (L)	1585	John S. Cutcliffe (L)	1718 (e)
R.L.G. MacPhail (PC)	1588 (e)	John P. Matheson (PC)	1492

Prince Edward Island Historical Review of Provincial Election Results, Elections PEI, 2001

3rd Queens

Eugene P. Cullen (L)	1460	Cecil A. Miller (L)	1561 (e)
J. Russell Driscoll (PC)	1614 (e)	Andrew B. MacRae (PC)	1518

4th Queens

Harold P. Smith (L)	1030 (e)	J. Stewart Ross (L)	1026 (e)
Bennett Carr (PC)	991	Daniel J. Compton (PC)	1001

5th Queens

J. Elmer Blanchard (L)	2925 (e)	Gordon L. Bennett (L)	3115 (e)
A. Walthen Gaudet (PC)	2632	J. Thomas Davis	2455

6th Queens

Eddy Brown (L)	2132	Mrs. B.E. MacDonald (L)	2163
M. Alban Farmer	2549 (e)	J. David Stewart (PC)	2530 (e)

1st Prince

Robert E.Campbell (L)	2171 (e)	Prosper A. Arsenault (L)	2016 (e)
Burton J. Rix (PC)	1690	Gerald Rooney (PC)	1832

2nd Prince

Thomas D. Adams (L)	961	Neil R. MacLeod (L)	890
Robert A. Grindlay (PC)	1111 (e)	Lloyd G. Dewar (PC)	1163 (e)

3rd Prince

William H. Burns (L)	1034	J. Léonce Arsenault (L)	982
Keith S. Harrington (PC)	1372 (e)	Henry W. Wedge (PC)	1433 (e)

4th Prince

Frank Jardine (L)	2515 (e)	G.M. Thompson (L)	2298 (e)
Eric Jessome	2006	R.J. MacDonald (PC)	2234

5th Prince

Alexander B. Campbell	2167 (e)	Thomas E. Hickey (L)	2118 (e)
A.E. MacLennan (PC)	1884	Hubert B. McNeill (PC)	1918

GENERAL ELECTION, May 11, 1970

PARTY STANDINGS
Liberals, 27
Progressive Conservatives, 5

COUNCILLOR		ASSEMBLYMAN	
1st Kings			
Daniel J.MacDonald (L)	1333 (e)	Bruce L. Stewart (L)	1387 (e)
Peter J. MacAulay (PC)	1140	Keith MacKenzie (PC)	1089
2nd Kings			
Brian E. McGuire (L)	817	Don Anderson (L)	813
Leo F. Rossiter	871 (e)	James W. Dingwell (PC)	876 (e)
3rd Kings			
Albert E. (Bud) Ings (L)	984 (e)	W. Bennett Campbell (L)	966 (e)
Preston D. MacLure	882	Thomas A. Curran (PC)	893
4th Kings			
Gilbert R. Clements (L)	1324 (e)	Mark L. Bonnell (L)	1516 (e)
Douglas McGowan (PC)	945	James W. King (PC)	776
5th Kings			
George J. Ferguson (L)	920 (e)	Arthur J. MacDonald (L)	885 (e)
George E. Carver (PC)	631	Joseph C. Sinnott (PC)	664
1st Queens			
Ralph W. Johnston (L)	1391 (e)	Ella J. Canfield (L)	1451 (e)
Knud Jorgensen (PC)	1242	Frank S. Myers (PC)	1180
2nd Queens			
Horace B. Willis (L)	1851	John S. Cutcliffe (L)	1904 (e)
R.L.G. MacPhail (PC)	1891 (e)	Bennett Carr (PC)	1831
3rd Queens			
John L. McNally (L)	1927 (e)	Cecil A. Miller (L)	2079 (e)
J. Russell Driscoll (PC)	1837	Ivan G. Kerry (PC)	1660
4th Queens			
Harold P. Smith (L)	1050	J. Stewart Ross (L)	1108 (e)
Daniel J. Compton (PC)	1153 (e)	Vernon MacIntyre (PC)	1087
5th Queens			
J. Elmer Blanchard (L)	4714 (e)	Gordon L. Bennett (L)	4681 (e)
Mary McQuaid (PC)	2472	Gerald R. Foster (PC)	2478

6th Queens

John H. Maloney (L)	3750 (e)	Allison G. MacDonald (L)	3711 (e)
M. Alban Farmer	2394	J. David Stewart (PC)	2419

1st Prince

Robert E. Campbell (L)	3066 (e)	J. Russell Perry (L)	2953 (e)
Kenneth Pridham (PC)	1731	Clifford Bernard (PC)	1837

2nd Prince

Joshua G. MacArthur (L)	1185 (e)	Ralph K. Adams (L)	1105
George Key (PC)	1177	Lloyd G. Dewar (PC)	1279 (e)

3rd Prince

Edward W. Clark (L)	1605 (e)	William M. Gallant (L)	1544 (e)
Keith S. Harrington (PC)	1119	Henry W. Wedge (PC)	1175

4th Prince

Robert Schurman (L)	3272 (e)	Frank Jardine (L)	3299 (e)
Norman L. Reeves (PC)	2218	E.W. Champion (PC)	2169

5th Prince

Alex B. Campbell (L)	2989 (e)	Thomas E. Hickey (L)	2904 (e)
Claude Ives (PC)	1410	Charlie Hogan (PC)	1489

BY-ELECTION, November 23, 1970

5th Queens, Councillor

J. Patrick Gaudet (PC)	2132	Peter McNeil (L)	3197 (e)

BY-ELECTION, December 4, 1972

1st Kings, Councillor

Melvin J. McQuaid (PC)	1271 (e)	Francis C. White (L)	1007
Fred Cheverie (NDP)	143		

4th Kings, Assemblyman

John C. Bonnell (L)	1095 (e)	John MacNeill (PC)	968
Barrie Harris (NDP)	197		

2nd Queens, Assemblyman

Bennett H. Carr (PC)	1910 (e)		
Henry D. Ford (L)	1609	Margaret Large (NDP)	144

GENERAL ELECTION, April 29, 1974

PARTY STANDINGS
Liberals, 26
Progressive Conservatives, 6

Councillor		**Assemblyman**	

1st Kings

Francis C. White, (L)	1236	Bruce L. Stewart (L)	1350 (e)
Melvin J. McQuaid (PC)	1314 (e)	A. (Brodie) Dixon (PC)	1121
W. Tyrell Pearson (NDP)	70		

2nd Kings

Brain E. McGuire (L)	778	John C. Matheson (L)	789
Leo F. Rossiter (PC)	911 (e)	James W. Dingwell (PC)	840 (e)
C.C. MacKinnon (NDP)	71		

3rd Kings

Albert E. (Bud) Ings (L)	1080 (e)	W. Bennett Campbell (L)	1002 (e)
Reg MacLaren (PC)	880	Albert Fogarty (PC)	957
Garth A. Gillis (NDP)	81	D.J. Carmichael (NDP)	76

4th Kings

Gilbert R. Clements (L)	1619 (e)	Charles J. Fraser (L)	1288 (e)
Bert J. Hankoop (PC)	807	John MacNeill (PC)	1039
Bob Miller (NDP)	120		

5th Kings

James Waldron Lavers	816 (e)	A.J. MacDonald (L)	858 (e)
Lowell S. Johnston	708	G.N. MacPherson (PC)	667
Gerald Cormier (NDP)	25		

1st Queens

Ralph W. Johnston (L)	1406 (e)	Ella J. Canfield (L)	1464 (e)
Knud Jorgensen	1172	Bruce Douglas (PC)	1123

2nd Queens

Arthur H. Howard (L)	2142	Henry D.Ford (L)	2127 (e)
R.L.G. MacPhail (PC)	2171 (e)	Bennett Carr (PC)	2010
R. MacKinnon (NDP)	235		

3rd Queens

John L. McNally (L)	2042 (e)	Cecil A. Miller (L)	2095 (e)
J. Russell Driscoll (PC)	1801	Horace B. Carver (PC)	1905
Aquinas Ryan (NDP)	669	Harry G. Kielly	496

4th Queens

Kenneth R. Emery (L)	1030	Frank A. Mutch (L)	1010
Daniel J. Compton (PC)	1070 (e)	V.J. MacIntyre (PC)	1073 (e)
Jan P. Vos (NDP)	107	William G. Worth (NDP)	113

5th Queens

George A. Proud (L)	3692 (e)	Gordon L. Bennett (L)	3851 (e)
James M. Lee	3003	N.H. Carruthers (PC)	2919
P.A. MacLeod (NDP)	848	Ruth R. Smith (NDP)	783

6th Queens

John H. Maloney (L)	3472 (e)	Allison G. MacDonald (L)	3438 (e)
Michael A. Farmer (PC)	2286	Lucille E. Hogg (PC)	2255
Andrew Robb (NDP)	513	Margaret I. Large (NDP)	541

1st Prince

Robert E. Campbell (L)	3245 (e)	J. Russell Perry (L)	3141 (e)
Cameron Trail (PC)	1524	David E. Harper (PC)	1622
Peter A. Ahern (NDP)	187	Cletus Shea (NDP)	175

2nd Prince

J.G. MacArthur (L)	1307 (e)	George R. Henderson (L)	1220 (e)
Hubert D. Joy (PC)	1008	Lloyd G. Dewar (PC)	1100

3rd Prince

Edward W. Clark (L)	1707 (e)	William M. Gallant (L)	1547 (e)
Keith S. Harrington (PC)	967	J.E. Arsenault (PC)	1098

4th Prince

Frank Jardine (L)	2974 (e)	Catherine Callbeck (L)	3289 (e)
Albert E. McCardle (PC)	2093	Doris MacWilliams (PC)	1838
Sidney Murray (NDP)	756	Doreen Sark (NDP)	684

5th Prince

Alex B. Campbell (L)	2582 (e)	Thomas E. Hickey (L)	2397 (e)
Peter M. Pope (PC)	1333	George R. McMahon (PC)	1700
Robert A. Rankin (NDP)	236		

BY-ELECTION, February 17, 1975

5th Queens, Assemblyman

James M. Lee (PC)	2343 (e)	David McLane (L)	2250
Madrien Ferris (NDP)	735		
Susan Partridge (Garden Party)	53		

BY-ELECTION, November 3, 1975

3rd Prince, Assemblyman

J.G. Léonce Bernard (L) 1571 (e)   J. Robert Brown (PC)   961

BY-ELECTION, November 8, 1976

2nd Prince, Councillor

Lloyd G. Dewar (PC)   1165 (e)   Robert A. Ellis (L)   1150

5th Prince, Assemblyman

G.R. McMahon (PC)   2131 (e)   George Olscamp (L)   1311

4th Queens, Assemblyman

J. Angus MacLean (PC)   1257 (e)
John Brehaut (L)   1005

1st Kings, Councillor

James B. Fay (L)   1472 (e)   Reg Peters (PC)   1045

GENERAL ELECTION, April 24, 1978

PARTY STANDINGS
Liberals, 17
Progressive Conservatives, 15

Councillor		Assemblyman	
1st Kings			
James B. Fay (L)	1687 (e)	R. (Johnnie) Young (L)	1479 (e)
Charles J. MacInnis (PC)	976	Arnold Dixon (PC)	1185
2nd Kings			
James MacAulay (L)	786	John C. Matheson (L)	827
Leo F. Rossiter (PC)	1004 (e)	Roddy B. Pratt (PC)	865 (e)
Aquinas Ryan (NDP)	102		
3rd Kings			
A.E. (Bud) Ings (L)	1211 (e)	W. Bennett Campbell (L)	1251 (e)
Peter B. MacLeod (PC)	1018	Emmett A. Power (PC)	977

4th Kings

Gilbert R. Clements (L)	1249	Charles J. Fraser (L)	1179
J. (Johnnie) Williams (PC)	1273 (e)	Patrick G. Binns (PC)	1254 (e)
Garry W. Herring (NDP)	88		

5th Kings

James W. Lavers (L)	804	Arthur J. MacDonald (L)	961 (e)
Lowell S. Johnston (PC)	853 (e)	Ivan K. Bartlett	699

1st Queens

Ralph W. Johnston (L)	1398 (e)	Ella J. Canfield (L)	1425 (e)
F.M. Leone Bagnall (PC)	1348	Marion L. Reid (PC)	1316

2nd Queens

Lawson Drake (L)	2558	Henry D. Ford (L)	2646 (e)
R.L.G. MacPhail (PC)	2794 (e)	Gordon Lank (PC)	2586
Anco Hamming (Ind)	128		

3rd Queens

John L. McNally (L)	2328	Cecil A. Miller (L)	2309
Fred L. Driscoll (PC)	3167 (e)	Horace B. Carver (PC)	3177 (e)

4th Queens

Kenneth R. Emery (L)	1138	William A. Drake (L)	1139
Daniel J. Compton (PC)	1323 (e)	J. Angus MacLean (PC)	1317 (e)

5th Queens

George A. Proud (L)	4298 (e)	Edward Watters (L)	3538
Harry H. Cook (PC)	3804	James M. Lee (PC)	4246 (e)
A. Neil Harpman (Ind)	129	Leo McCormack (NDP)	474

6th Queens

John H. Maloney (L)	3320 (e)	Allison MacDonald (L)	3120
A.J. Larkin (PC)	3027	Barry R. Clark (PC)	3232 (e)

1st Prince

Robert E. Campbell (L)	3265 (e)	J. Russell Perry (L)	2977 (e)
Frances M. Ready (PC)	2154	David E. Harper (PC)	2429

2nd Prince

Robert A. Ellis (L)	1490 (e)	George Henderson (L)	1499 (e)
Darlene Collicut (PC)	1101	Lloyd G. Dewar (PC)	1102

3rd Prince

Edward W. Clark (L)	1856 (e)	J.G. Léonce Bernard (L)	1834 (e)
Bernard McCabe (PC)	1095	Pierre A. Doiron (PC)	1066
Joseph Gallant (NDP)	59		

4th Prince

J. Stavert Huestis (L)	3057	Allison M. Harper (L)	3249
Prowse Chappell (PC)	3268 (e)	William MacDougall (PC)	3283 (e)
Doreen Sark (NDP)	236		

5th Prince

Alex B. Campbell (L)	2376 (e)	Wally MacGillivray (L)	1859
Peter M. Pope (PC)	1605	George McMahon (PC)	2334 (e)
John M. Murphy (NDP)	214		

INDEX

Numbers in italics denote photographs or graphics

Canadian Brotherhood of Railway Trainmen and General Workers Union, 65-68,

Canadian Civil Liberties Association, 145

Canadian constitution, 182

Canadian Coast Guard, 67

Canadian Magazine, 233, 252

Canadian National (CN), 65, 66, 67, 71

Canadian Science Council, 246

Canadian Wildlife Federation, 246

Canfield, Jean, 28, 136

Carson, Rachel, 231

Catmur, David, 165, *241*

causeway, *see* fixed link

Cavenagh, Patrick, 40, 48

C.D. Howe Co., 43

Centennial Commission, 203, 204, 208, 228

Central Academy, 86, 87

CFB Summerside, 76, 129, 135

CFCY Radio, 126, 210

CFCY Television, 15, 29, 33, 78

Chant, Donald, 248

Charlottetown City Council, 146-47

Charlottetown Guardian, 32, 33, 34, 52, 61, 66, 70, 125, 134, 137, 145, 152, 167, 186, 208, 226, 249, *260*, 262, 265, 267

Charter of Rights and Freedoms, 9

Chatelaine, 235

Chrétien, Jean, 151

Churchill, Col. Edward, 75, 76

Civil Service Act, 14, 163, 192, 193

Civil Service Commission, 192, 197

civil service reform, 191-97. *See also under* Comprehensive Development Plan

Clark, Edward, 169, *266*

Clark, Keir, 28, *37*, 67, 88, 107, 109, 130

Clark, Dr. Marvin, 90

Clark, Merlin, 265

Clements, Gilbert, 152, *135*, 164, 187, *227*, 265

Cockburn, Bruce, 139, 146

Coles, George, 216

Commercial Marine International, 43

Commission of Inquiry into Gulf Garden Foods Limited and Bathurst Marine Limited, 43, 44, 46, 47, 53, 56, 59, 60, 61

Committee of Inquiry into Land Acquisition and Land Transfers, 179

community schools, 157, 161

Comprehensive Development Plan, 14, 31, 76-79, 97-113, 115-37, 151, 155-60, 164-69, 183, 187, 188, 197, 204, 222, 226, 227, 240, 255, 264

agriculture, 116-17, 118, 119, 171-89, 205, 209-11,

Moe, Jens, 32, 39-63

Moe Industries, 47

Monkley, Lorne, 20, 22

Montague Eastern Graphic, 159, 167

Morgan, Richard, 181

Morrison, Bill, 259, 264, 265

Mullally, John, 5, 6, 29, 30

Mullally, Philip, *144*

Mumford, Lewis, 231, 239

municipal infrastructure, 166. *See also under* Comprehensive Development Plan

Murphy, Elmer, 90, 135

Murray, Lowell, 31

Mutch, Jean, 166, 169

Myrdal, Gunnar, 99

National Farmers Union (NFU), 186, 209-11, 223, 225

national parks, 31, 149-55. *See also* East Point National Park; PEI National Park

National Research Council of Canada, 246

National Sea Products, 43

Natural Areas Advisory Committee, 187

Nemetz, Donald, 164, 198, 199

Nestlé Alimentana S.A., 42

Nestlé Canada, 54

New Alchemy Institute, 231, 233, 234, 250, 251

New Democratic Party (NDP), 145, 226-27, 256

Newman, Peter, 74, 257

New York Times, 235

Nicholson, Jack, 25, 26

Norinvest AS, 54, 57

Norris, Kenneth, 90

Northumberland Strait Crossing, 74

O'Connell, Harry, 166, 167

Old Home Week, 140

Olsen & Ugelstad, 48, 57

OPEC, 237

Ottawa Journal, 183

Pantry, Lou, 141

patronage, 3-5, 163, 192-97, 201

Peake, Arthur, 25, 88

Pearson, Lester, 6, 7, 21-22, 62, 65, 72, 74, 75, 76, 95, 101, 111

Pearson, Tyrrell, 150

PEI Federation of Agriculture, 12, 242

PEI Heritage Foundation, 228-29

PEI Human Rights Commission, 225

PEI Industrial Development Corporation, 41, 43, 48, 53, 54, 56

PEI Labour Act, 141

PEI Lending Authority, 119

PEI Medical Society, 140-141

PEI National Park, 18, 149

pensions, 4, 30

Peters, Arthur, 87